The Political Economy of Bilateral Aid

The social and economic consequences of the COVID-19 pandemic and of extreme climate events have brought into sharp relief the serious deficiencies of our political economies. The dominant global ideology of neoliberalism and its architects and beneficiaries are responsible for this. Bilateral development assistance is an integral part of the neoliberal grand design. However, while the deficiencies of neoliberalism have been starkly exposed by the pandemic, its collapse is unlikely in the short term. Much bilateral assistance will therefore continue to be self-serving.

Within these confines, and on the basis of a sharply critical analysis of the functioning of technical assistance at the point of the design and delivery of programmes and projects, this book identifies crucial supply-side nodes of power and influence where feasible and relatively straightforward 'functional' reforms – strategy, structure, selection, training – would make genuinely developmental results for recipients more likely and enhance donor interests at the same time. It argues that more authentic, empathetic, and altruistic technical assistance will be essential to bringing this about.

The arguments are supported by primary, published evidence gathered by the author during 18 years of full-time employment as a team leader or programme manager of technical assistance programmes. The book will be of interest to students of development management, development economics, political economy and international relations, as well as policy-makers, development practitioners and supply- and demand-side government officials.

Peter Blunt is Adjunct Professor at the School of Business at the University of New South Wales, Canberra, Australia.

Cecilia Escobar holds a PhD and an MPhil in Economics from the University of Athens and a Master in Economic Development from the Carlos III University of Madrid.

Vlassis Missos is Research Fellow at the Centre of Planning and Economic Research, Athens, Greece, and a staff member of the Department of Economics, University of Athens.

Routledge Studies in Development Economics

6 **State Building and Social Policies in Developing Countries**
The Political Economy of Development
Rashed Al Mahmud Titumir

7 **Taxation in the Digital Economy**
New Models in Asia and the Pacific
Edited by Nella Hendriyetty, Chris Evans, Chul Ju Kim and Farhad Taghizadeh-Hesary

8 **Human Capital and Gender Inequality in Middle-Income Countries**
Schooling, Learning and Socioemotional Skills in the Labour Market
Elizabeth M. King and Dileni Gunewardena

9 **Digital Financial Inclusion and Regulation**
Ogochukwu Monye

10 **Household Demand for Consumer Goods in Developing Countries**
A Comparative Perspective with Developed Countries
Eliyathamby A. Selvanathan, Saroja Selvanathan and Maneka Jayasinghe

11 **Unlocking Private Investment in Sustainable Infrastructure in Asia**
Edited by Bhajan Grewal, Nella Hendriyetty, Iskandar Abdullaev, Chul Ju Kim, Naoyuki Yoshino and Eisa Khan Ayoob Ayoob

12 **The Political Economy of Bilateral Aid**
Implications for Global Development
Peter Blunt with Cecilia Escobar and Vlassis Missos

For more information about this series, please visit: www.routledge.com/Routledge-Studies-in-Development-Economics/book-series/SE0266

The Political Economy of Bilateral Aid

Implications for Global Development

Peter Blunt
with Cecilia Escobar
and Vlassis Missos

Routledge
Taylor & Francis Group
LONDON AND NEW YORK

First published 2023
by Routledge
4 Park Square, Milton Park, Abingdon, Oxon OX14 4RN

and by Routledge
605 Third Avenue, New York, NY 10158

Routledge is an imprint of the Taylor & Francis Group, an informa business

British Library Cataloguing-in-Publication Data
A catalogue record for this book is available from the British Library

Library of Congress Cataloging-in-Publication Data
Names: Blunt, Peter, author. | Escobar, Cecilia, author. | Missos, Vlassis, author.
Title: The political economy of bilateral aid : implications for global development / Peter Blunt with Cecilia Escobar, Vlassis Missos.
Description: Abingdon, Oxon ; New York, NY : Routledge, 2023. | Series: Routledge studies in development economics | Includes bibliographical references and index.
Identifiers: LCCN 2022025997 (print) | LCCN 2022025998 (ebook) | ISBN 9781032256412 (hbk) | ISBN 9781032256429 (pbk) | ISBN 9781003284352 (ebk)
Subjects: LCSH: Economics. | Economic development. | COVID-19 Pandemic, 2020—Social aspects. | COVID-19 Pandemic, 2020—Economic aspects.
Classification: LCC HB171 .B54155 2023 (print) | LCC HB171 (ebook) | DDC 362.1962/414400681—dc23/eng/20220811
LC record available at https://lccn.loc.gov/2022025997
LC ebook record available at https://lccn.loc.gov/2022025998

ISBN: 978-1-032-25641-2 (hbk)
ISBN: 978-1-032-25642-9 (pbk)
ISBN: 978-1-003-28435-2 (ebk)

DOI: 10.4324/9781003284352

Typeset in Bembo
by Apex CoVantage, LLC

For Alexander Dimitri whose generation has done nothing to deserve the imperilled Planet Earth bequeathed to them by the architects of Empire but who will, in the true spirit of neoliberalism, have to suffer the consequences anyway.

Peter Blunt

Contents

About the Author and Collaborators

Peter Blunt is Adjunct Professor, School of Business, University of New South Wales (Canberra), Australia (peter.blunt@adfa.edu.au; peterblunt1011@gmail.com). Before then, he had held a senior position with the World Bank in Jakarta, Indonesia, and tenured full professorships of management in universities in Australia (Charles Darwin University), Norway (University of Nordland) and the United Kingdom (Cardiff University). His experience includes more than 30 years (and 80 projects) as a consultant working for agencies such as the World Bank, UNDP, ADB, AusAID/DFAT, DfID, SDC, Sida, USAID and the EU in 35 countries, including eight fragile states. He is widely published and has served on the editorial boards of *The Journal of Applied Behavioural Science*; *Journal of Contemporary African Studies*; *International Journal of Human Resource Management* and *Public Administration and Development*. His commissioned publications for UNDP on governance and public sector management formed the basis of UNDP policy on these matters and have been well received in many countries around the world, and his books on management and organisation in Africa are widely considered to be among the standard works in their field.

Cecilia Escobar holds a PhD and an MPhil in Economics from the University of Athens and a master's in Economic Development from the Carlos III University of Madrid. She has worked as a lecturer and researcher for the Department of Economics of the Central American University (El Salvador) and as an independent consultant. Her publications include works on economic development, gender relations, economic crisis, political economy and various debates in the field of history of economic thought.

Vlassis Missos is Research Fellow, Centre of Planning and Economic Research, Athens, Greece, and a staff member of the Department of Economics, University of Athens. His main research interests are social policy, poverty, income inequality, political economy, and the history of economic thought. He has also worked as a consultant to the General Secretary of Fiscal Policy at the Greek Ministry of Finance and as a short-term consultant to the Government of Samoa on a development assistance project funded by the Government of Australia. His publications include (with Costis Vaitsos) *The Real Economy: Experience of Development, Crisis and Impoverishment in Greece* (2018, Athens: Kritiki, in Greek).

Preface

No doubt like many others who found their way into the development assistance industry, I was raised in the heart of the British Empire, in the so-called White Highlands of the then colony of Kenya. But even as a young boy, enchanted by the wonders and joys of living in what was surely the world's Garden of Eden and seduced by the privileges and pleasures of a colonial upbringing,[1] I could not help but notice the fundamental injustices of the imperialist enterprise. Perhaps as a way of atoning for the sins of our fathers and our complicity as beneficiaries, for people like me, those crucial formative years, and the conviction that there was something gravely wrong with the system, marked the beginnings of a sense of duty to make reparations.[2]

Years after independence in Kenya, in the late 1970s, when doing fieldwork there for my master's thesis, a statement by one of my sample informants about his experience of work crystalised what I had felt as a child to be unjust about, and would come to understand to be the hallmark of, the imperialist and neo-imperialist systems. His forlorn account of his employment – which he said was to '*mwaga maji kwa shamba ya wazungu*' or to 'pour water on the gardens of whites' – was a poignant and pithy metaphor for the distribution of power, and the indignity, encapsulated in the master–slave relations inherent in his job, and in the remnants of the British Empire, of which it was a part.

Being a product, and captive, of a strict upbringing and the Western Establishment's institutional 'manufacture of consent' – British boarding school and university followed by years of working in the engine rooms of neoliberal indoctrination and elite formation, university business schools – my early attempts at restitution were of the 'clerky and calculating' variety or 'reckless at slow speed' (Roy in Kumar, 2011). They took the form of books on management and organisation in Africa, which, while the first to be written on the subjects and critical of some Western theorising, were squarely within the Establishment's structural functionalist domain and therefore implicitly supportive of prevailing distributions of power and control (see Blunt, 1983; Blunt & Popoola, 1985; Blunt & Jones, 1992).

My questioning of the historical structural violence of imperialism and of the ideological packaging in neoliberalism of its neo-imperialist successors began to feature more prominently in my writing following my belated discovery of

Noam Chomsky's work in the 1990s (e.g. Chomsky, 1987, 1996, 1997; Herman & Chomsky, 1988; Blunt, 1995a, 1995b; Blunt & Jones, 1997; Blunt & Rondinelli, 1997). More rein, and fuller expression, came from my reading of Arundhati Roy's evocative and scathing essays on power and international relations published from the turn of the twenty-first century (e.g. Roy, 2003a, 2003b, 2004; Blunt & Lindroth, 2012). Soon thereafter, Yanis Varoufakis burst onto the scene with his laser-like gaze, his penetrating analyses of the global economy, and his damning account of Greece's mistreatment at the hands of the European Union (e.g. Varoufakis, 2015, 2016, 2017, 2020; Blunt, 2018; Blunt *et al.*, in press). What little was left of my 'normal scientific herding instincts' (Blunt & Khamoosh, 2016), of any lingering sense that there were no alternatives to the dominant ideology of neoliberalism, disintegrated under the red dot and was blown away.

In many ways, this book is the culmination of all of that. It is as full an expression as I can give of the misgivings about Empire that have their roots in the Kenya of my youth, my long experience of development assistance, the immediate and catastrophic threats of the climate crisis, the failings of neoliberal-induced complacency exposed by the COVID-19 pandemic, and the US Empire's complicity in creating and maintaining the conditions for what amounted to a proxy war in Ukraine. The latter so deepened and widened the geostrategic fissures between the United States and NATO and their declared adversaries – Russia and China – as to make the risks of a terminal nuclear war greater than at any time since the (1962) Cuban Missile Crisis.

As we demonstrate in the pages that follow, as a means of providing some form of reparation, to date, development assistance has proved to be a chronic source of disappointment, showing itself to be nothing more than a faithful emissary of Empire's latest incarnation, neoliberalism, an agent of its dirty work. It is of course necessary to expose exploitation, injustice and deceit wherever they are found even if, as in the case of much bilateral development assistance, the grubby little secrets have not always been that well kept. The more important task, however, is clearly to try to do something about them, which is the main purpose of this book.

I have been greatly assisted in this by my collaborators – Cecilia Escobar and Vlassis Missos – who were recommended to me by Yanis Varoufakis when I went to him in search of non-doctrinaire economists to provide technical assistance to the Government of Samoa.

Peter Blunt

Notes

1 An excellent account of some of these privileges and pleasures is provided by Connan (2015) in his analysis of private members' clubs in colonial Kenya, their role in 'assimilating Europeans to a race-based ruling community', and their use as an instrument of state power.

2 The full extent of the barbarism of colonial rule in Kenya, its basis in convictions of racial and civilisational supremacy, and Britain's 'cleansing of the records', particularly during the Mau Mau uprising that led to independence, are graphically exposed by Elkins (2005). Elkin's (2022) detailed and persuasive account of the historical structural violence of the British Empire more broadly is just as damning.

References

Blunt, P. (1983). *Organisational Theory and Behaviour: An African Perspective (Modern Management in Africa)*. Longman.

Blunt, P. (1995a). Cultural Relativism, 'Good' Governance and Sustainable Human Development. *Public Administration and Development, 15*(1), 1–9. https://doi.org/10.1002/pad.4230150102

Blunt, P. (1995b, January). *Public Sector Management, Governance and Sustainable Human Development: A Discussion Paper*. Management Development and Governance Division, Bureau for Policy and Programme Support, United Nations Development Programme. Retrieved February 24, 2022, from www.researchgate.net/publication/315727992_Public_Sector_Management_Governance_and_Sustainable_Human_Development

Blunt, P. (2018). Varoufakis Versus Europe's Deep Establishment: 'Frail Deeds', Apologias, and a Battle Lost before it Was Begun. *Journal of Interdisciplinary Economics, 30*(2), 210–225. https://doi.org/10.1177%2F0260107918769124

Blunt, P., Escobar, C., & Missos, V. (in press). Emergency Responses Under COVID-19: Development Assistance, 'Structural Violence', and 'Interpretive Labour' in Samoa. *Journal of Interdisciplinary Economics*.

Blunt, P., & Jones, M. (1992). *Managing Organisations in Africa*. Walter de Gruyter.

Blunt, P., & Jones, M. (1997). Exploring the Limits of Western Leadership Theory in East Asia and Africa. *Personnel Review, 26*(1/2), 6–23. https://doi.org/10.1108/00483489710157760

Blunt, P., & Khamoosh, S. (2016). Vexatious Voice: The Politics of Downward Accountability and Subnational Governance Reform in Afghanistan. *Progress in Development Studies, 16*(1), 81–100. https://doi.org/10.1177/1464993415608085

Blunt, P., & Lindroth, H. (2012). Development's Denial of Social Justice. *International Journal of Public Administration, 35*(7), 471–481. https://doi.org/10.1080/01900692.2012.655357

Blunt, P., & Popoola, O. (1985). *Personnel Management in Africa (Modern Management in Africa)*. Longman.

Blunt, P., & Rondinelli, D. (1997). *Reconceptualising Governance* (Discussion Paper DP(05)/D611/No. 2). Management Development and Governance Division, United Nations Development Programme. http://digitallibrary.un.org/record/268781

Chomsky, N. (1987). *On Power and Ideology: The Managua Lectures*. South End Press.

Chomsky, N. (1996). *Powers and Prospects: Reflections on Human Nature and the Social Order*. South End Press.

Chomsky, N. (1997). *Democracy in a Neoliberal Order: Doctrines and Reality*. University of Cape Town Press.

Connan, D. (2015). *Race for Distinction: A Social History of Private Members' Clubs in Colonial Kenya* [Unpublished doctoral dissertation]. Florence: European University Institute. https://cadmus.eui.eu/bitstream/handle/1814/40809/2015_Connan.pdf?sequence=1

Elkins, C. (2005). *Imperial Reckoning: The Untold Story of Britain's Gulag in Kenya*. Henry Holt and Company.

Elkins, C. (2022). *Legacy of Violence: A History of the British Empire*. Knopf.

Herman, E. S., & Chomsky, N. (1988). *Manufacturing Consent: The Political Economy of the Mass Media*. Pantheon Books.

Kumar, A. (2011, February 15). The Un-Victim. *Guernica*. www.guernicamag.com/roy_2_15_11/

Roy, A. (2003a, January 27). Confronting Empire [Speech audio recording, print edition February 14, 2003]. *Frontline*. https://frontline.thehindu.com/world-affairs/article30215627.ece

Roy, A. (2003b, May 13). *"Instant-Mix Imperial Democracy" (Buy One, Get One Free)* [Speech audio recording]. Retrieved February 24, 2022, from http://jonsenglishsite.info/Class%20Docs%205/6_InstantMix.pdf

Roy, A. (2004). *The Ordinary Person's Guide to Empire*. HarperCollins Publishers.

Varoufakis, Y. (2015). *The Global Minotaur: America, Europe and the Future of the World Economy* (3rd ed.). Zed Books.

Varoufakis, Y. (2016). *And the Weak Suffer What They Must? Europe, Austerity and the Threat to Global Stability*. The Bodley Head.

Varoufakis, Y. (2017). *Adults in the Room: My Battle With Europe's Deep Establishment*. The Bodley Head.

Varoufakis, Y. (2020, September 4). Yanis Varoufakis: Capitalism isn't Working. Here's an Alternative. *The Guardian*. www.theguardian.com/books/2020/sep/04/yanis-varoufakis-capitalism-isnt-working-heres-an-alternative

Acronyms

ADB	Asian Development Bank
AUD	Australian dollar
AUKUS	Australia, United Kingdom, United States
AusAID	Australian Aid
BEC	Bid Evaluation Committee
CDA	Community Development Agreement
CEO	Chief executive officer
CIA	Central Intelligence Agency
COP	Chief of party
CPD	Contractor's programme director
CPP	Cambodian People's Party
CSO	Civil society organisation
DCOP	Deputy chief of party
DfID	Department for International Development
DM	Deputy master
DSF	Decentralisation Support Facility
EITI	Extractive Industries Transparency Initiative
EU	European Union
FCO	Foreign and Commonwealth Office
GDP	Gross domestic product
GHG	Greenhouse gas
GOA	Government of Afghanistan
GOI	Government of Indonesia
GOM	Government of Mongolia
GSDRC	Governance and Social Development Resource Centre
GPM	Governance programme manager
GoTL	Government of Timor-Leste
HIV	Human Immunodeficiency Virus
IBL	Integrated budget law
IDLG	Independent Directorate for Local Governance
IFI	International financial institution
IMF	International Monetary Fund
IPCC	Intergovernmental Panel on Climate Change

KRG	Kurdistan Regional Government
LDF	Local development funds
LDI	Latter-day imperialist
LG	Local government
LGP	Local Government Programme
M	Master
MES	Messenger
NATO	North Atlantic Treaty Organization
NCD	Non-communicable disease
NGO	Non-governmental organisation
OECD	Organisation for Economic Cooperation and Development
PC	Prime contractor
PD	Paris Declaration of 2005
PMO	Prime Minister's Office
POM	Programme operations manual
PTL	Programme team leader
SDC	Swiss Agency for Development and Cooperation
SNG	Subnational governance
UN	United Nations
UNDP	United Nations Development Programme
UNESCO	United Nations Educational, Scientific and Cultural Organisation
UNICEF	United Nations Children's Fund
UNIDO	United Nations Industrial Development Organisation
US/USA	Unites States of America
USAID	United States Agency for International Development
VP	Vice president
WB	World Bank

1 Introduction

Global warming is the most pressing and serious problem that humanity has ever had to face (Chomsky in Casleton, 2019).[1] The great calamity in waiting of the modern world has come about at the hands of *Homo sapiens*. It is almost entirely of our own making.[2] But it is a minuscule fraction of humankind, mainly in the rich countries, that is largely responsible for the planet's perilous condition. Elites comprising coalitions of government and business interests have devised and enforced policies that have resulted in the ruthless exploitation, to the point of extinction, of the planet's natural resources, ecosystems, plants and animals.[3] Prospects for a decent life on Earth have been put in serious jeopardy by their actions.

The Dominant Ideology of Neoliberalism

These elites are the architects and beneficiaries of the ideology of neoliberalism, the dominant global political economy (e.g. Harvey, 2007; Saad-Filho & Johnston, 2005; Shaikh, 2006) that, since the late 1970s, has threatened to seal our fate. It is the means by which those in power have instigated and overseen our wild gallop towards the precipice (Chomsky in Polychroniou, 2021). Their sole purpose in doing so has been self-enrichment. Enrichment founded on the exploitation not just of nature but also of the people of the world. During the neoliberal era, the wages of hundreds of millions of middle- and lower-income earners have stagnated, and income inequality has risen sharply, pushing many into poverty (e.g. Piketty, 2014, 2015; Chancel *et al.*, 2021).[4] Levels of alienation and anomie among affected populations have risen accordingly (e.g. Hedges, 2015, 2018, 2020), to the point where, in the United States, they pose a serious threat to public order (Chomsky, 2021; Roy, 2021).

Since its declaration in mid-March 2020, these, and other, severe and chronic deficiencies of our already weakened political economies (Hedges in Livesey, 2020) have worsened and been magnified by the COVID-19 pandemic. The worth of national and international systems of governance can be gauged by the huge social and economic costs of the disease, and by the global spread of easily ignited civil unrest that has shattered the brittle veneer of the neoliberal political and social order, exposing the extent of pent-up anger and anomie

DOI: 10.4324/9781003284352-1

among the poor and disempowered. The social and economic effects of the pandemic are more pronounced and severe than any experienced in the past century and impossible to ignore, to conceal or to rationalise (Blunt *et al.*, in press).[5]

Poorer and browner people, and the disempowered everywhere, have suffered the most from the virus because they age faster, are generally less healthy, and are therefore more vulnerable to disease.[6] At the same time, state-induced and state-supported monopolies have allowed big business to prosper and enhance its privileged status (Varoufakis, 2020).

But, as Roy (2020b) points out, we should not be surprised by any of this. The symptoms of the catastrophe are not new. They are the culmination and detritus of a slow-motion tragedy that has been playing out in full view for decades.

Neoliberalism and Development Assistance: The New Imperialism

Development assistance has been, and remains, an important part of the neoliberal grand design, being both a product of neoliberalism and a crucial means for its maintenance and spread (Chomsky in Mitchell & Schoeffel, 2002). It is what a poor country gets when it has something that a rich country needs or wants. Natural resources, cheap and passive labour, markets and geopolitical advantage are among the most sought-after commodities (Klein, 2007). A defining characteristic of such 'assistance' is subterfuge and deceit: exploitation posing as altruism.[7] Put into effect by technical advisors who create 'conducive investment climates' whose principal purpose is to facilitate corporate predation, access to compliant labour, tax evasion,[8] and the unlimited repatriation of profits (Blunt *et al.*, in press). In short, development assistance serves as the Trojan horse for the 'neoliberal economic evangelists' (Roy, 2020a) of imperial and corporate penetration (e.g. Wallace, 2004), and their accumulation by dispossession (Harvey, 2004).[9] An integral part of neoliberalism's 'highly evolved, intricate way of pulverising a people behind the genial mask of democracy' (Roy, 1999).

The exchanges between the givers and takers of bilateral development assistance are of course unequal. The rich country 'giver' possesses vastly superior financial, economic and technical resources and brute force. Often on threadbare grounds, the rich country also presumes that it has moral – even cultural – ascendancy, in terms of human rights, 'good' governance, and the much-trumpeted values of the so-called free world, a kind of all-embracing civilisational pre-eminence (e.g. Said, 1978/2003; Elkins, 2005, 2022). Bilateral donors who behave in this way clearly place their own values, institutions and interests above all others, frequently with a palpable sense of entitlement, of almost divine right (Roy, 2003c). Aid recipients are expected to comply meekly, to accept what is offered without question. In poor and aid-dependent countries, it is a Mafia-like offer that cannot be refused. For critical theorists like Escobar (1995, 2004), the whole enterprise of development assistance therefore constitutes a new form of imperialism, that is, a largely Western post-colonial means for enabling rich countries to exploit poor countries.[10]

Chomsky (in Mitchell & Schoeffel, 2002) considers the global leader in these respects to be the United States, whose 'assistance' is designed to make sure that other countries are obedient members of the US-devised global system. For developing countries, this entails providing markets and resources and other advantages to US corporations. Aid recipients are thereby made compliant subjects of post-colonial empires. As suggested earlier, soft and alluring words like 'democracy' – Empire's euphemism for neoliberalism (Roy, 2003b) – are used as flimsy cover for hard-faced self-interest.

The first two decades of the twenty-first century have shown no let-up in the US's pursuit of Empire, marked by a trail of destruction that began at the end of the Second World War. Since then, the United States has embarked on military expeditions to secure control of (non-white) country after country; toppled governments; killed and wounded millions; backed militias; supported tyrants and brutal military dictatorships; and toppled fledgling democracies. In all this, it has used the modern equivalent of the familiar – 'selfless', 'civilising' – rhetoric of British colonialism, as it did in Vietnam and in Afghanistan (Roy, 2021).[11]

Along with the United States, the vanguard, and bulk, of the new imperialism comprises the 'old money' of former colonial powers like the United Kingdom, Germany, France, the Netherlands and Belgium and the 'new money' of big and small countries, and former colonies, like Australia, Canada and New Zealand. Other countries like Switzerland make up the numbers. Collectively, and following Browne (2006), we refer to them here as 'latter-day imperialists' (LDIs).[12]

We do not argue these assertions in detail by reference to the considerable literature that addresses them, partly not only because we (see Blunt *et al.*, 2011, 2013, in press; Blunt & Lindroth, 2012; Blunt, 2021a), and many others before us (see, for example, Meier, 1974; Todaro, 1981; Maizels & Nissanke, 1984; Griffin, 1986; Roy, 2003a, 2003b; Harvey, 2003), have already done this at some length but also because these days the arguments are much more widely known and accepted than they were, even 10 years ago. Long overdue popular appreciation of human culpability for global warming during the Anthropocene[13] has contributed to this.

Motivations and Aims

Our interest in analysing bilateral development assistance and, before it is too late, reformulating it, arises, first, from our conviction that we have a duty to do what we can within the bounds of our knowledge and experience to prevent the looming catastrophe of global warming. And, second, it stems from a wish to improve as soon as possible the 'deals' that are presented to poor countries by LDIs – in the interests of a more equitable and sustainable distribution of development benefits within and between countries. The full realisation of this will require a complete transformation of the current inhumane, irrational and unsustainable ruling paradigm.

But, third, our interest springs also from a strong sense that we would be complicit in the subterfuge and exploitation if we did not try to do something about them – by, so to speak, examining both sides of the master–slave relationship discussed by Graeber (2012) and the structural violence and interpretive labour that characterise it. That is to say, the unquestioning obedience of the slave is as deserving of analysis as the use of arbitrary and absolute power by the master. What does 'unquestioning' mean? What does it imply for the slave and how does it shed light on the ways in which the slave manages her awareness of the weaknesses of the master's reasoning (and its often-calamitous consequences) with her inability to speak out about, or even hint at, it? How much time and energy must the slave devote to navigating these treacherous waters? Graeber's (2012) point is that if we do not examine these questions and, instead, focus solely on the behaviour of the master, are we not in some way simply accomplices of those who hold the whip?

These are questions that we examine more thoroughly in Chapter 2 and throughout the book.

Our fourth reason for writing this book is that the significant amount of money that is spent annually on bilateral assistance by the LDIs suggests that even marginal improvements to the way that they do business would be worthwhile. In 2019, official bilateral development assistance by LDI donors was worth about US$150 billion annually, and comprised approximately 88% of the global total of about US$170 billion (World Bank, n.d.). According to the OECD, the COVID-19 pandemic has brought official bilateral development assistance to a record high.[14] In 2020, the 'big five' LDIs in rank order (in US$ billions rounded to the first decimal place) were the United States (35.5), Germany (28.4), the United Kingdom (18.6), Japan (16.3) and France (14.1) (OECD, 2021).

In terms of what we think can be done to make LDI development assistance better, we have argued elsewhere (e.g. Blunt *et al.*, in press) that we do not foresee the sudden collapse of neoliberalism, because its replacement by climate- and people-friendly policies in the countries that are the greatest offenders will vary significantly over time and between countries. Development assistance policy and practice will be an important part of the rear-guard action in neoliberalism's disorderly retreat: its cover blown, yet defiantly persistent in its empty protestations, clinging desperately and in vain to its false claims of altruism.

We therefore accept that for the short period that remains for humanity to avert climate catastrophe[15] and the breaching of the tipping points that will make it inevitable (at most, 10 to 20 years) (IPCC, 2021), LDI donor self-interest will continue to predominate.[16] Accordingly, in these pages, we confine our attention to analysing what can be done within those narrowly defined limits to improve such assistance and, thereby, to help stave off catastrophe and enhance the development prospects for recipients at the same time.[17]

In doing so, we concentrate on what we have found to be a small number of critical factors affecting the design and implementation of – in particular – technical assistance.[18] The most important of these is the question of who really decides what gets done and why, and the nature of the advice and other forms of technical assistance that are provided. This is largely a matter of 'ownership', and whose interests are served as a consequence of the advice that is given and heeded.

We show that typically there is no clearly articulated donor strategy regarding country or government ownership. However, as one might expect, donor behaviour in this regard is consistent with the *historical* structural violence (see Chapter 2 for further discussion of the concept), or the economic and social oppression and 'obedience training' inflicted by foreign powers as a prelude to development assistance. Further, our data reveal that the form and manner of the expression of bureaucratic structural violence are nearly always decided at the lowest levels of the organisations involved on the supply-side, at nodes of influence or concentrations of power that are often in the hands of single individuals – the little-studied 'subalterns' of development assistance (Sogge, 2001). It is their personalities, attitudes to authority, commitment, risk aversion, fears, ambitions, knowledge and capability that can exert a determining influence on what takes place. The evidence that we present demonstrates that this is largely serendipitous. In most cases, the luck of the draw decides who you get in these respects (e.g. Blunt & Sainkhuu, 2015; Blunt *et al.*, in press). The wide variations of personality that result can be detrimental to both donor and recipient interests. We argue that this need not be the case and that at least some of the problems that cause these things to happen are soluble.

In short, the principal author's experience of working on development questions in 35 countries for more than 30 years shows that a great deal could be done at these nodes of influence to achieve genuinely developmental results for the recipient, results that do not threaten, and may indeed enhance, the interests of the donor. The two are not mutually exclusive. The data analysed in Chapters 4 and 5 indicate where this might be possible.

Notes on Method

The sample of LDI bilateral donor programmes that are the main source of our primary evidence and argument were funded[19] by two of the three biggest of the 'big five' – the United States and the United Kingdom – and four of the smaller, but still significant, camp followers: Australia (US$2.6 billion), the Netherlands (US$5.4 billion), Canada (US$5 billion) and Switzerland (US$3.6 billion) (see Table 1.1). We also draw on some of our experience of programme implementation carried out under the auspices of the World Bank (WB) and the Asian Development Bank (ADB) with grant funding from LDIs (the United Kingdom, Australia, Canada and the Netherlands) that was either clearly earmarked for specific programmes or projects of technical assistance and thereby subject to donor control (Cambodia), or where the principal donor intervened if the programme was perceived to be providing technical assistance that it did not like (Indonesia), in these important respects making the assistance essentially bilateral.

As can be seen in Table 1.1, our primary data are derived from programmes of LDI technical assistance funded by six LDI donors in seven countries at very different stages of development over a period of 18 years, from 2003 to 2021. In all save the project in Iraq – where he was a senior technical adviser – the principal author was either programme team leader or programme manager of these projects for the full periods set out in Table 1.1. Importantly, in Indonesia and Mongolia, he was employed as a staff member of a development assistance agency, which afforded him an insider's view of the technical assistance that was provided. In the case of Indonesia, his employer was the World Bank, and, in the case of Mongolia, it was the Swiss Agency for Development and Cooperation (SDC).

Table 1.1 Primary Data Sources

Donor	*Country*	*Programme Dates*	*Years*	*Role of Principal Author*	*Sources*
Netherlands, Sweden (via ADB)	Cambodia	04/2003 – 07/2006	**3**	Team leader – consultant	Blunt (2004a, 2004b), Blunt and Samneang (2005), Blunt and Turner (2005, 2007)
Australia	Timor-Leste	08/2006 – 07/2008	**2**	Programme manager – consultant	Blunt (2009)
United Kingdom, Australia, Canada (via WB)	Indonesia	08/2008 – 10/2011	**3.2**	Bank staff – trust fund manager	Blunt and Lindroth (2012), Blunt *et al.* (2012a, 2012b, 2013)
United States	Iraq	11/2011 – 01/2012	**0.25**	Senior technical adviser – consultant	Blunt (2012)
Switzerland	Mongolia	08/2012 – 11/2013	**1.3**	SDC staff – programme manager	Blunt (2013, 2014a) Blunt and Sainkhuu (2015)
United Kingdom	Afghanistan	04/2014 – 03/2016	**2**	Team leader – consultant	Blunt (2014b, 2015), Blunt *et al.* (2015), Blunt and Khamoosh (2016), Blunt *et al.* (2017)
Australia	Samoa	09/2016 – 08/2021	**5**	Team leader – consultant	Blunt (2019, 2021a, 2021b), Blunt *et al.* (in press)

Accordingly, like those of Mosse (2005), Li (2007) and Farmer (2004), the data and analyses presented here are both empirical investigation and 'lived experience', or what Mosse (2013, p. 228) calls 'reflective observant participation'. That is, they are personal analyses or ethnographies in which the authors are the principal informants (Mosse, 2005).

The sample of projects and countries upon which we rely is arbitrary in the sense that it comprises a sizable chunk of the development experience of the principal author. Despite this, we believe that the sheer amount and richness of the primary evidence that we present, the variety of development settings and LDI donor programmes from which it is drawn, and the different perspectives afforded by the positions held by the principal author, enable us to make a well-founded case for the reformulations of bilateral technical assistance that we propose.

In all cases, we are able to draw on published analyses of what took place. However, the principal uses to which we put the data contained in those papers are new and confined to these pages.

In all of these papers, and this book, our methods of data collection and analysis (epistemology) were informed primarily by the 'interpretive' paradigm of social analysis and 'radical humanism', which regard social reality as being a function of individual perceptions, interpretations and meanings. It is an approach that relies on the close examination of distributions of power and their effects on social and economic domination and exploitation. It is the polar opposite of structural functionalism, which accepts the *status quo* in these respects and supports the dominance and self-aggrandisement of state-capitalist elites and the maintenance by them of social and economic inequality (Burrell & Morgan, 1979).

Then and now, our approach is similar to that of the 'power in institutions' matrix employed by Kashwan *et al.* (2019) to examine power relations in international development under neoliberalism. It is compatible also with Edgley's (2015) 'critical realism', Parker's (1995) account of 'critical modernism', and with the views of critical anthropologists like Mosse who regard development as 'the cloak of power' (Mosse, 2013, p. 229) and see development policy much as we do, namely, as a technical discourse that is used to rationalise and conceal donor self-interests (Mosse, 2005).

These views inform our discussion of the empirical evidence that we use to support our arguments and recommendations, and are evident in our earlier critiques of other forms of Western intellectual and ideological hegemony (e.g. Blunt, 1995a, 1997; Blunt & Jones, 1997).

Structure of the Argument

Our argument is structured as follows. Chapter 2 extends our discussion of power, from its manifestations in neoliberalism and development assistance to other forms of historical structural violence and to the lower reaches of the organisation of such assistance, at the point of design and delivery of programmes and projects. In accordance with our embrace of the interpretive paradigm of organisational analysis noted earlier, our view of power relations, jobs and organisational behaviour at that level draws on critical theorists like Graeber (2015, 2018), Kafka (1926/1997), Farmer (2004) and Gupta (2012). We use insights from such theory to examine the principal features of supply-side behaviour at the coalface and to explain what transpires there – particularly in Chapter 3, which addresses 'Historical Structural Violence, Donor Strategy and the 'Ownership' Problem', and Chapter 4, where we discuss 'Critical Interfaces of [Supply-Side] Bureaucratic Structural Violence: Masters, Messengers and Minions'. Our analysis of how to improve matters draws on functionalist contingency theory and, in particular, the pioneering work of Henry Mintzberg. Chapter 2 sets out the principal features of contingency theory and explains how we reconcile our use of it with our critical theory approach to problem identification and analysis.

In Chapter 3, we argue that donor strategy that is characterised by domination and control runs counter to its own interests as well as those of aid recipients. In particular, we present empirical case studies that demonstrate that the fiction of 'government ownership', which is such a conspicuous and well-known aspect of LDI assistance, is frequently used simply as convenient cover to mask the realisation of supply- and demand-side non-developmental purposes.

Chapter 4 expands the discussion to the principal nodes of supply-side influence, namely, the supervising donor official and the managing contractor or implementing agent (the programme director) and their most critical interfaces – with programme team leaders, government members of programme steering committees, and so-called principal counterparts. The discussion reveals the ways in which the conventions and construction of the relationships and transactions involved have traits that are not dissimilar to those that are characteristic of certain psychological disorders. The principal traits are a marked lack of empathy and self-insight, deceitfulness and an unconcern for others. These traits produce different forms of 'structural violence' and demand extensive 'interpretive labour' on the part of supplicants (Gupta, 2012; Graeber, 2015; Kafka, 1926/1997). At least some of the jobs held by the principal power holders at this level are also shown to bear the 'bullshit' hallmarks identified by Graeber (2018).

Also in Chapter 4, we consider demand-side constraints, associated predominantly with the imbalance of power between donors and recipients, which prevent effective resistance by recipient governments. Where recipient government intentions are genuinely developmental, such imbalances are most evident in the degree of the recipient's aid dependence; the recipient's ability to tell good advice and project performance from bad and to push back; and the prevalence of what might be called a 'cargo cult' mentality ingrained by years of colonial rule or other forms of external domination. Power imbalances are at their most extreme where senior government officials have been co-opted or bought off by corporations from the LDI countries, or pressured in other ways, and, effectively, have become LDI proxies, the sponsors, architects and defenders of the LDI-friendly 'investment climates' that pave the way for their country's exploitation.

However, despite our sympathy for the dystopian accounts of organisation given by the likes of Graeber, Kafka and Gupta, we do not accept an 'all or nothing' version of such accounts. That is to say, we believe that domination and control can come in different shapes and sizes. This means that where the holders of power can be persuaded that relieving some of the pressure might be in their own interests as much as the recipient's, the amount of harm that is done can be reduced significantly and opportunities can arise for mutual and genuinely developmental results.

This leaves room for us to propose a number of essentially functionalist, reformulations – strategy, structure, selection, training and development – of the generally counter-productive organisation and behaviour of donor petty officials and others analysed in Chapters 3 and 4. Among the principal actors involved in programme and project design and delivery on both the supply- and the demand-sides, the aim is to provide conditions for building organisational cultures that are much more authentic, empathetic and altruistic than they have been in the past. This is the subject of Chapter 5.

Audiences

In the concluding chapter, Chapter 6, we consider who will have to be persuaded of the merits of what we have to say for it to make a difference, and the chances of this happening. Most critical of all will be the short-term fate of the US Empire, which we discuss following Chomsky, Hedges, Roy and Varoufakis. In the light of this, we speculate briefly about the extent to which the scale of the impending disasters associated with climate change and the certainty of COVID-19-like (or worse) pandemics to come are likely to make LDIs more motivated to look for alternatives to the dominant ideology of neo-liberalism and to current technical assistance convention.

And we ask whether the rise of China and the emergence of Chinese aid in places considered until now to be the 'back-yards' or exclusive domains of the LDIs – their 'traditional partnerships' – will do more than raise hackles or provoke outbursts of breast-beating and sabre-rattling.[20] Can the complacent, presumptuous, condescending (Prashad, 2007) self-serving ways of the LDIs be persuaded in these circumstances to change even slightly (that is, while maintaining self-interest)? Or will they continue to display a cavalier disregard for anything but the form of notions like government 'ownership and leadership', as they have done for so long with international declarations like those of Paris (2005) and Busan (2011) (e.g. Blunt & Samneang, 2005; Blunt *et al.*, 2012a, in press).

We naturally hope that the book will find a (even if only reluctantly) receptive audience among supply-side policy-makers who decide these matters. The risk is, of course, that the people on the supply-side whom we most want to persuade will dismiss our criticisms as 'donor bashing' and 'anti-development perspectives', as Establishment scholars like Brinkerhoff and Brinkerhoff (2010) have done in their defence of development professionals against claims that they are simply the agents of the new imperialism.

But our main target comprises the principal agents on the demand-side of technical assistance. The large numbers of government officials who serve on technical assistance steering and management committees are the principal counterparts of agencies that are the recipients of such assistance. For our arguments to succeed, these people will need to be made aware of them and be convinced, and emboldened, by them.

The book's biggest audiences are likely to be found among students of educational programmes on international development, international relations, political economy and development studies, and among development practitioners and consultants. This long and winding road to reform may be a luxury that we can only afford if our arguments, and those of like-minded others mounting pressure from below, manage to persuade policy-makers to act more or less immediately in the ways that we (and they) suggest.

Notes

1 The ever-present threat of nuclear conflagration is of course in close attendance. Together, these threats – of neoliberal-induced global warming and nuclear war – presage an era of extinction and annihilation (Prashad, 2018).

2 According to the IPCC (2021), human activity has caused global warming at a rate that is faster than any experienced in at least the last 2000 years. Moreover, economists working at the IMF highlight the difficulties of predicting precisely how bad the calamity will become, and when. Difficulties that are magnified greatly by the fact that as the climate changes it will inevitably reveal 'previously hidden interdependencies between the economy and natural systems', some of which may carry significant, and previously unforeseen, 'disruptions and costs'. On the basis of growing consensus among economists and scientists, they conclude that the so-called tail risks are real and that 'the risk of catastrophic and irreversible disaster is rising, implying potentially infinite costs of unmitigated climate change, including, in the extreme, human extinction' (Krogstrup & Oman, 2019, p. 11).

3 In 2017, The Carbon Majors Database found that fossil fuels are the largest source of anthropogenic greenhouse gases. In 2015, the fossil fuel industry and its products produced 91% of global industrial GHGs, and accounted for about 70% percent of all GHG emissions (Griffin, 2017). See also Chancel *et al.* (2021), who, among other things, argue that to date the burden of climate policies like carbon taxes has been borne largely by low- and middle-income groups, while the excessive consumption of the rich has been unaffected. It is clear that climate change and the COVID-19 pandemic are increasing the divide between the already rich and the poor.

4 For example, after more than half a century as the world's largest 'democracy', in 2010, more than 800 million Indians struggled to survive on less than 20 rupees (or 50 US cents) a day (Barsamian, 2011; Mundkur, 2011). In 2018, about half the world's population lived on less than US$2.50 per day (Prashad, 2018).

5 In the United States, where 112 million people cannot afford proper health care, life expectancy fell in both 2020 and 2021, from 78.86 years in 2019 to 76.99 years in 2020 and 76.60 years in 2021, a net loss of 2.26 years (Corbett, 2022).

6 In the United States, COVID-19 death rates in poor counties were found to be twice those in wealthier counties (Dolan, 2022).

7 The language of development assistance has always seemed a little overdone and a little too good to be true, designed no doubt to bolster its political acceptance among donor-country taxpayers and its appeal to the objects of its attentions. Fundamental

entitlements that have been withheld from large segments of their own populations (Blunt *et al.*, 2011) – 'empowerment' and 'voice', 'sustainable human development', 'poverty elimination' and 'inclusion' – are proffered by donors as prospects for the poor and the 'marginalized' in developing countries. 'Democracy', 'free trade', 'good governance', 'institution building' and 'environmental protection' are promoted as the bases of national development. This is the language of development assistance – expressed with almost evangelical conviction and zeal, and sealed with false promises of 'partnership' and 'win-win' solutions. It is a language that asserts the donor's right to 'help', its proprietorial interests, and its possession of 'best-practice' know-how, moral ascendancy and good will (Blunt & Lindroth, 2012). For the unwary, warning signs at the gates of development heaven should read 'to all ye who enter, beware of "development partners" bearing gifts'.

8 For example, in Papua New Guinea, from the year 2000, just in the timber industry, a conservative estimate of losses to transfer pricing is 100 million US$ per year (Blunt *et al.*, 2018).

9 The dispossession to which Harvey (2004) refers is inflicted by Empire on its own citizens as well as people in foreign lands. However, as we demonstrate in Chapter 3, the dispossession of foreign lands – and the historical structural violence to which they are subjected – nearly always entails extensive and prolonged bloody conflict, subjugation, cultural abasement and the destruction of physical as well as institutional infrastructure. This paves the way for establishing the conditions for imperial predation (e.g., Smith, 2016), which, during the neoliberal era, among others, has been accomplished via privatisation, deregulation (labour flexibility, fiscal paradises, etc.), reductions in the size of government, media control, the dismantling of the commons, the commodification of nature and development assistance. Domestic dispossession can be bloody as well of course and no less predatory (Harvey, 2004), but there is much less scope domestically for using physical violence to achieve these ends or to protect the ruling classes from 'the trampling and the roar of [the] bewildered herd' (Walter Lippmann, quoted in Chomsky, 2012).

10 We were making very similar points around the same time, and in the unlikeliest of places. In 1995, for example, the principal author was commissioned to write a discussion paper for the Management Development and Governance Division of UNDP in New York. The paper's core argument held that the pragmatic concerns of human development in poor countries should outweigh the preoccupations of richer, industrialised countries and that for too long the architecture of development has been dominated by the interests and ideological preferences of the rich and powerful countries. The same discussion paper had argued (just as fruitlessly) that the notion of sustainable human development, as well as the means for attaining it (state governance), should be subject to interpretation according to different national circumstances (Blunt, 1995b). Two years later, in a second discussion paper commissioned by UNDP, among other things, we argued that economic growth should not be viewed as an end in itself and that the social and environmental effects of unconstrained economic growth should be critically examined otherwise extensive, and irreparable, damage to the environment was likely (Blunt & Rondinelli, 1997).

11 Since the Second World War, in addition to Iraq and Afghanistan, countries attacked by the United States include Korea, Guatemala, Cuba, Laos, Vietnam, Cambodia, Grenada, Libya, El Salvador, Nicaragua, Panama, Somalia, Sudan and Yugoslavia. This list does not include covert operations in Africa, Asia and Latin America, or the countries where it has sponsored coups (Roy, 2003d).

12 For Browne (2006, p. 137) 'latter-day imperialism' applies where there is a weak relationship between aid and the needs of the recipient country and aid tends to favour the interests of the donor. On the basis of an empirical analysis of aid flows, Berthélemy (2006) describes our sub-category of donors as 'egoistic' or non-altruistic.

13 The Anthropocene Epoch refers to the period during which the activities of human beings have been the dominant or determining influence on climate and the environment. Many scientists believe that the Anthropocene Epoch should follow the Holocene Epoch (11,700 years ago to the present) and that it should begin in the year 1950. In 2019, the Anthropocene Working Group of the International Union of Geologic Sciences voted in favour of designating the Anthropocene Epoch as a formal geological period starting in the mid-twentieth century (Subramanian, 2019).

14 At about US$25 billion per year, the costs of implementing policies (e.g., the monitoring of wildlife trade, early detection and control, and reducing deforestation by half) to prevent the occurrence of zoonotic disease are a small fraction of the trillions that have been spent by governments to cope with just some of the effects of the COVID-19 pandemic and, most importantly, lower than the amount that LDIs such as the United States and Germany donated in 2020 to address the pandemic (Dobson *et al.*, 2020).

15 For example, Lenton *et al.* (2019) assert that the Greenland ice sheet could melt at 1.5 °C of warming, and by as early as 2030.

16 In many ways, COVID-19 vaccine production and distribution show how resilient such self-interest can be, even in the face of incontrovertible evidence of the harm that will be done to rich country populations if poor countries are prevented from vaccinating their populations to the same extent and at the same time. Immediate, almost certain, and lethal penalties on a grand scale, are not enough it seems to override corporate interests and make COVID-19 vaccinations a global public good. Even the World Bank has been critical of what it calls 'zero-sum Vaccine Nationalism' (Evenett *et al.*, 2021).

17 This is consistent with what Chomsky argued in a 2021 interview (Pâkzâd & Magnussen, 2021), namely, that the crises we face now are ones of survival that will have to be addressed largely within the existing institutions, which can be modified in the time available but not changed fundamentally.

18 Technical assistance is simply non-financial assistance rendered by technical specialists. It can entail the exchange of knowledge and expertise, training and development and consultancy services (UNESCO, n.d.). The GSDRC (Lucas, 2009) notes the long history of technical assistance in development aid and that it has frequently been criticised for being supply-driven (and therefore in conflict with country ownership), too costly, and badly designed and implemented. These criticisms have had little effect on the prevalence or character of technical assistance, which comprises at least one-quarter of global aid, with some estimates suggesting that it could be as much as 50% percent of all aid.

19 Annual spend according to OECD (2021) figures.

20 A trilateral security pact between Australia, the United Kingdom and the United States signed in September 2021 suggested not, and escalated tensions in the Indo-Pacific region dramatically. The pact will enable Australia to build a fleet of nuclear-powered submarines using technology supplied by the United States. The move was seen as a direct response to China's growing influence and presence in the Indo-Pacific. To join the pact, Australia reneged on an agreement with France (worth AUD 90 billion) to build a fleet of diesel-powered submarines, which it did just hours before the announcement in the media of the trilateral pact. France described this as a 'stab in the back' and withdrew its ambassadors to Canberra and Washington. The French foreign minister then accused Australia and the United States of 'lying' and 'duplicity, a major breach of trust and contempt'. Australian Prime Minister Scott Morrison retorted that he had acted in Australia's national interests, as if this was enough to excuse anything (see *Aukus*, 2021a; Tingle, 2021; *Aukus*, 2021b). The tension between the allies eased a little when, immediately (28 September) after Australia's refusal to complete the purchase, France closed a number of arms deals with other countries. For example, despite its extremely fragile fiscal condition, Greece committed to purchasing three French warships with an option for a fourth (Nikas & Nussbaum, 2021). This is a telling example because it illustrates the lengths to which LDI countries will go to maximise self-interest. Just

months before Australia reneged on the deal with France, Prime Minister Morrison and President Macron had been embracing and 'elbow-bumping' at the presidential palace in Paris. Warm-word blandishments filled the air: 'We are good friends. We are good partners'. 'We share common goals and we share common values', Morrison said. Hollow words that now hang there suspended in time, hovering reminders of Australian ('fair dinkum') duplicity and government proclivity for deal-breaking, even with supposed 'good mates'. Australians are fond of proclaiming their 'fair dinkumness' and the importance to national identity of 'mateship' (with heavy undertones of 'we are much more like this than anyone else'), steely values, forged it is said in the trenches of Verdun and Gallipoli. Such blatant and public disavowal of 'core values' when 'good mates' are involved clearly bodes ill for those in less-favoured positions, making more comprehensible the findings outlined in this book and strengthening our general argument.

References

Aukus: UK, US and Australia Launch Pact to Counter China (2021a, September 16). BBC News. www.bbc.com/news/world-58564837

Aukus: French Minister Condemns US and Australia 'Lies' Over Security Pact (2021b, September 19). BBC News. www.bbc.com/news/world-europe-58610234

Barsamian, D. (2011, May 17). Revolts and Rebellions: India in Upheaval, from Kashmir to the 'Red Corridor'. Arundhati Roy Interviewed by David Barsamian. *ISR*, 77. https://isreview.org/issue/77/revolts-and-rebellions/index.html

Berthélemy, J.-C. (2006). Bilateral Donors' Interest vs. Recipients' Development Motives in Aid Allocation: Do All Donors Behave the Same? *Review of Development Economics, 10*(2), 179–194. https://doi.org/10.1111/j.1467-9361.2006.00311.x

Blunt, P. (1995a). Cultural Relativism, 'Good' Governance and Sustainable Human Development. *Public Administration and Development, 15*(1), 1–9. https://doi.org/10.1002/pad.4230150102

Blunt, P. (1995b, January). *Public Sector Management, Governance and Sustainable Human Development: A Discussion Paper.* Management Development and Governance Division, Bureau for Policy and Programme Support, United Nations Development Programme. Retrieved February 24, 2022, from www.researchgate.net/publication/315727992_Public_Sector_Management_Governance_and_Sustainable_Human_Development

Blunt, P. (1997). Prisoners of the Paradigm: Process Consultants and 'Clinical' Development Practitioners. *Public Administration and Development, 17*(3), 341–349. https://doi.org/10.1002/(SICI)1099-162X(199708)17:3<341::AID-PAD954>3.0.CO;2-N

Blunt, P. (2004a, February). *Explanatory Note on Decentralisation and Deconcentration* [Briefing Note]. Commune Council Development Project, Cambodia. Retrieved February 24, 2022, from www.researchgate.net/publication/354597887_Explanatory_Note_on_Decentralisation_and_Deconcentration

Blunt, P. (2004b, March 15). *Cambodia Decentralisation and Deconcentration: Note on Outstanding Policy Issues, and Policy Proposals* [Policy Brief]. Commune Council Development Project, Cambodia. Retrieved February 25, 2022, from: www.researchgate.net/publication/316391562_CAMBODIA_DECENTRALISATION_AND_DECONCENTRATION_NOTE_ON_OUTSTANDING_POLICY_ISSUES_AND_POLICY_PROPOSALS

Blunt, P. (2009). The Political Economy of Accountability in Timor-Leste: Implications for Public Policy. *Public Administration and Development, 29*(2), 89–100. https://doi.org/10.1002/pad.522

Blunt, P. (2012). Toxic Technical Assistance in Conditions of State Fragility: Field Notes From Iraq. *Progress in Development Studies, 12*(4), 337–352. https://doi.org/10.1177/146499341201200405

Blunt, P. (2013, October). *Rural Mongolia's Early Experience With Local Development Fund Utilisation Under the Integrated Budget Law: Findings and Recommendations* (Discussion Paper 1/2013). SDC/GDP. Retrieved February, 24, 2022, from www.researchgate.net/publication/265300899_Rural_Mongolia%27s_Early_Experience_with_Local_Development_Fund_Utilisation_under_the_Integrated_Budget_Law_Findings_and_Recommendations

Blunt, P. (2014a). Whose Resources Are They Anyway? 'Development Assistance' and Community Development Agreements in the Mongolian Mining Sector. *Progress in Development Studies, 14*(4), 383–399. https://doi.org/10.1177/1464993414521491

Blunt, P. (2014b, October). *Civilian Casualties Caused by Military Operations and the Foundational Legitimacy of the State in Afghanistan* [Draft Project Concept Note]. Retrieved February 24, 2022, from www.researchgate.net/publication/329643190_CIVILIAN_CASUALTIES_CAUSED_BY_MILITARY_OPERATIONS_AND_THE_FOUNDA TIONAL_LEGITIMACY_OF_THE_STATE_IN_AFGHANISTAN

Blunt, P. (2015, February). *Sub-National Governance in Afghanistan* [Briefing Paper]. Retrieved February 24, 2022, from www.researchgate.net/publication/355335535_SNG_Briefing_Paper

Blunt, P. (2019). *Public-Private Partnership for the Establishment in Samoa of a World-Class Tertiary Referral Centre* [Discussion Paper]. Samoa Governance Support Programme.

Blunt, P. (2021a). Development Undone: Weber, Kafka, and the Organisation of Supply-Side Vested Interests. *Journal of Interdisciplinary Economics, 33*(1), 74–102. https://doi.org/10.1177/0260107919896879

Blunt, P. (2021b). *Fateful Synergies: Climate Change and Non-Communicable Diseases in the Pacific Island Countries* [Discussion Paper]. Retrieved February 25, 2022, from www.researchgate.net/publication/354597783_Fateful_Synergies_Climate_Change_and_Noncommunicable_Diseases_in_the_Pacific_Island_Countries_1

Blunt, P., Anuk, J., & Nema, K-H. (2018, March). *Communique on Public Policy and SDG Utilisation in Papua New Guinea* [Discussion Paper]. Department of National Planning & Monitoring & UNDP Papua New Guinea. Retrieved February 24, 2022, from www.researchgate.net/publication/325988433_Public_Policy_and_SDG_Utilisation_in_Papua_New_Guinea_DISCUSSION_PAPER

Blunt, P., Escobar, C., & Missos, V. (in press). Emergency Responses Under COVID-19: Development Assistance, 'Structural Violence', and 'Interpretive Labour' in Samoa. *Journal of Interdisciplinary Economics.*

Blunt, P., & Jones, M. (1997). Exploring the Limits of Western Leadership Theory in East Asia and Africa. *Personnel Review, 26*(1/2), 6–23. https://doi.org/10.1108/00483489710157760

Blunt, P., & Khamoosh, S. (2016). Vexatious Voice: The Politics of Downward Accountability and Subnational Governance Reform in Afghanistan. *Progress in Development Studies, 16*(1), 81–100. https://doi.org/10.1177/1464993415608085

Blunt, P., & Lindroth, H. (2012). Development's Denial of Social Justice. *International Journal of Public Administration, 35*(7), 471–481. https://doi.org/10.1080/01900692.2012.655357

Blunt, P., Mamundzay, F., & Nasary, M. (2017). The Long and the Short of Policy Pantomime in Afghanistan. *Progress in Development Studies, 17*(1), 67–88. https://doi.org/10.1177/1464993416674303

Blunt, P., Mamundzay, F., Yama, N., & Afghan, H. (2015). Policy Paradigms, Subnational Governance and the State Sovereignty Gap in Afghanistan. *Progress in Development Studies, 15*(3), 270–285. https://doi.org/10.1177/1464993415578981

Blunt, P., & Rondinelli, D. (1997). *Reconceptualising Governance* (Discussion paper DP(05)/D611/No. 2). Management Development and Governance Division, United Nations Development Programme. http://digitallibrary.un.org/record/268781

Blunt, P., & Sainkhuu, G. (2015). Serendipity and Stealth, Resistance and Retribution: Policy Development in the Mongolian Mining Sector. *Progress in Development Studies, 15*(4), 371–385. https://doi.org/10.1177/1464993415592763

Blunt, P., & Samneang, M. (2005, October). *Aid Effectiveness and Aid Coordination in Cambodia: Stakeholder Perceptions*. The Asia Foundation. Retrieved February 24, 2022, from http://webarchive.nationalarchives.gov.uk/+/www.dfid.gov.uk/mdg/aid-effectiveness/newsletters/cambodia-report.pdf

Blunt, P., & Turner, M. (2005). Decentralisation, Democracy and Development in a Post-Conflict Society: Commune Councils in Cambodia. *Public Administration and Development, 25*(1), 75–87. https://doi.org/10.1002/pad.349

Blunt, P., & Turner, M. (2007). Decentralisation, Deconcentration and Poverty Reduction in the Asia Pacific. In G. S. Cheema & D. A. Rondinelli (Eds.). *Decentralized Governance: Emerging Concepts and Practices* (pp. 115–130). Brookings Institution Press. www.jstor.org/stable/10.7864/j.ctt1261v1.10

Blunt, P., Turner, M., & Hertz, J. (2011). The Meaning of Development Assistance. *Public Administration and Development, 31*(3), 172–187. https://doi.org/10.1002/pad.592

Blunt, P., Turner, M., & Lindroth, H. (2012a). Patronage's Progress in Post-Soeharto Indonesia. *Public Administration and Development, 32*(1), 64–81. https://doi.org/10.1002/pad.617

Blunt, P., Turner, M., & Lindroth, H. (2012b). Patronage, Service Delivery and Social Justice in Indonesia. *International Journal of Public Administration, 35*(3), 214–220. https://doi.org/10.1080/01900692.2011.641050

Blunt, P., Turner, M., & Lindroth, H. (2013). Morton's Fork: 'Democracy' Versus Neopatrimonialism in Developing Countries. *International Journal of Public Administration, 36*(1), 45–62. https://doi.org/10.1080/01900692.2012.713293

Brinkerhoff, J. M., & Brinkerhoff, D. W. (2010). International Development Management: A Northern Perspective. *Public Administration and Development, 30*(2), 102–115. https://doi.org/10.1002/pad.557

Browne S. (2006). *Aid and Influence: Do Donors Help or Hinder?* Earthscan from Routledge.

Burrell, G., & Morgan, G. (1979). *Sociological Paradigms and Organisational Analysis: Elements of the Sociology of Corporate Life* (1st ed.). Routledge. https://doi.org/10.4324/9781315242804

Casleton, S. (2019, June 4). Choosing Hope: Noam Chomsky and Scott Casleton Discuss Socialism, Anarchism, and the Fight for Progress in U.S. Politics Today. *Boston Review*. http://bostonreview.net/politics/noam-chomsky-scott-casleton-choosing-hope

Chancel, L., Piketty, T., Saenz, E., Zucman, G. *et al.* (2021). *World Inequality Report 2022*. World Inequality Lab. https://wir2022.wid.world/

Chomsky, N. (2012, July 22). Destroying the Commons. *TomDispatch*. https://tomdispatch.com/noam-chomsky-the-great-charter-its-fate-and-ours/

Chomsky, N. (2021, September 24). The Future of American Power: Noam Chomsky on The Cruelty of American Imperialism. *The Economist*. www.economist.com/by-invitation/2021/09/24/noam-chomsky-on-the-cruelty-of-american-imperialism

Corbett, J. (2022, April 10). Life Expectancy in US Declined in 2021. Many High-Income Nations Saw It Recover. *Truthout*. https://truthout.org/articles/life-expectancy-in-us-declined-in-2021-many-high-income-nations-saw-it-recover/

Dobson, A. P., Pimm, S. L., Hannah, L., Kaufman, L., Ahumada, J. A., Ando, A. W., Bernstein, A., Busch, J., Daszak, P., Engelmann, J., Kinnaird, M. F., Li, B. V., Loch-Temzelides,

T., Lovejoy, T., Nowak, K., Roehrdanz, P. R., & Vale, M. M. (2020). Ecology and Economics for Pandemic Prevention. *Science, 369*(6502), 379–381. https://doi.org/10.1126/science.abc3189

Dolan, K. (2022, April 16). A Pandemic of the Poor. *Scheerpost.* https://scheerpost.com/2022/04/16/a-pandemic-of-the-poor/

Edgley, A. (2015). Method, Methodology and Politics. In A. Edgley (Ed.). *Noam Chomsky* (pp. 99–120). Palgrave Macmillan. https://doi.org/10.1007/978-1-137-32021-6

Elkins, C. (2005). *Imperial Reckoning: The Untold Story of Britain's Gulag in Kenya.* Henry Holt and Company.

Elkins, C. (2022). *Legacy of Violence: A History of the British Empire.* Knopf.

Escobar, A. (1995). *Encountering Development: The Making and Unmaking of the Third World* [1st printing]. Princeton University Press.

Escobar, A. (2004). Beyond the Third World: Imperial Globality, Global Coloniality and Anti-Globalisation Social Movements. *Third World Quarterly, 25*(1), 207–230. https://doi.org/10.1080/0143659042000185417

Evenett, S. J., Hoekman, B., Rocha, N., & Ruta, M. (2021). *The Covid-19 Vaccine Production Club: Will Value Chains Temper Nationalism?* Policy Research Working Paper No. 9565, World Bank. http://hdl.handle.net/10986/35244

Farmer, P. (2004). An Anthropology of Structural Violence. *Current Anthropology, 45*(3), 305–325. https://doi.org/10.1086/382250

Graeber, D. (2012). Dead Zones of the Imagination: On Violence, Bureaucracy, and Interpretive Labour. The Malinowski Memorial Lecture, 2006. *HAU: Journal of Ethnographic Theory, 2*(2), 105–128. https://doi.org/10.14318/hau2.2.007

Graeber, D. (2015). *The Utopia of Rules: On Technology, Stupidity, and the Secret Joys of Bureaucracy.* Melville House.

Graeber, D. (2018). *Bull Shit Jobs: A Theory.* Simon and Schuster.

Griffin, K. (1986). Doubts About Aid. *IDS Bulletin, 17*(2), 36–45. https://doi.org/10.1111/j.1759-5436.1986.mp17002006.x

Griffin, P. (2017, July). *The Carbon Majors Database: CDP Carbon Majors Report 2017.* CDP Worldwide. https://cdn.cdp.net/cdp-production/cms/reports/documents/000/002/327/original/Carbon-Majors-Report-2017.pdf?1501833772

Gupta, A. (2012). *Red Tape: Bureaucracy, Structural Violence, and Poverty in India.* Duke University Press.

Harvey, D. (2003). *The New Imperialism.* Oxford University Press.

Harvey, D. (2004). The 'New' Imperialism: Accumulation by Dispossession. *Socialist Register, 40,* 63–87. https://socialistregister.com/index.php/srv/article/view/5811/2707

Harvey, D. (2007). *A Brief History of Neoliberalism.* Oxford University Press

Hedges, C. (2015). *The Wages of Rebellion: The Moral Imperative of Revolt.* Nation Books.

Hedges, C. (2018). *America: The Farewell Tour.* Simon & Schuster.

Hedges, C. (2020, August 10). Chris Hedges: America's Death March. *Scheerpost.* https://scheerpost.com/2020/08/10/chris-hedges-americas-death-march/

Intergovernmental Panel on Climate Change. (2021). Summary for Policymakers. In V. Masson-Delmotte, P. Zhai, A. Pirani, S. L. Connors, C. Péan, S. Berger, N. Caud, Y. Chen, L. Goldfarb, M. I. Gomis, M. Huang, K. Leitzell, E. Lonnoy, J. B. R. Matthews, T. K. Maycock, T. Waterfield, O. Yelekçi, R. Yu, B. Zhou (Eds.). *Climate Change 2021: The Physical Science Basis. Contribution of Working Group I to the Sixth Assessment Report of the Intergovernmental Panel on Climate Change.* www.ipcc.ch/report/ar6/wg1/downloads/report/IPCC_AR6_WGI_SPM_final.pdf

Kafka, F. (1997). *The Castle* (J. A. Underwood, Trans.). Penguin Books (Original work published 1926).

Kashwan, P., MacLean, L. M., & García-López, G. A. (2019). Rethinking Power and Institutions in the Shadows of Neoliberalism: (An Introduction to a Special Issue of World Development). *World Development, 120*, 133–146. https://doi.org/10.1016/j.worlddev.2018.05.026

Klein, N. (2007). *The Shock Doctrine: The Rise of Disaster Capitalism*. Metropolitan Books.

Krogstrup, S., & Oman, W. (2019, September 4). *Macroeconomic and Financial Policies for Climate Change Mitigation: A Review of the Literature* (IMF Working Paper. No. 19/185). www.imf.org/en/Publications/WP/Issues/2019/09/04/Macroeconomic-and-Financial-Policies-for-Climate-Change-Mitigation-A-Review-of-the-Literature-48612

Lenton, T. M., Rockstrom, J., Gaffney, O., Rahmstorf, S., Richardson, K., Steffen, W., & Schellnhuber, H. J. (2019). Climate Tipping Points – Too Risky to Bet Against. *Nature, 575*, 592–595. https://doi.org/10.1038/d41586-019-03595-0

Li, T. M. (2007). *The Will to Improve: Governmentality, Development, and the Practice of Politics*. Duke University Press.

Livesey, B. (2020, September 10). End Times for American Democracy? An Interview With Chris Hedges. *National Observer*. www.nationalobserver.com/2020/09/10/analysis/end-times-american-democracy-interview-chris-hedges

Lucas, B. (2009, April 24). *Helpdesk Research Report: Changing Approaches to Technical Assistance*. Governance and Social Development Resource Centre. www.gsdrc.org/docs/open/hd586.pdf

Maizels, A., & Nissanke, M. K. (1984). Motivations for Aid to Developing Countries. *World Development, 12*(9), 879–900. https://doi.org/10.1016/0305-750X(84)90046-9

Meier, G. (1974). *Problems of Cooperation for Development*. Oxford University Press.

Mitchell, P. R., & Schoeffel, J. (Eds.). (2002). *Understanding Power: The Indispensable Chomsky*. The New Press.

Mosse, D. (2005). *Cultivating Development: An Ethnography of Aid Policy and Practice*. Pluto Press.

Mosse, D. (2013). The Anthropology of International Development. *Annual Review of Anthropology, 42*(1), 227–246. https://doi.org/10.1146/annurev-anthro-092412-155553

Mundkur, B. (2011). Incredible India: The Inconvenient Truth. *Asian Affairs, 42*(1), 83–97. https://doi.org/10.1080/03068374.2011.539330

Nikas, S., & Nussbaum, A. (2021, September 28). *Macron Back With Greek Defense Pact After Submarine Crisis*. Bloomberg. https://www.bloomberg.com/news/articles/2021-09-28/greece-buys-warships-from-france-signs-major-defense-pact?leadSource=uverify%20wall

Organisation for Economic Cooperation and Development. (2021, April 13). *COVID-19 Spending Helped to Lift Foreign Aid to an All-Time High in 2020* [Detailed Note]. www.oecd.org/dac/financing-sustainable-development/development-finance-data/ODA-2020-detailed-summary.pdf

Pâkzâd, P., & Magnussen, B. (2021, November 19). Noam Chomsky: Ending Climate Change 'Has to Come From Mass Popular Action', Not Politicians. An Interview with Noam Chomsky. *Jacobin*. www.jacobinmag.com/2021/11/noam-chomsky-climate-change-afghanistan-anarchism-china

Parker, M. (1995). Critique in the Name of What? Postmodernism and Critical Approaches to Organisation. *Organisation Studies, 16*(4), 553–564. https://doi.org/10.1177/017084069501600401

Piketty, T. (2014). *Capital in the Twenty-first Century* (A. Goldhammer, Trans.). Harvard University Press.

Piketty, T. (2015). *The Economics of Inequality* (A. Goldhammer, Trans.). Harvard University Press.

Polychroniou, C. J. (2021, July 29). Chomsky: We Need Genuine International Cooperation to Tackle the Climate Crisis. *Truthout*. https://truthout.org/articles/chomsky-we-need-genuine-international-cooperation-to-tackle-the-climate-crisis/

Prashad, V. (2007). *The Darker Nations: A People's History of the Third World*. The New Press.

Prashad, V. (2018, March 1). *In the Ruins of the Present*. Tricontinental Working Document No. 1. https://thetricontinental.org/working-document-1/

Roy, A. (1999). *The Cost of Living* [Jawaharlal Nehru Memorial Lecture No. 22, Trinity College, Cambridge]. Cambridge Trust. www.cambridgetrust.org/assets/documents/Lecture_22.pdf

Roy, A. (2003a, January 27). Confronting Empire [Speech audio recording, print edition February 14, 2003]. *Frontline*. https://frontline.thehindu.com/world-affairs/article30215627.ece

Roy, A. (2003b, May 13). *"Instant-Mix Imperial Democracy" (Buy One, Get One Free)* [Speech audio recording]. Retrieved February 24, 2022, from http://jonsenglishsite.info/Class%20Docs%205/6_InstantMix.pdf

Roy, A. (2003c). Noam Chomsky, Neoliberalism, and the New War on Iraq. *Contemporary Justice Review*, *6*(4), 321–327. https://doi.org/10.1080/1028258032000144767

Roy, A. (2003d, August 24). The Loneliness of Noam Chomsky. *The Hindu*. www.thehindu.com/todays-paper/tp-features/tp-sundaymagazine/the-loneliness-of-noam-chomsky/article28523764.ece

Roy, A. (2020a, February 12). *The Graveyard Talks Back: Arundhati Roy on Fiction in the Time of Fake News* [Text of the 2020 Clark Lecture in English Literature, Trinity College, Cambridge]. Literary Hub. https://lithub.com/the-graveyard-talks-back-arundhati-roy-on-fiction-in-the-time-of-fake-news/

Roy, A. (2020b, April 3). Arundhati Roy: 'The Pandemic Is a Portal'. *Financial Times*. www.ft.com/content/10d8f5e8-74eb-11ea-95fe-fcd274e920ca

Roy, A. (2021, September 3). The Future of American Power: Arundhati Roy on America's Fiery, Brutal Impotence. *The Economist*. www.economist.com/by-invitation/2021/09/03/arundhati-roy-on-americas-fiery-brutal-impotence

Saad-Filho, A., & Johnston, D. (Eds.). (2005). *Neoliberalism: A Critical Reader*. Pluto Press. https://doi.org/10.2307/j.ctt18fs4hp

Said, E. (2003). *Orientalism*. Penguin Books (Original work published 1978).

Shaikh, A. (2006). *Globalization and the Myths of Free Trade: History, Theory and Empirical Evidence* (1st ed.). Routledge. https://doi.org/10.4324/9780203966389

Smith, J. (2016). *Imperialism in the Twenty-First Century: Globalization, Super-Exploitation, and Capitalism's Final Crisis*. Monthly Review Press, NYU Press. www.jstor.org/stable/j.ctt15zc7jb

Sogge, D. (2001). Subalterns on the Aid Chain. In Humanitarian Studies Unit (Ed.). *Reflections on Humanitarian Action: Principles, Ethics and Contradictions* (pp. 120–141). Pluto Press. https://doi.org/10.2307/j.ctt18fs9tr.10

Subramanian, M. (2019, May 21). Anthropocene Now: Influential Panel Votes to Recognize Earth's New Epoch. *Nature*. https://doi.org/10.1038/d41586-019-01641-5

Tingle, L. (2021, September 17). Australia's Nuclear Submarine Deal Fundamentally Changes Our Relationship with the World. *ABC News*. www.abc.net.au/news/2021-09-18/australia-nuclear-submarine-deal-aukus-change-relationship-world/100471990

Todaro, M. (1981). *Economic Development in the Third World* (2nd ed.). Longman.

United Nations Educational, Scientific and Cultural Organization. (n.d.). *What Is Technical Assistance?* Retrieved February 24, 2022, from www.unesco.org/new/en/culture/themes/cultural-diversity/cultural-expressions/programmes/technical-assistance/what-is-technical-assistance/

Varoufakis, Y. (2020, September 4). Yanis Varoufakis: Capitalism Isn't Working. Here's an Alternative. *The Guardian*. www.theguardian.com/books/2020/sep/04/yanis-varoufakis-capitalism-isnt-working-heres-an-alternative

Wallace, T. (2004). NGO Dilemmas: Trojan Horses for Global Neoliberalism? *Socialist Register, 40*, 202–219. https://socialistregister.com/index.php/srv/article/view/5818/2714

World Bank. (n.d.). *Net Official Development Assistance and Official Aid Received (Current US$)* [Data set]. World Bank Open Data. https://data.worldbank.org/indicator/DT.ODA.ALLD.CD

2 Theoretical Framework

Introduction

This chapter establishes a theoretical basis for the empirical analyses and proposals for change that are the subjects of Chapters 3, 4 and 5. It does so, first, by reconciling what some might consider to be the philosophical incompatibility between, on the one hand, our critical theory approach to identifying the organisational shortcomings of LDI technical assistance and, on the other, our structural functionalist proposals for rectifying them.

Second, in much the same way as we do in Chapter 1 when we distinguish between the overarching ideology of neoliberalism and the organisation of LDI technical assistance at the 'lower reaches' of its bureaucracy, in this chapter we identify two corresponding levels of structural violence. The first is *historical* structural violence, which comprises the consequences of the imposition on societies of a burden of colonial and other forms of foreign oppression, exploitation and injustice, and which finds expression to the present day in social, political and economic institutions, conditions and practices. The second level is that of the *bureaucratic* structural violence of everyday life, which perpetuates and reinforces the historical structural violence of the environment in which it is found. Both levels of structural violence are relevant to all human endeavour. But in the Anthropocene, they undoubtedly weigh most heavily on the people of developing countries and poor and disempowered people everywhere.

Third, in a separate section, we consider Graeber's notions of 'interpretive labour' and 'bullshit jobs', which are integral to a full understanding of the nature and effects of bureaucratic structural violence.

Fourth, we discuss briefly the (structural functionalist) contingency theory approach to questions of organisation and management, which we employ to suggest where and how to make the design and delivery of technical assistance by LDIs less counter-productive for developing countries than it has been to date.

Reconciling the Irreconcilable?

One of the issues that we have had to contend with in writing this book is a seeming incommensurability between the two main strands of our argument.

DOI: 10.4324/9781003284352-2

In the first strand, we employ the critical theory of the likes of Graeber (2012, 2015, 2018), Gupta (2012), Farmer (2004) and Kafka (1926/1997) to explain why the organisation of grassroots development assistance is inherently and intrinsically structurally violent. The effects of this discussion are to shatter the thin veneer of niceties and platitudes of development rhetoric; and to reveal in some detail the extent of the domination and control exercised by donor petty officials and other supply-side actors that such rhetoric attempts to conceal.

Donor officials in charge of development assistance at the point of delivery bear the brunt of our criticism. For example, we characterise their roles as having a kind of immaculate omniscience and omnipotence, and infallibility, a reflection of power stemming from overwhelming economic and military might and the presumptions of civilisational superiority referred to in Chapter 1.[1] This, we suggest, is a function of both the inherent ('genetic') nature of the bureaucratic system of which they are a part and the Skinnerian-like positive reinforcements of their daily interactions with those over whom they have authority, which includes the power to inflict material harm. If everyone around you treats you as if you were all-knowing, all-powerful and incapable of error, it is hardly surprising that before long you start to believe it to be true. As we shall see, this combination of strong 'genetic' or structural predisposition and daily reinforcement of behaviour is a formidable mix.[2]

However, in the second strand of our argument, we employ structural functional means (which we refer to in Chapter 1 as the 'polar opposite' of critical theory) to pick up and put together again some of the pieces of the edifice that we have just torn down using critical theory. You may well ask how can we justify this cake-and-eat it approach to the task that we have set ourselves?

For at least part of the answer, there is perhaps no better place to start than Graeber's (2015) account of one of his own experiences of bureaucratic structural violence, which arose from his having to deal with the consequences of a series of debilitating strokes suffered by his mother. In the aftermath, nearly everything that he had to do entailed engaging with different organisations, such as British Medicaid, commercial banks and notary publics. The experience was time-consuming and frustrating, for reasons that will be familiar to most people in developed and developing countries alike. It involved a repeated 'coming-and-going' to the same bureaucrat or office because a form had not been filled in correctly. Or because he had contacted the wrong person following poor advice given by someone who should have known better. Or because his fear of offending an official and making things worse, or getting some relatively powerless lower-level functionary into trouble, made him suspend his own good judgement and any suggestion of overt criticism of the people or system that he was dealing with.

The universality of Graeber's experience is reflected in a fictitious case study written many years ago by the principal author as the opening chapter to a book titled *Personnel Management in Africa* (Blunt & Popoola, 1985). It concerned the attempts made by the main character – Joe – to gain access to a large private corporation in the hope of finding work as a management trainee. Though not expressed in the same terms, it is a story about bureaucratic structural violence. Here is an excerpt from Blunt and Popoola (1985, p. 3):

> The first barrier he had to overcome was getting into the firm's fenced compound. Two smartly uniformed guards patrolled behind a pair of large iron gates doing their best it seemed to ignore everyone. When a vehicle approached, they would saunter to the guard house for a visitors' book and then dawdle across to the lorry or car to have it signed; all the while hoping to be distracted *en route* so as to keep the by now impatient driver waiting for as long as possible. Eventually they would get around to swinging the gates open. This was their way of showing the driver and whoever else happened to be watching who was boss in that situation. Joe was not to know it then but later he would find that this attitude was prevalent throughout the public service, and indeed wherever individuals were accorded a certain amount of power and status, and the trappings to go with them. Their attitude became one of 'I am in a position where I can be of help to you. I have the power to make things happen, so show due deference and tread carefully or else'.

Joe complied meekly and eventually gained entry. But as he penetrated deeper into the bowels of the organisation, he encountered more of the same, and worse (Blunt & Popoola, 1985, pp. 4–5):

> There, seated behind a desk and an electric typewriter, studying her finger nails, was a secretary. She did not look up as Joe entered.
>
> 'Excuse me, I would like to arrange to see the Assistant Personnel Officer'.
>
> The secretary glanced at her watch. It was precisely 11.55; Joe knew because he had just had another elaborate look at his own timepiece seconds before.
>
> 'Mr Akedji is out to lunch'.
>
> 'Well perhaps I could see him after lunch. When will he be back?'
>
> The secretary had now shifted her attention to that day's newspaper, and was inspecting the ads. Not looking up: 'It's difficult to say when he will be back'.
>
> 'Well would it be possible to arrange an interview with him later in the week? Perhaps I could make an appointment now?' Joe continued patiently.
>
> 'Mr Akedji will be away next week'.
>
> 'What about the following week then?' asked Joe, his hopes dwindling fast.
>
> 'Mr Akedji never makes definite appointments more than a week in advance. You will have to come back next week'.
>
> He had returned the following week as instructed, but had been greeted with more excuses, and the suggestion that he 'go and come' once more. It was not until his third visit that the secretary enquired as to why he

wished to arrange an appointment with her boss. On being told that Joe was interested in becoming a management trainee, she informed him that only the Personnel Director took such decisions, and that Mr Akedji could not therefore be of any assistance.

This was the *coup de grace*. Comprehensively defeated, Joe had pursued his enquiries no further.

Graeber's and Joe's bureaucratic encounters suggest that many employees of both public and private bureaucracies are encouraged or allowed not to perform their formal duties as prescribed by their organisations or in accordance with the reasonable expectations of customers or clients (Graeber, 2012).

The examples also reveal the threats of harm of one form or another that are integral to the experience of bureaucratic structural violence – what Graeber (2015, p. 58) refers to as 'systemic inequalities' that are enforced by explicit or implicit threats of harm. In their attempts to cope, both Joe and Graeber found themselves continually having to compromise and behave in ways that they otherwise might not have imagined possible. It made them feel decidedly foolish and uncomfortable. And it all required a lot of effort. Effort expended mainly in trying to understand what was going on so they could avoid making a false step (Graeber, 2012).

Though thousands of miles apart geographically and separated by decades and great chasms of culture, poverty and wealth (historical structural violence), our accounts of Graeber's and Joe's experiences are uncannily similar. They demonstrate how the power, domination and control that are inherent in systems of bureaucracy are evident in even the most mundane of day-to-day transactions, in some respects at least, independent of time and space, national wealth or poverty (though, of course, the one percent will have others doing their dirty work for them, insulating them from the drudgery and indignities that everyone else is forced to endure).

The relevance of all of this to our being able to reconcile the seemingly irreconcilable is that while the two examples of bureaucratic structural violence that we have given do what we have just said, they also point to some of the critical interfaces between Graeber and Joe (as supplicants) and the agents of the oppressive and unyielding bureaucratic systems that they were dealing with. These interfaces show where relatively minor functional adjustments could have made a big difference for the better. Such changes would not have altered the generally domineering natures of the bureaucratic beasts in question but they could have softened their blows. That is, they could have made the transactions much less stressful and unpleasant for Graeber and Joe, and produced much better results for them more quickly. We assume that the functioning of all bureaucracies can be improved at the margins in these respects, but also more profoundly, as we argue in Chapter 5.

The other rationale for our use of structural functionalist, or managerial, remedies for the problems that we identify is that the people who control the bureaucratic systems that need to be reformed, and whom we therefore have to persuade, are only likely to be impressed by suggestions that come in a form that they are familiar and comfortable with.

The prosaic, piecemeal conventions of organisational development and change that could have been used to help to resolve at least some of the difficulties that Graeber and Joe had to contend with accord much more with Establishment notions of social engineering and are much less alarming to those in charge than wholesale so-called utopian attempts to produce an ideal alternative to Weberian bureaucracy or any other form of social control. They are, as Popper suggests, therefore much more likely to be accepted by decision-makers and those subjected to change. Indeed, in this book, our argument proceeds in principle very much as Popperian critical rationalism and piecemeal social engineering might dictate (e.g. Popper, 1962, 1971).

More than incidentally, we also show that it is not just the perpetrators of structural violence on the supply-side who must be held to account for what the iniquities of the system induce in supplicants, or 'force' them to do. Graeber himself, as he freely admits, (and Joe) could have been a little more attentive to detail and a little less cowed by the bureaucratic bullying than they were, thereby limiting what the system was able to get away with. But while there is clearly room for improvement on both sides of the power equation, just as clearly, most attention must be given to those who pull the strings or have the whip hand.

The validity of our critical theory analyses of the problems that need to be fixed in bureaucracies, and our general view of them and their genesis, are unaffected by any of our functionalist remedies, making for a perhaps uneasy, but workable, rapprochement between these otherwise unlikely bedfellows. That is to say, whatever its theoretical underpinnings, valid diagnosis is essential to effective treatment.

We are not alone in this. In the field of public health, for example, Farmer *et al.* (2006, p. 1689) do much the same in advocating both day-to-day and structural (proximal and distal) reformulations for health care directed at HIV prevention in the United States and Rwanda, while accepting that historical structural violence is often a major determinant of the distribution and outcome of disease. Their understanding of the historical structural violence in these countries led them to what they called 'proximal interventions' (like the functionalist organisational measures referred to in this book) that had little or nothing to do with clinical medicine *per se* but had significantly positive effects on morbidity and mortality. One such intervention gave greater power or 'agency' to the poor and greatly reduced their chances of contracting or dying from HIV. In the same way, they argued that a valid analysis and treatment of alcoholism among Native (US) Americans, or crack cocaine addiction among African (US) Americans, had to include a thorough understanding of the history of genocide and slavery in the United States.

Structural Violence

Graeber conceives of bureaucracy as a symbiosis of private profit-making and state power. Bureaucracies are created by governments but are shaped by, and primarily benefit, private (elite) interests. Like Kafka (1926/1997), he rejects the Weberian ideal of bureaucracy as constituting rule-based neutrality, instead arguing that elite connivance in its own interests is its dominant feature. Weber and scholars like Merton (1940), on the other hand, view the 'pain' associated with 'domination' as a necessary cost that it is the duty of workers (and customers) to bear and that this is in the interests of all employees because it maintains the organisational 'apparatus' and the 'rational' order that it imposes (Weber, 1946, p. 216). Departures from the formal order and rationality that Weber ascribes to bureaucracy were dysfunctional aberrations to be avoided and, where they occurred, stamped out (Blunt, 2021).

Kafka's emphasis is on resistance from within the bureaucratic apparatus, that is, resistance on the part of lower-level workers in particular to the application of rules that Kafka saw as deliberately inconsistent, personalised and abusive. He regarded as illusory the protections from 'arbitrary action' claimed by Weber to be prevented by rules that were designed to constrain or prevent 'impulsive' actions (Merton, 1940, p. 560). Kafka's 'bottom-up' perspective depicts bureaucracy as being in a state of perpetual internal conflict, between those in charge and those, mainly within the organisation, who suffer at their hands (Hodson *et al.*, 2013; Warner, 2007).[3]

For these reasons, for Kafka and Graeber and others like Marglin (1974), Weber's hierarchies and divisions of labour are instruments of oppression and alienation that should be resisted, and their formal goals and statements of purpose should be regarded as fig leaves for vested interests and frequently harmful intentions (Blunt, 2021).

However, unlike Kafka, Graeber's main interests, and ours, have to do with the violence inflicted by bureaucracies on those who seek to obtain services or legitimate benefit from them, as in our examples earlier. As we do here, Graeber acknowledges that the genesis of bureaucratic structural violence is rooted in historical, political, social and economic processes of domination and control.

Bureaucratic structural violence is universal. It is something that afflicts us all, wherever we are and whatever our circumstances might be (save, as we have suggested, for the one percent). Equally clearly, huge differences between people's circumstances and innate characteristics – power, poverty, health, education, age, race and gender – mean that their vulnerability to the structural violence inflicted by bureaucracies varies accordingly. The ability of poor people in developing countries in particular, but poor people everywhere, to cope with bureaucratic structural violence and to bear the financial and other costs involved is clearly much less than that of, say, comfortable middle-class people in rich countries.

To reiterate, in the pages that follow, we shall show that bureaucratic structural violence is a refashioned perpetuation of historical structural violence. As suggested in Chapter 1, since the late 1970s, the ideology of neoliberalism has been the principal means of subjugation – including the 'disciplining' of the so-called working classes (e.g. Bhattacharya, 2017) – and of exploitation and self-enrichment wielded by elites of privilege and power mainly in the LDIs. In fundamental ways, neoliberalism has assumed the mantle of colonialism and maintained its historical structural violence (e.g. Kohli, 2020), which in turn has spawned the bureaucratic structural violence that we discuss in this book. In the weasel words of public relations, it has been a 'seamless transition'. Former colonies in the West (the United States, Canada, etc.) have joined forces with the old hands of colonialism, like the United Kingdom and France, to make the most of what is on offer – by, in one way or another, compelling developing countries to perform their 'assigned functions' (Chomsky in Mitchell & Schoeffel, 2002). The so-called international community has profited greatly in the process. Development assistance has been integral to this and complicit.

For the poor in developing countries, combined, these two levels of structural violence are a crushing weight. No more so than during times of international and national emergency such as those brought about by the COVID-19 pandemic, as Mills *et al.* (2020) make clear in their discussion of the experience of Palestine where colonialism and neoliberalism have 'fragmented' the Palestinian people and their health systems, and made them aid-dependent and subject to the whims and vagaries of donor politics. In addition, since 2007, the 1.4 million Palestinians of the Gaza Strip have been victims of the structural violence of an Israeli-imposed air, sea and land blockade, which has disrupted medical supply chains, constrained the movement of patients and health workers, retarded the development of the public health system, and produced high levels of poverty, food insecurity and unemployment. Combined, these streams of historical structural violence have made Palestine extremely vulnerable to external shocks like the COVID-19 pandemic.

All of the countries in our sample are victims of historical structural violence, from its most extreme expression in the invasions, occupations and ongoing devastation of Afghanistan and Iraq, through the less immediate, but no less destructive, experiences of conquest and oppression by colonial regimes in Cambodia, Indonesia, Timor-Leste and, more distally and perhaps to a lesser degree, Samoa.

Our discussion of the delivery of technical assistance by LDIs in these countries uses the perspective afforded by historical structural violence to analyse, understand and explain the structurally violent bureaucratic behaviour of the different supply-side actors involved in the design and delivery of technical assistance, and to devise functional means for its improvement.

Interpretive Labour and Bullshit Jobs

It is plain from the examples given earlier, and our experiences of everyday life, that in order to extract benefit from bureaucracies, the populations that they claim to serve must engage in copious amounts of what Graeber (2012, 2015) refers to as 'interpretive labour'.

For bureaucratic customers or clients, the fruits of such labour are clearly a function of the bureaucracy that they are dealing with, and what demands it makes of supplicants. However, as suggested earlier, returns to interpretive labour will also be a function of supplicant characteristics. Gupta (2012), for example, shows that among those he studied in India, knowledge regarding who to bribe and how and when is unequally, and arbitrarily, distributed among system supplicants. Another illustration of such variability is evident in Chayes' (2021) bureaucratic encounters in Afghanistan:

> 'Come back tomorrow', barked the clerk, with a toss of his head, just as clerks had been telling my colleague for the past nine months. The subtext was clear: 'Come back tomorrow – with the money'.
>
> Abruptly, I found myself on top of the clerk's desk, sitting cross-legged amid all the documents and paperwork. 'Fine', I told him. 'Take as long as you want. But I'm staying right here until you complete our forms'. Eyes wide, the clerk got to work.

Such qualities are indeed unlikely to be distributed equally among system supplicants, implying as we might expect that there is variability in supplicant 'power'.[4]

The amount and nature of interpretive labour required of supplicants vary also according to the degree of power imbalance. As Graeber (2015, pp. 67–68) suggests, supplicants are forced to spend a great deal of time and 'imaginative energy' in their attempts to come to terms with the social dynamics of their circumstances and, in particular, how to divine and contend with the whims and wishes of those whom they serve. Their masters, on the other hand, can remain 'largely oblivious' to what transpires beneath them and are very rarely concerned with understanding the position of supplicants (that is, a complete absence of empathy, to which we shall return).

As the force or power available to supply-side masters increases, their need to engage in interpretive labour diminishes or disappears completely. The effect is that interpretive labour is almost entirely the work of subordinates, who are compelled to engage in it by the threat of psychological or physical violence inherent in the relations of domination and control. These presuppose and demand obedience, often thinly veiled by euphemisms like 'cooperation', 'coordination' or 'communication'.[5] Such interpretive labour is not a matter of choice. It is a structural feature of bureaucracy under neoliberalism.

Another effect of such conditions is that they are inimical to critical thinking, creativity and imagination. Indeed, the aim appears to be to stamp them out because they are seen as threats to the *status quo,* because they undermine subservience and presage change. Such denial entails what Graeber (2018) refers to as 'spiritual violence' whereby the pleasures of imaginative labour are the sole province of masters. This produces in supplicants or workers feelings of alienation, as if the work that they do belong to those who control them.[6]

Clearly, also, the consequences of failures of interpretive labour for supplicants vary enormously, from the relatively benign – as in the Nigerian (Joe) and British (Graeber) cases discussed earlier – through the seriously damaging to the fatal, as in the public health cases. A particularly tragic and poignant example of the latter, and of the confluence of historical and bureaucratic structural violence, is that of Anite, who, in Farmer's painstaking account, made fruitless visits to 14 clinics in Haiti to find treatment for a breast tumour that had become a 'fungating mass' (Farmer, 2004, p. 306).

Anite's experience and that of countless others like her in poor and oppressed countries, or the consequences for ordinary Afghans of the historical and bureaucratic structural violence discussed by Chayes (2021), are the most representative.

The examples of bureaucratic structural violence that we give later in this book do not have the same dramatic, tragic immediacy of Anite's case. They are more distal and indirect, but in many instances no less lethal or seriously damaging in the same or other ways.

In his 2018 work, Graeber addresses the question of 'bullshit' jobs and their prevalence. These are jobs that have been deliberately created to reinforce hierarchy and control within public and private organisations so as to optimise profits or attain political objectives, and so on. For Graeber (2018, p. 79), capitalism creates such jobs in order to maintain the form or character of its bureaucratic apparatus. Frequently, they are jobs in which the incumbent has nothing useful to do. Jobs that could vanish without trace, that is, without damaging the organisation's performance or without anyone noticing that they had gone. Or jobs that are so pernicious that their disappearance would actually improve performance. Holders of such jobs therefore spend much of their time pretending to be doing something useful when they are not and cannot. In a vain search for real purpose and meaning, 'bullshit' job holders therefore adopt the perspectives and interests of their superiors. They substitute rule enforcement and micromanagement for 'meaning', while resenting those who have real work to do.

At the same time, bullshit jobs can cause feelings of 'hopelessness, depression, and self-loathing' among incumbents, who sense the iniquity and pointlessness of what they do (Graeber, 2018, p. 132).[7] Such jobs are frequently prestigious, held by well-paid, ambitious, professionals who 'secretly' recognise these aspects of their work and feel undeserving of the benefits they have enjoyed as a result. As if everything they have achieved is 'based on a lie', which in Graeber's (2018, p. 32) view, it is.

Our discussion of the data presented in the chapters that follow views them through a multi-focal lens of historical and bureaucratic structural violence, interpretive labour and bullshit jobs.

Functionalist Remedies – Contingency Theory

Contingency theory forms the basis of our functional analysis of what can be done to reduce bureaucratic structural violence and to make the functioning of the lower reaches of LDI technical assistance more authentic, empathetic and altruistic. This approach to questions of organisation and management requires that the strategy, structure, staffing and culture of organisations be adapted to their internal and external operating environments.

A pioneering and eminent contingency theorist of organisational structure and design, strategic management, leadership and organisational change is Henry Mintzberg (e.g. Mintzberg, 1979, 1983, 1989a, 1989b), whose work we draw on extensively later, as we have done before in our discussions of management and organisation in developing countries (e.g. Blunt, 1991; Blunt & Jones, 1992).

In contingency theory, how the operating environments of organisations are viewed of course is a function of explicit or implicit theories about the world that we hold. Social facts are interpreted through a lens made up of these theories, making one person's perception of drowning another's perception of waving. That is, we do not perceive worldly phenomena as they are, but as we are (Blunt, 2021, p. 76). As the years have gone by and our experiences of mostly bad technical assistance have piled one upon the other, we have become more and more convinced of the validity of critical theories' assessment of its grim realities and of its sponsors and perpetrators. Our perceptions of what matters in organisational environments in developing countries clearly reflect this. Poverty and inequality reduction, sustainability and the environment are central to our thinking. As the sheen of development rhetoric, these for so long empty words are on everyone's lips. Nevertheless, our aim in the pages that follow is to reduce the gap between such rhetoric and the behaviour of (in particular) the supply-side actors who espouse it, and to persuade the holders of power that greater authenticity (less hypocrisy and deceit), empathy and altruism is needed urgently and is in everyone's interests.

We say 'mostly bad technical assistance' because, occasionally, we have managed, through a combination of exhaustive interpretive labour and good fortune, to achieve some genuinely developmental results in oppressive bureaucratic conditions. It was these rare chinks in the armour of bureaucratic structural violence that made us think that more general repair of supply-side bureaucracies might be possible as well as worthwhile.

Notes

1 The Eurocentric view is challenged persuasively by Graeber and Wengrow (2021) by taking serious account of what they call 'indigenous critique', that is, contributions to social thought that fall outside of the European canon.

2 This is the received wisdom for explaining aberrant human behaviour. The American Psychological Association (n.d.) refers to it as 'diathesis-stress' theory, meaning that psychological and physical illnesses are caused by a combination of genetic or biological predisposition for a condition (diathesis) and environmental stressors that precipitate onset.

3 Merton (1940, p. 565) regarded 'vested interests' solely as the bureaucrat's attempt to protect his/her own position within the system from the effects of formal change, rather than the misuse of the authority of the position to satisfy personal or other external interests.

4 It is also possible of course that, in our example earlier, Chayes may not have been perceived as a genuine supplicant, but more as an oppressor masquerading as one, a wolf in sheep's clothing.

5 This is Orwellian *Newspeak* – a language so bland and impoverished that there are no words that can even hint at the idea of dissent, as if to render impossible other thoughts or forms of expression (Orwell, 1949/2000, p. 312).

6 Some of the cases of structural violence discussed later in this book in part were also designed to constrain critical thinking and creativity (and altruism) in workers whose lives, it could be said, had been devoted to them. For many of the supplicants, their notions of self revolved around 'imaginative labour', making its denial even more likely to provoke alienation, resentment and feelings of injustice.
7 We say 'can' because our experience shows that some holders of bullshit jobs seem to relish them precisely because they are able to exercise control through rule enforcement and micromanagement.

References

American Psychological Association. (n.d.). Diathesis-Stress Model. In *APA Dictionary of Psychology*. Retrieved February 23, 2022, from https://dictionary.apa.org/diathesis-stress-model

Bhattacharya, T. (Ed.). (2017). *Social Reproduction Theory: Remapping Class, Recentering Oppression*. Pluto Press. https://doi.org/10.2307/j.ctt1vz494j

Blunt, P. (1991). Organizational Culture and Development. *International Journal of Human Resource Management*, *2*(1), 55–71. https://doi.org/10.1080/09585199100000051

Blunt, P. (2021). Development Undone: Weber, Kafka, and the Organisation of Supply-Side Vested Interests. *Journal of Interdisciplinary Economics*, *33*(1), 74–102. https://doi.org/10.1177/0260107919896879

Blunt, P., & Jones, M. (1992). *Managing Organisations in Africa*. Walter de Gruyter.

Blunt, P., & Popoola, O. (1985). *Personnel Management in Africa (Modern Management in Africa)*. Longman.

Chayes, S. (2021, September 3). Afghanistan's Corruption Was Made in America: How Self-Dealing Elites Failed in Both Countries. *Foreign Affairs*. www.foreignaffairs.com/articles/united-states/2021-09-03/afghanistans-corruption-was-made-in-america

Farmer, P. (2004). An Anthropology of Structural Violence. *Current Anthropology*, *45*(3), 305–325. https://doi.org/10.1086/382250

Farmer, P. E., Nizeye, B., Stulac, S., & Keshavjee, S. (2006). Structural Violence and Clinical Medicine. *PLOS Medicine*, *3*(10), 1–6. https://doi.org/10.1371/journal.pmed.0030449

Graeber, D. (2012). Dead Zones of the Imagination: On Violence, Bureaucracy, and Interpretive Labour. The Malinowski Memorial Lecture, 2006. *HAU: Journal of Ethnographic Theory*, *2*(2), 105–128. https://doi.org/10.14318/hau2.2.007

Graeber, D. (2015). *The Utopia of Rules: On Technology, Stupidity, and the Secret Joys of Bureaucracy*. Melville House.

Graeber, D. (2018). *Bull Shit Jobs: A Theory*. Simon and Schuster.

Graeber, D., & Wengrow, D. (2021). *The Dawn of Everything: A New History of Humanity*. Allen Lane.

Gupta, A. (2012). *Red Tape: Bureaucracy, Structural Violence, and Poverty in India*. Duke University Press.

Hodson, R., Martin, A. W., Lopez, S. H., & Roscigno, V. J. (2013). Rules Don't Apply: Kafka's Insights on Bureaucracy. *Organization*, *20*(2), 256–278. https://doi.org/10.1177/1350508412443581

Kafka, F. (1997). *The Castle* (J. A. Underwood, Trans.). Penguin Books (Original work published 1926).

Kohli, A. (2020). *Imperialism and the Developing World: How Britain and the United States Shaped the Global Periphery*. Oxford University Press. https://doi.org/10.1093/oso/9780190069629.001.0001

Marglin, S. A. (1974). What Do Bosses Do?: The Origins and Functions of Hierarchy in Capitalist Production. *Review of Radical Political Economics*, *6*(2), 60–112. https://doi.org/10.1177/048661347400600206

Merton, R. K. (1940). Bureaucratic Structure and Personality. *Social Forces*, *18*(4), 560–568. https://doi.org/10.2307/2570634

Mills, D., Wispelwey, B., Muhareb, R., & Gilbert, M. (2020, March 27). Structural Violence in the Era of a New Pandemic: The Case of the Gaza Strip. *The Lancet*. https://doi.org/10.1016/S0140-6736(20)30730-3

Mintzberg, H. (1979). *The Structuring of Organisations*. Prentice-Hall.

Mintzberg, H. (1983). *Structure in Fives: Designing Effective Organisations*. Prentice-Hall.

Mintzberg, H. (1989a). *Mintzberg on Management: Inside Our Strange World of Organizations*. Free Press.

Mintzberg, H. (1989b). The Structuring of Organizations. In D. Asch & C. Bowman (Eds.). *Readings in Strategic Management* (pp. 322–352). Palgrave. https://doi.org/10.1007/978-1-349-20317-8_23

Mitchell, P. R., & Schoeffel, J. (Eds.). (2002). *Understanding Power: The Indispensable Chomsky*. The New Press.

Orwell, G. (2000). *Nineteen Eighty-Four*. Penguin Books (Original work published 1949).

Popper, K. R. (1962). *Conjectures and Refutations: The Growth of Scientific Knowledge*. Basic Books Publishers.

Popper, K. R. (1971). *The Open Society and Its Enemies, Volume 2: The High Tide of Prophecy: Hegel, Marx, and the Aftermath*. Princeton University Press.

Warner, M. (2007). Kafka, Weber and Organization Theory. *Human Relations*, *60*(7), 1019–38. https://doi.org/10.1177/0018726707081156

Weber, M. (1946). Bureaucracy. In H. H. Gerth and C. Wright Mills (Eds). *From Max Weber* (pp. 196–244). Oxford University Press.

3 Historical Structural Violence, Donor Strategy and the 'Ownership' Problem

Introduction

In the so-called aid community, it is widely held that the idea of 'ownership' in development assistance is difficult to define and put into effect (e.g. Carothers, 2015; Martinez-Alvarez, 2018).[1] Authoritative Establishment organisations like the OECD (2011) explain the disappointing results by asserting that for both donors and recipients, 'fulfilling responsibilities' has simply been a 'tough challenge'(!). A tough challenge made tougher it is said because it has not been clear which agency in a recipient country makes the decisions about the uses to which aid should be put; because recipient-country development strategies and 'operational frameworks' are not strong enough; and because there is too much corruption and not enough transparency. Neither has enough been done to combat (demand-side) corruption: while anticorruption measures have been devised and formalised, it has not been possible to discern 'tangible progress'. Donors, on the other hand, are said not to have been sufficiently transparent about aid flows.

Nowhere in such evaluations is it ever suggested that perhaps a little too much is made of the conceptual difficulties, that donor protests may be overdone. Equally hard to find is any suggestion that donors may not always really mean, or do, what they say, for reasons of political or economic or geostrategic self-interest.

On the other hand, our experience in the field over the last 30 years has shown that donors have no difficulty whatsoever in deciding what *they* 'own', that is, what might constitute an infringement of their interests or state sovereignty, no matter how slight or tangential it may be. In the examples that we give later and in the chapters that follow (particularly Chapter 4), we show repeatedly how sensitive donors can be to the crossing of *their* 'red lines' and how trigger-happy they are with 'red flags' when something is not to their liking. For empathetic development 'partners', transposing this experience to recipient governments, by putting themselves in their shoes, would be routine. When it is not, and when weak excuses are made for inaction or poor performance in this regard, we must wonder why.

The reasons for these contrasting observations are not difficult to find. To begin with, wonder at the muted and anodyne criticism of donors and the

DOI: 10.4324/9781003284352-3

proclivity for victim blaming by organisations like the OECD vanishes as soon as we recognise that all of the LDIs are major financial contributors to the OECD and to other multilateral development assistance organisations.[2] By far the largest contributor to the OECD, the United States, is also one of the worst offenders. Analysis and attribution of fault or blame, in such evaluations, are therefore always likely to be muted and circumscribed and to bear little resemblance to the distribution of power, or responsibility for poor performance, between donors and recipients.

Most of all, however, such partial evaluations reflect a deeper and more serious malaise. Some time ago, referring particularly to the United States, Chomsky and Herman (1973) showed that attribution of meaning to social events by LDIs, and unprincipled behaviour generally, have a long and duplicitous history. In particular, concern about violence and bloodbaths has been highly selective (in the United States, but also in Moscow and Beijing), meaning that some bloodbaths are treated as 'benign' or even beneficial, while others are widely and publicly condemned.

Roy (2004, p. 49) makes the same point when she says that in the Establishment lexicon the meaning of terms like *freedom* has little, or nothing, to do with freedom as we would want it, as opposed to freedom to do pretty much anything you please. When LDI interests are at stake, it seems plain that self-serving 'flexibility' of interpretation and meaning regarding such terms as bloodbaths and freedom will transpose effortlessly to no less a degree of flexibility regarding 'ownership'.

Our discussion later of the principal agents of donor power and their behaviour regarding a commonsensical notion of recipient government ownership[3] is set against a background of historical structural violence and of LDI donor self-interest and opportunism. The weight and direction of the historical structural violence are so overwhelming that we should be astonished if the subsequent behaviour of LDIs (the perpetrators of historical structural violence), or donor 'strategy', was anything other than self-interested. Unsurprisingly, our evidence confirms this.

We begin, first, by outlining the main reference point for the definitions of the related terms of 'ownership', 'harmonisation' and 'alignment' (the Paris Declaration of 2005, hereafter PD), and briefly discussing some of their limitations.

Second, from 2003 up until the declaration of the COVID-19 pandemic in mid-March 2020, we provide examples from our sample of programmes and projects that demonstrate that LDI behaviour regarding such questions appears to have had little to do with definitional problems or a lack of understanding about ownership agency,[4] and much more to do with questions surrounding the maintenance of donor power and control, administrative convenience and self-interest.

Third, we show how for one programme in our sample such LDI behaviour continued, and in some ways worsened, after the declaration of the COVID-19 pandemic.

And, finally, fourth, we consider what the 'ownership' case studies that we have discussed tell us about the forms of bureaucratic structural violence involved and reform possibilities.

The Paris Declaration Benchmark

More than 100 countries and international organisations signed the PD and endorsed its principles of 'ownership', 'alignment', 'harmonisation', 'managing for results' and mutual accountability. According to Lundsgaarde and Engberg-Pedersen (2019), the PD was designed to do away with the 'donor-driven approaches' of the past and to give control of development 'cooperation' to developing countries.

To this day, the PD continues to be one of the principal reference points for the idea of national or government ownership. In 2011, we concluded that the PD and other declarations like it are so loosely stated that they can accommodate a wide range of donor self-interest (Blunt *et al.*, 2011). We demonstrated that these qualities were most pronounced when it came to the notions of 'national ownership and government leadership' and 'harmonisation'. For example, the PD sets targets in these respects for all signatory countries. Yet, at the same time, it leaves room for 'choice', 'adaptation', 'interpretation' and 'judgement' in relation to those targets. We pointed to two possible interpretations of these findings. A 'sceptical' interpretation that would regard the internal inconsistencies as deliberate designed to give the appearance of a desire to achieve one aim while intentionally allowing 'complete *laissez-faire*'. And a 'more benign' interpretation of the document's limitations, namely, that they were merely what one might expect from drafting done by a committee constrained by consensus decision-making. We concluded that both interpretations were convenient for donors whose principal interests were 'maximising control and aid distinctiveness'.

Our discussion of the empirical evidence from the seven countries in our sample examines the validity of these conclusions over time and in a wide variety of development settings.

Whose Ownership and for What Purposes?

In the following paragraphs, we discuss evidence of donor behaviour regarding government ownership of technical assistance programmes and projects, and attempt to explain its expression and character by analysing the interests and relative power of the principal stakeholders. We do so against background snapshots of the often extremely destructive historical structural violence experienced by each of the seven countries in our sample, the 'iron in the soul of imperialism' referred to by Prashad (2018).[5]

The evidence is discussed in the chronological order in which the programmes were implemented, as set out in Table 1.1 of Chapter 1. All of the cases clearly demonstrate that government ownership is circumscribed by donor power, self-interest and control. For the donors in question, government ownership was mostly part of the window dressing for technical assistance, a standard adornment of project documents. All of the programmes and projects that we discuss made formal statements of commitment to the notions of government ownership, alignment and harmonisation, sometimes by explicit reference to the PD.

Cambodia (2003–2006)

Few countries have experienced such recent and extreme historical structural violence as Cambodia. From the mid-nineteenth to mid-twentieth centuries, the country was under French colonial rule. Generations of colonial coercion, forced assimilation and human rights violations prepared the ground for what was to come (Blakemore, 2019).

US involvement came in the form of a CIA-sponsored right-wing coup in Cambodia in March 1970 that installed the Lon Nol military dictatorship. A regime that quickly sought to gain (Cambodian) peasant support by carrying out a pogrom of local Vietnamese. The subsequent invasion by the United States and its client government in Saigon was not intended to stop further bloodshed but to support the perpetrators who were close to being overthrown. Three years later, this was followed by extensive bombing of densely populated areas in an attempt to prevent the fall of the US-backed regime, which was on the point of collapse (Chomsky & Herman, 1973).[6]

Soon after, Cambodia was subjected to arguably its most devastating period of historical structural violence, at the hands of the Khmer Rouge. During the short period from their seizure of power in 1975 to 1979, when the country was invaded by Vietnamese forces, the Khmer Rouge (the Communist Party of Kampuchea) reduced the state to ruins. Their aim was to wipe the slate clean. A goal they achieved by the evacuation of city populations to rural areas; the suspension of education and the abolition of government institutions; forced labour; re-education programmes; the abolition of private property; religious repression; and the neglect of infrastructure. Tens of thousands of Cambodians were executed and hundreds of thousands died of starvation. All told, 'excess mortality' was greater than 1.7 million. Millions lost relatives, homes and livelihoods. On their arrival, the Vietnamese found an institutional *tabula rasa* – no legal framework, no organised religions, no public administration, no private networks, no military or police and no hospitals or schools (Gottesman, 2002).

When the Vietnamese withdrew 10 years later, in 1989, they left behind a state that was relatively stable but whose economy was weak and constrained by collective agriculture. Poverty was widespread and hundreds of thousands of refugees lived in border camps. Aid flows had dried-up following the collapse of the Soviet bloc, and government revenues were insufficient to support anything but the most rudimentary of services (Blunt & Turner, 2005).

The United Nations Transitional Authority arrived soon after and provided 'an edgy incomplete pause in war-making' (Kamm, 1998, p. 39). It departed in 1993 without having improved political stability or governance. A coup led by the Cambodian People's Party (CPP) followed in 1997. Two years later (in 1999), the CPP was elected to govern and has been in power ever since. Twenty years after the defeat of the Khmer Rouge, the country was still in turmoil. Ruled by political elites who were more concerned with dividing and defending the spoils of office than they were with good governance (Blunt & Turner, 2005).

Such political opportunism – on both the supply- and demand-sides – is the defining feature of ownership of the technical assistance discussed in this case study.[7] As we shall see, it is an interesting example of the ways in which both donor and government self-interests can be served by the technical assistance that is given.

The case examines ownership questions surrounding the provision of technical assistance to a programme of administrative and political decentralisation to the lowest level of government in the country, commune councils (the Programme). Following Blunt and Turner (2005), there were five features of the technical assistance that stood out.

First, there was strong, largely ideological, support among donors for decentralisation programmes that involved extensive community participation and delegation of decision-making power to the lowest levels of local government. Donor interest stemmed entirely from the plausible conceptual links that could be drawn between such programmes and democratic governance.[8] At the time, decentralisation programmes were in fashion and an easy sell to superiors in headquarters, as well as to the recipient government (the CPP), who were just as interested in the maintenance of politically correct appearances and were heavily dependent on development assistance.

Second, there was a generally low level of knowledge (and interest) among donors regarding comparative and Cambodian evidence of the realities of decentralisation and deconcentration and their effects on poverty reduction. The research evidence clearly showed that decentralisation was not a good idea, and rarely worked, where state governance at the centre was weak, as was clearly the case at the time in Cambodia. In addition, within government, there was already considerable tension and conflict over power and resources connected with the institutional arrangements surrounding it.

Deconcentration would have made a lot more sense in the circumstances. But the differences between deconcentration and decentralisation were not sufficiently, or at all, understood by donors. Attempts to raise the subject in conversation tended to elicit blank stares because anything that was seen to weaken the cosmetic links between the Programme and the promotion of democratic governance was off-limits. Written advice in the form of explanatory briefing notes also had little or no effect (e.g. Blunt, 2004a). Goal displacement was inevitable in these circumstances, towards easily delivered and measurable outputs such as 'capacity building' (training) and away from (unattainable) outcomes like poverty reduction.

Third, at the vanguard of the donor-sponsored 'decentralisation produces democratic governance' movement in Cambodia was the well-established, and large, Seila programme.[9] Seila was well liked by donors because of its efficient delivery of country-wide training for decentralisation to all of the 1,621 commune councils in the country, and because its financial management procedures were sound. Attaching a smaller programme to it, and implementing 'lessons learned', was therefore an appealing low-risk strategy for donors, whereas questioning Seila's whole *raison d'etre* by debating the virtues of decentralisation would have threatened substantial financial and reputational sunk costs. The contemplation of alternatives was ruled out.

Fourth, combined, the first three points constituted a strong 'push' effect for decentralisation from donors. Packaged in this way, the Programme ticked all of the (donor) boxes. It appeared to be helping to deliver an important component of democratic governance found in many Western countries, decentralisation. The existing and much-loved Seila programme on decentralisation was a convenient bandwagon for the Programme to attach itself to. And 'progress' could be measured straightforwardly by recording training body counts. The Programme set sail on these grounds with government support. This was a triumph of form over substance in the face of strong counter-evidence and argument, which were simply suppressed or ignored.[10]

Government (the CPP) supported the Programme for two reasons. First, because it entailed very little dilution of central control, government was content to play along.[11] Second, government's principal interest was the consolidation of the political power of the CPP. One feature of the Programme was particularly helpful to this end because it entailed the construction of commune council office buildings in every commune. This provided locally elected officials (many of whom were CPP members) with opportunities for predation and personal gain through the award of contracts.[12] And the buildings themselves became highly visible and enduring concrete symbols of the reach and national presence of the CPP.

The political consolidation of the ruling party undoubtedly contributed to much-needed stability at the time. But the long-term cost has been the entrenchment of the CPP and a political system built by its strong-man leader, Hun Sen, on increasing levels of 'control, coercion, and co-option' (Peou, 2019, pp. 46, 57) combined with implacable opposition to reform that might weaken the position of the ruling party.

On the question of 'whose ownership and for what purposes?', it is clear that government and donor interests were largely satisfied. Donor interest in the surface appearance of being seen to promote democratic governance by supporting decentralisation was largely met. Government acceded to donor pressure in this regard because the weak form of decentralisation involved did not threaten central control by the CPP and, at the same time, presented opportunities for establishing the CPP's presence nationwide and rewarding party member loyalty in the communes. The intervening years have demonstrated unequivocally what the research evidence on decentralisation at the time would have predicted, namely, that development circumstances like those of Cambodia at the turn of the century are not fertile grounds for the growth of authentic democratic institutions and governance. Donors were aware of this but chose to ignore it for reasons that we have suggested earlier.

At the time and since, most Cambodians are likely to have benefitted very little from any of this. Meanwhile, authoritarian rule under the CPP and Hun Sen has prospered.

Timor-Leste (2006–2008)

For hundreds of years before the Indonesian invasion in 1975, East Timor had been subject to Portuguese colonial rule (from 1702). By the time of the landmark plebiscite held in 1999, in which 75% of the population voted for independence, East Timor had been under the control of Indonesia for 24 years. Despite their geographical colocation on the island of Timor, there was a considerable ethnic, linguistic and religious divide between East Timor and Indonesia. More than 95% of East Timorese are Roman Catholics, and one of the main Indigenous languages, Tetum, is spoken in parts of Indonesian West Timor, but nowhere else in the Indonesian archipelago. More than 30% of the population of Timor-Leste are native speakers of the language. The Tetum language became an important symbol and rallying point for independence when it was adopted by the Catholic Church as its official liturgical language.

US- and Australian-backed Indonesian rule of East Timor was brutal and resulted in the deaths of more than 200,000 East Timorese, equivalent at the time to a near-genocidal 25% to 30% of the population. Further slaughter and expulsion followed the 1999 vote. Much of the country was devastated and within a matter of weeks more than 10,000 might have been killed (Chomsky, 1999). In addition, more than 250,00 were forced across the border into Indonesian West Timor, in what amounted to a 'scorched earth policy' (Rourke, 2019).

Before the 1999 vote, explicit threats by senior Indonesian military officers told of what was to come. If the pro-independents won, everything was to be destroyed. Army orders were to massacre people in every village. The independence movement was to be wiped out, from top to bottom. All of this was understood by Indonesia's 'foreign friends' (Chomsky, 1999). Those countries that might have been able to prevent this tragedy – the United States, the United Kingdom and its 'subimperialist' offspring Australia (Chomsky in Polychroniou, 2022; Roberts, 2022) – chose instead to actively support Indonesia (Robinson, 2011).

The ramifications of this historical structural violence were still playing out when the programme that is the subject of our discussion here commenced operations. Among these ramifications, and particularly for young men, the history of occupation and repression recounted earlier, the long freedom struggle and periodic violence since independence had created a culture in which violence was regarded as a legitimate form of retribution and fulfilment of social obligation. Another ramification was that fledgling government institutions and weak law enforcement meant that during this period criminals (including those responsible for crimes of high treason) were not held to account, which seriously undermined respect for the law (Blunt, 2009).

It was in these volatile and unpredictable circumstances that development assistance to an independent Timor-Leste was soon being delivered by the very countries that had rendered material support to Indonesia in its invasion of the country. During the occupation, the same countries had then turned a blind eye to the atrocities that were being committed by Indonesian forces and Indonesian-backed militias. This willingness to 'switch horses' opportunistically, as soon as it was convenient to Australia's and the US's interests to do so, would not have been lost on the new government. But, as we shall see later, Timor-Leste's condition at the time was such that it was in no position to refuse outside 'help'.

Meanwhile, Australia, in its development assistance mode, reverberating with all the bells and whistles of the PD, appeared in the vanguard of donor support and set about its business, straight-faced. That is, without any apparent sense of hypocrisy or guilt and with no break in step. The transition from partner-in-crime with a brutal oppressor to 'development partner' of the victim observed a well-worn routine of LDI 'best practice', established in places like Vietnam, the Philippines and Guatemala (Chomsky & Herman, 1973), soon to be followed in Iraq, and threatening now with the Taliban government in Afghanistan. Yet another example of the selective attribution of meaning by LDIs noted at the beginning of this chapter.

The conditions in Timor-Leste at the time were of course bleak, characterised by episodic and sometimes serious civil disturbance in the capital, Dili, and by a pervasive atmosphere of chronic lawlessness (and transgressor impunity) and political uncertainty and discord.

In March 2007, the security situation deteriorated to the point where it became necessary to evacuate all foreign Programme personnel from the country for a period of 12 days. Thereafter, the increased presence in the country of UN police and foreign defence force personnel combined with the gradual rebuilding of local security forces reduced the scale and frequency of outbreaks of violence. Both the presidential and parliamentary election periods were relatively peaceful and, following reportedly free and fair elections, a new government was formed in early August. Immediately following the announcement of the new Government of Timor-Leste (GoTL), there were a number of violent protests in Dili involving arson and attacks against UN police. Dozens of UN vehicles were damaged by stoning. By mid-August, the security situation in Dili had been brought under control, but there were serious sporadic outbreaks of violence and arson elsewhere in the country, particularly in and around Viqueque and Baucau.

The governance context generally was fraught with violence and complex. Its principal characteristics were as follows: first, chronic, widespread and severe poverty affecting the mass of the population, but with marked regional disparities. Second, high expectations among ordinary people everywhere of rapid poverty reduction and development following independence. Third, perceptions that government was failing to fulfil expectations; combined with rumours of elite enrichment, political and ethnic partiality, and so on.

Fourth, there were widespread fears that poverty and unemployment might not improve, or worsen, and other problems would become apparent (e.g. inter-regional disparities, and threats to land tenure). Fifth, the social strains of poverty and unemployment, combined with perceptions of government partiality and failure, produced perceptions of social exclusion – and, therefore, divisions – along ethnic lines. Sixth, such ethnic divisions were sharpened and crystallised by a number of 'triggers' (one involving the army) that led to serious civil disturbance. Seventh, government's ability to cope unaided was tested to the limit, making outside assistance necessary. And eighth, political discord was heightened by the opportunities created for acquiring political power and control over resources.

The legacies of Indonesian administration during the occupation also meant that corruption in government would be likely to be regarded as standard practice (e.g. Blunt *et al.*, 2012a). And it was not very long before patronage-based systems of social exchange and obligation began to emerge in the new government. When combined with generally weak loyalties to the state, high levels of poverty and inequality, and the availability of rich pickings for ruling elites, the likelihood was that patronage would be strongly defended and largely immune to the conventions of technocratic reform (Blunt, 2009, p. 90).

These were the conditions that prevailed at the time for a programme that sought (conventionally) to help provide for a sustainable and effective system of governance and public administration for the delivery of high-quality public services, and to strengthen the capacity-building institutions and processes to build individual and institutional capacity, that is, to 'build back better' a country that you had helped to destroy in the first place.[13] The fragile, helpless condition of the state meant that the GoTL had no choice but to accept whatever assistance was on offer.

For reasons that we shall discuss more fully in Chapter 4 (and, as we shall see, more by chance than design), in this case, donor supervision of the Programme was relatively hands-off and seemed almost empathetic, allowing the Programme manager (the principal author) considerable latitude in the design, with the GoTL, of projects of assistance. The organisational culture that resulted was marked by mutual respect and trust combined with healthy and undefensive critical debate of high quality concerning the development and management issues confronting the Programme. Moreover, Programme performance was not hindered by an over-emphasis on control but, rather, was characterised by support for the positions taken by the Programme on sometimes difficult issues and by acceptance of the professional advice it gave. The principal author can recall saying at the time that the Programme was thankful (to the donor) for humanising the management relationship with good humour, thoughtful consideration, warmth and courtesy.[14]

These relatively benign and unusual conditions allowed for – indeed encouraged – government ownership. But it was ownership borne of exhaustion from decades of historical structural violence, repeated betrayal by the 'international community', chronic civil unrest since independence, desperate and urgent need, no choice, and a government that knew little about the business of governing and had no experience of it. In short, a government that was on its knees. The Programme was simply an offer that could not be refused.

It is likely also, however, that, like their Australian counterparts, the most senior officials in the recipient government were preoccupied with other things, not least those associated with Timor-Leste's substantial natural resource wealth. When there is a high concentration of power in the hands of small ruling elites and this is combined with an abundance of natural resources, comparative evidence indicates that 'personal aggrandisement' is inevitable and is regarded as a prerogative of political power (Blunt, 2009).

One might well ask, where in any of this is there a suggestion that the donor did not really understand what the 'national interest' might mean or what 'ownership' of it might entail? Understanding only becomes a problem it seems when it applies to the interests of others, when any old excuse will do for behaving as you please. Or you simply assert, as your reason, what development assistance claims not really to understand – as Prime Minister Morrison did after reneging on the French submarine deal in 2021 and Gareth Evans (Evans, 2011), the former Australian foreign minister, did in response to Chomsky's criticisms of Australia's actions regarding East Timor – namely, that you were acting in the 'national interest'.

Indonesia (2008–2011)

Like many of its neighbours in the region, Indonesia has a long history of colonial rule. From 1603, when it established its first trading post in Banten on the Indonesian island of Java, to its bankruptcy in 1800, the Dutch East India Company had trading posts throughout what is now the Indonesian archipelago. The subsequent colonisation by the Dutch government of what was referred to as the Dutch East Indies expanded throughout the nineteenth century, peaking in the early twentieth century.

As with other colonies, the social order was based on strict racial and social segregation, with a Dutch elite living separately from their native subjects. Dutch conquest at the time was portrayed, according to well-established colonial standards, as a 'civilizing mission' of primitive and backward Indigenous Indonesians. It was accompanied by the familiar pogroms seen in other European colonies. There were frequent atrocities that included the torture, rape and execution of Indonesian civilians (Tasevski, 2020). Slavery was widespread (Minasny, 2020). Even in its final years, Dutch colonialism imprisoned thousands of supporters of independence (Tasevski, 2020).

These were fertile conditions for authoritarian rule in an independent Indonesia and for the creation of competing local elites. This is reflected in Indonesia's development journey since independence in August 1945, which has been characterised by lengthy periods of political turbulence and authoritarian rule. From 1955 to 1966, the Sukarno presidency was one of political instability and economic stagnation. This was followed by more than 30 years of economic development and political repression under the Suharto dictatorship (1966–1998) (Mourer, 2021). Attempts to introduce more democratic forms of government since then have been stronger in form than substance (Blunt *et al.*, 2012a, 2012b). In today's Indonesia, Mourer (2021, p. 10) observes 'clear signs of democratic regression'.

Throughout, of course, Indonesia's critical geostrategic position at the crossroads of the Indo-Pacific, its status as a Western-friendly Muslim democracy (the world's third largest), its close proximity to Australia, the large size of its economy and internal market and its immense natural resource wealth have made it a prime target of LDIs. We have shown in our discussion of historical structural violence in Cambodia and East Timor how far LDIs like the United States, the United Kingdom and Australia were prepared to go to realise such interests. Just as damning was the way in which the United States and the 'international community' refused to condemn and, in many cases, explicitly condoned the massacre by the Suharto regime of half a million Indonesian Communists and sympathisers or people suspected of being, or supporting, either.

Now-released classified documents show that US officials were aware that most of (Suharto's) victims were innocent of any crime, other than being communist or somehow vaguely associated therewith (Falcone, 2017). Representative of the prevailing LDI view was that of the late Prime Minister of Australia, Harold Holt, who told the River Club of New York City in July 1966 that the killing of 500,000 to 1 million Communist sympathisers made it safe to assume that a 'reorientation' had taken place. Clearly, once identified as Communists, these people became legitimate targets for any form of inhumane treatment. It was a 'constructive bloodbath' also because it reinforced the imperialist system and opened the door to US investment (Chomsky & Herman, 1973).

In addition to the extreme self-interest and unprincipled opportunism evident in the earlier, it also conveys the sense of LDI civilisational superiority and entitlement, which we suggested in Chapter 1 has carried over into LDI development assistance. Subject nations must be kept in their place. They must be kept 'stable' and in 'political equilibrium', meaning passive and subdued. Achieving these states via atrocities and bloodbaths is presented as necessary and desirable 'readjustments' (Chomsky & Herman, 1973).

Against this backdrop, the form of government ownership (and bureaucratic structural violence) regarding LDI technical assistance to Indonesia that comprised the programme that is the subject of our discussion here appears as a natural extension of the historical structural violence discussed earlier. Indeed, the history of LDI involvement in Indonesia demonstrates so clearly and unequivocally that the principle of LDI self-interest trumps all others that it would come as a great surprise if LDI technical assistance was not just as cavalier and opportunistic in its pursuit of self-interest.

The following discussion demonstrates that this was the case.

The programme in question was a multi-donor facility under a US$40 million trust fund managed by the World Bank known as the Decentralisation

Support Facility (DSF). The principal LDI financial contributor to the fund was the United Kingdom (more than 90%), with smaller financial contributions from Australia and Canada. So, while the assistance was channelled through a multilateral agency, the financial and (therefore) decision-making dominance of the principal donor enables us to classify it as bilateral aid in principle.

The principal author's appointment by the World Bank to the position of manager of the DSF trust fund in late 2008 came at a time of acute crisis for the Facility. The principal donor, the Department for International Development (DfID), had threatened to withdraw funding from the DSF because of its strong dissatisfaction with the direction it was taking under its founding manager.[15] DfID insisted that if its financial support to the DSF was to continue, the existing DSF manager would have to be replaced and a completely new direction set for the Facility. In an atmosphere of palpable donor hostility, a World Bank senior management, in one of its biggest offices outside of Washington DC,[16] bristling at the 'reputational risk' of DSF failure, and a demoralised DSF staff, the principal author was given 4 months in which to engineer a turnaround. This was accomplished to the satisfaction of the principal donor and the other financial donors within the allotted period.

The purpose, activities and something of the 'ownership' politics of the Facility following its turnaround can be described as follows. The Facility's comprehensive programme of support addressed aspects of public service delivery, fiscal decentralisation, governance capacity building and planning. Prominent features of its work comprised support to the development of local government borrowing (bond issuance), data provision to the regional financial information system, and monitoring and evaluation of the use of specific purpose grants to local governments. Other activities included contributions to spatial planning and to the strengthening of the capacity of local government legislatures and local public service providers.

However, Facility reports noted that the most important development had been the 'deepening' of government ownership and leadership of the DSF. The Facility's mode of operation was clearly in accordance with the Jakarta Commitment's (an aid effectiveness declaration) emphasis on government-led capacity building.

Another notable feature of the Facility was that much of its work was executed using government procurement and financial management systems ('on budget' and 'on treasury'). This feature of the DSF, which had required close collaboration between the DSF Executive and different units of government, and sometimes between government agencies, set it apart from other (particularly bilateral) development assistance to decentralisation. Facility reports declared it to have been a time-consuming and sometimes complex process, but one that had yielded considerable benefit, in terms of both government capability enhancement and ownership. The same reports noted that this was a cornerstone of international aid effectiveness declarations – which emphasised the need to 'strengthen and use developing country systems to the maximum extent possible' and for donors 'to use country systems as the first option for aid programmes' (DSF, 2010).

These were seen as important and 'heartening' developments, which demonstrated that multi-donor facilities like the DSF, which took seriously the aspects of government ownership referred to previously, were vital to aid effectiveness in strong middle-income countries like Indonesia (DSF, 2010).

The positive overtones regarding government ownership in Facility reports were not all 'spin' or a simple recitation of what we thought government and donors would want to hear. Again, this was a case of real government ownership, but likely for mostly non-developmental reasons. Donor self-interest was satisfied as well, as we explain later, by addressing the positions and interests of the principal stakeholders: the World Bank; the principal donor, DfID; and the Government of Indonesia (GOI).

While quite large by bilateral technical assistance standards, trust funds like the DSF *per se* are somewhat peripheral to the (lending) core business of the World Bank. Often, grant support through trust funds or other means is rationalised as a vehicle for helping borrowers to make the best use of the money that they borrow for major capital works and other purposes.

The World Bank's position on the DSF had three main elements. First, its most immediate and pressing concern was to avert serious reputational damage that would arise if the principal donor to the DSF was to withdraw its funding. The implications of a DSF failure were significant and far-reaching because it would have involved three of the Bank's top ten member countries in terms of subscriptions and voting power for the World Bank as a whole (the United Kingdom, Canada and Germany).[17] Second, local embarrassment and questions of 'face' were important because of the Bank's visibility and standing and the large size of its local loan portfolio. Any form of public humiliation would have been seen locally as very damaging to the Bank's credibility.[18] In addition, as an insider, it soon became apparent to the principal author that the Bank saw itself as a cut above other members of the development industry.[19] The fact that major LDIs were willing to hand over quite large sums of grant funding for the Bank to manage supported this perception. DSF failure would therefore have been galling and irksome to Bank staff on a personal level. Third, once the DSF had been turned around and a plausible programme of assistance had been designed, protection against further possible embarrassment was achieved by allowing project execution to be managed by the GOI, thereby insulating the Bank from project implementation problems such as 'patronage predation', which was highly likely at the time (Blunt *et al.*, 2012a, 2012b).

From the principal donor's standpoint, it is unlikely in the first place to have wanted to deal with the administrative messiness and inconvenience that inevitably would have accompanied a withdrawal of funding from the DSF. Like the World Bank, 'escalation' of the DSF problem was to be avoided, if possible. One of the principal virtues of a reformed DSF was that it enabled the principal donor to supply visiting ministers from the United Kingdom with succinct technical assistance good news stories to decorate their conversations with their Indonesian counterparts.[20] Many of the desirable ingredients and soothing words for such exchanges were evident in the reports referred to above.

The GOI, on the other hand, was interested to use support for decentralisation to consolidate political power. Decentralisation enabled patronage to spread nationwide and was employed by government at the centre as a means of 'appeasement' that enhanced political stability (Blunt *et al.*, 2012a, p. 70). Patronage predation was essential to this, and government-executed technical assistance projects were rich targets of such predation. External technocratic reform was easily assimilated, deflected or neutralised by skilful patronage networks. The relationship between such predation and development assistance was 'symbiotic' in that patronage networks depended partly on development for illicit 'sustenance', while donors were keen to achieve visible and distinctive results quickly that served their own non-altruistic purposes (Blunt *et al.*, 2012a, pp. 77–78). Blunt *et al.* (2012a, 2012b) provide numerous empirical examples of the ways in which DSF projects were thus subverted.

In so far as government ownership and the niceties of harmonisation and alignment were concerned, the DSF was able to present a picture of authentic compliance, which all parties were happy to endorse for the reasons given earlier. Largely non-developmental self-interests on the part of all of the principal stakeholders were realised behind the customary 'dense fog of development-babble and cliché', which was also designed to 'soft-soap' those of its victims who were not aware of what was really going on (Blunt *et al.*, in press).

Iraq (2011–2012)

The desecration and dismemberment of Iraq that followed the invasion by the United States and its allies in 2003 defiled a nation that was the origin of many of the very qualities (civilisational, 'democratic values', etc.) that its invaders proclaimed to be introducing to the Iraqi people. As Simons (2002, p. 1) points out, it has always been difficult to find words to express adequately the extent to which:

> the geographical region that the ancient Greeks called Mesopotamia ('land between the rivers') and that we know today as Iraq was a fount of civilization. Historians search for original metaphors – a womb, cradle, crucible – as they try to convey the scale of the contribution that the people of the region made to the development of human society. The ancient Iraqis built the first cities on earth, created writing, and devised the first codified legal systems. Here – through such ancient lands as Sumer, Akkad, Babylonia, and Assyria – the cultural brew was stirred from which Western civilization would emerge.

However, like their colonial predecessors, the modern invaders of course did not care about such tragic ironies – of what came before or how their own 'civilisations' paled in comparison – or were ignorant of them. As in Cambodia, East Timor, Indonesia and Afghanistan, the historical structural violence inflicted by imperialists paid no heed to the Indigenous cultures or civilisations that were trampled, which were assumed to be intrinsically inferior to their own.

Some of the bloodiest hallmarks of Western (European) historical structural violence against Muslims in the Middle East can be traced back to the Christian Crusades that were launched in 1094. Representative is the testimony of Raymund of Aquiles on the Christian conquest of Jerusalem (in Simons, 2002, p. 4):

> Wonderful sights were to be seen. Some of our men . . . cut off the heads of our enemies; others shot them with arrows . . . others tortured them longer by casting them into the flames. Piles of heads, hands and feet were to be seen in the streets . . . men rode in blood up to their knees and bridle reins . . . it was a just and splendid judgment of God that this place should be filled with the blood of the unbelievers.

More of the same was to come at the hands of the Mongols under Genghis Khan, starkly illustrated in the fate of the survivors of the attack on Baghdad in 1258 where around 800,000 men, women and children were killed and their corpses displayed for all to see. European Christians were said to have been overjoyed at the slaughter and the sacking of the city (Simons, 2002).

Undoubtedly, these European actions and sympathies will have left indelible marks on the Muslim collective unconscious.

Western interest in the region re-emerged following the collapse during the First World War (WW1) of the Ottoman Empire – of what had become known as the 'sick man of Europe' – thereby ending its long period of control over Iraq, which had begun in the mid-seventeenth century. British interest had been ignited in the late nineteenth century by the discovery of oil in Kuwait, which was properly part of Iraq, but which it was convenient for Britain to pretend otherwise.

By the end of WW1, Britain was in control of most of Iraq and, together with France, sought to monopolise all Middle Eastern oil, excluding the United States because it had done the same in areas that it controlled. Promises regarding Arab independence made by France and Britain were not kept. Understandably resentful at the betrayal and their new colonial status, the Indigenous people resisted the occupation. In what was always an unequal contest, Arab casualties were counted in the thousands. For their part, the British did not allow squeamishness to inhibit their barbarism, as conveyed in the words of the always bombastic and bellicose Winston Churchill who famously claimed not to comprehend the 'squeamishness' of using poisoned gas, declaring that he was 'strongly in favour' of its use against 'uncivilized tribes' (Simons, 2002, p. 6).

The dispensing of British 'civilisational' largesse, behavioural correction and 'justice' was not confined to the Arabs however. Other 'beneficiaries' included the Kurds. Senior British military officers boasted how 'bottoms' had been 'spanked' with the use of bombs and guns so that the 'Arab and the Kurd' would appreciate what 'real bombing' meant (Simons, 2002, p. 6).

But the British soon tired of the difficulties and financial costs of controlling their new colony, leading them instead to install an Arab 'puppet' monarch, King Faisal I. During Faisal's reign, Iraq became an independent state that was accepted as a member of the League of Nations (1932). However, the country's political economy remained firmly under British control, which was increasingly resented and resisted by Iraqis. The enormously volatile political circumstances, Britain's brutal responses to civil demonstrations, and wide social discontent sparked the coup of the Free Officers (a secret organisation of high-ranking Iraqi army officers), known as the Revolution of July 1958. During the late 1960s, successive coups led to the accession of Saddam Hussein, whose declaration of war against Iran in 1980 was strongly supported by the United States and its allies and was financially backed by Kuwait. The collaboration was short-lived, however. Within 10 years, diplomatic relations between Iraq and Kuwait had soured because Saddam refused to repay the large debt owed to the latter. Soon after – in 1990 – Saddam invaded Kuwait (Batatu, 1978; Farouk-Sluglett & Sluglett, 2001).

Saddam's recalcitrance and misbehaviour led to the imposition of severe US-led sanctions, culminating in 2003 in the invasion of Iraq by the United States and its allies.

We can perhaps best illustrate the desperate condition of the Iraqi state at the time of this project's implementation, and the immediacy and destructiveness of the historical structural violence it had endured in the years leading up to 2011, by setting out some of the raw statistics. These convey the social costs of the pre-2003 sanctions on Iraq imposed by the United States and its 'natural allies'; by the subsequent US-led invasion, on weak pretext,[21] of an Iraq enfeebled by those sanctions; and by Iraq's subsequent occupation by 'the coalition of the willing'.

The 12 years of crippling sanctions imposed before the invasion are estimated to have resulted in the deaths of half a million Iraqi children. The invasion itself caused the death of up to a further one million Iraqis with millions more wounded, maimed and disabled. Between 3.5 million and 5 million became refugees or were internally displaced and lost their homes and livelihoods. The economy and most government institutions were destroyed. Other social costs included two million widows and more than four million orphans, with hundreds of thousands of children living on the streets; an increase in the percentage of the population living in slum conditions from 17% to 50%; and, since 1990, a tripling of maternal mortality rates (Tirman, n.d.; Chomsky, 2010).[22]

In the light of such horrors of historical structural violence, it will come as little surprise that the project of US-funded technical assistance discussed here (the Project)[23] paid no heed to the niceties of government or national ownership. The extent and blatancy of the Project's complete disregard for government interests was the main reason for the resignation from his senior adviser position by the principal author less than 3 months into his 2-year contract. The main reasons – from the first half of an attachment to the letter of resignation – were as follows.

Government Ownership Not Sought or Obtained

Perhaps the most telling and damaging aspect of the project was that it had been designed with little or no apparent consultation with the Government of Iraq. In a now sovereign country, the project therefore had no legitimacy, meaning that in the absence of formal authorisation from central government it should not commence operations. But it also meant that the project's design was likely to be seriously deficient.

By the end of December 2011, more than three months after project commencement in Iraq, formal government approval of the project had not been obtained and no invitation had been extended to government to comment on or to influence the project's design.

Faulty Project Design

The most serious shortcoming in relation to project design was that mentioned above, namely, that it had been produced without consulting government.

But the project seemed deficient – politically naïve – in other crucial respects. A striking example of this was that Component 1 of the project was designed to 'resolve' anomalies and contradictions in the national legislation governing decentralisation in Iraq, the assumption being that a 'strong' form of decentralisation would be implemented. Some of the latest and best thinking on precisely this subject in Iraq demonstrates that this assumption was unsafe (Visser, 2011a). For example, the evidence shows that cases concerning federalism or decentralisation recently brought before the Supreme Court of Iraq had resulted in rulings that clearly favoured increasing centralisation of authority (outside of Kurdistan). It is widely known that the Supreme Court is strongly influenced by the Prime Minister's Office and that the Prime Minister is in favour of 'a centralised form of government south of Kurdistan' (Visser, 2011b). Moreover, as Visser (2011a) makes clear, the idea of federalism or decentralisation in Iraq is of recent (2003/4) and largely foreign invention, there having been no historical evidence of demand for it from within Iraq, going back more than a century. Pressing for decentralisation in these circumstances – that is: where there is no tradition of demand for decentralisation; where the idea has been introduced recently into legislation by an occupying force; and where, in a now sovereign country, the effects of a strong externally-driven push for decentralisation would be highly likely to be counterproductive from the point of view of national peace and stability – is at best imprudent, at worst reckless.

It was as if the project documents had been written by people who knew little about governance, about decentralisation, or about the rapidly changing development context of Iraq. The project's designers seemed to be applying what amounted to a standard *technocratic* formula based on the work of previous projects such as USAID's LGP.

> Decentralisation is a highly volatile subject politically in all development settings, but particularly so now in Iraq. It clearly lies at the heart of bitter sectarian divides over power and resources in the country. The project documents were written as if these problems did not exist, as if the tired *technocratic* rhetoric of decentralisation and development would apply whatever the political governance context. Despite the obvious significant changes to governance conditions since the original design, the prime contractor seemed not to be prepared to contemplate modifications let alone to discuss them with the donor or, more importantly, with government.

It seemed highly likely at the time that the Project was a small part of some grander design to bolster the security and geostrategic imperialist interests of the United States and its allies.[24] A view since confirmed by Kathem (2020) in his analysis of one of the largest projects in USAID history (worth half a billion US$), which was implemented from 2003 to 2011 and had been designed to establish decentralisation by constructing 1,000 local councils.[25] Kathem (2020) shows that in sharp contrast to USAID's official statements, this project was important to the achievement of the strategic objectives of the occupation, the major one being to reduce Iraq to the status of a client state in the US imperial design.

In the Project, the question of government ownership was simply dismissed by the supply-side contractor. Oral and written requests to seek government involvement and approval made by the principal author and other senior project staff were ignored.

Invariably, contractor behaviour conforms strictly to donor wishes. In accordance with the 'if you break it, you own it' maxim, it is clear that the donor in question felt that Iraq was, or was soon to be, a vassal state and that it (the donor) could do as it pleased. The Project was to do as directed without question, which the managing contractor ensured that it did.

Project benefits for the Iraqi people were derisory in the circumstances. It was almost certain, however, that the Project would inflame a tinder-dry and unpredictable political environment by imposing (no matter how ineptly) the idea of decentralisation (Blunt, 2012). If internal dissension was seen by the donor as a means for facilitating control and compliance, then its interests will have been well served by the Project.

Mongolia (2012–2013)

In our account of historical structural violence in Mongolia, we begin with a thumbnail sketch of the country and its 'shock therapy' transition from Soviet satellite to neoliberal 'democracy'. This includes a brief discussion of the aetiology and persistence to the present day of high levels of poverty and social injustice. However, for three reasons, the major part of our discussion of historical structural violence focuses on corporate predation in the mining sector over the last 20 years. We do so, first, because mining is, and will remain for the foreseeable future, the most important sector of the Mongolian economy. Second, because the exploitation of Mongolia by foreign mining corporations, associated LDI technical assistance, and co-opted local elites arguably constitutes the dominant force of historical structural violence in the country. And third, because the primary data from our Mongolian case are drawn from technical assistance provided to the mining sector.

The Mongols comprise three groups: the Khalkha of the southern or middle territory, the Oirats of the west and the Buryats of the north. While their traditional political organisation has been fluid, and based on tribal affiliations, they have similar cultural practices, languages and lifestyles, which distinguish them from neighbouring ethnic groups. The idea of a Mongol nation began to take shape with the consolidation of these tribes by Chinggis Khan in the thirteenth century (Porter, 2009).

Since its independence in 1924, the Mongolian state has placed great stress on the principal of Mongol national unity. Even during the period of Soviet influence (from 1924) socialist revolution reflected Mongolia's unique qualities. Lodged geographically between its two powerful neighbours, Russia and China, since the fall of the Qing Dynasty in China in 1911, Mongol national identity has been the foundation for the development of an autonomous nation-state (Porter, 2009).

For some analysts, the much remarked upon peaceful mass protests that brought about the 'smooth and bloodless' transition from Soviet satellite to democratic state capitalism were more an expression of a strong sense of nationalism and concern about the erosion of Indigenous culture than they were a longing for democracy or capitalism (Shaw, 2016).

The 'big-bang' transition from a centrally planned, communist, Soviet-dependent economy to an independent, state-capitalist economy, was accompanied 'overnight' by 'disorderly' privatisations of almost all state-owned assets (including predation by the local elites that sprung up to take advantage of what was on offer); by the immediate cessation of Soviet subsidies and aid to energy, food, raw materials, capital equipment market access and state-owned enterprises; by severe curtailments to social services like education, health and pensions; and by chronic and widespread disruptions to power and other basic utility services. This caused immediate and widespread unemployment and hardship. Living standards fell precipitously, making Mongolia's economic contraction one of the most severe among the post-Soviet economies (Helble *et al.*, 2020, p. 2). These were fertile conditions for the rapid growth of income inequality, corruption and elite formation and predation on the fruits of state capitalism.

With almost half of the population of 3.31 million living on less than two (US) dollars per day (Ariunzaya *et al.*, 2020), to the present day, the patience and national unity of the Mongol people referred to by Shaw (2016) continue to be tested to the limit.

Mongolia is the world's least densely populated country. Its immense natural resource wealth includes substantial proven mineral reserves of gold, silver, copper, iron ore, zinc, coal and oil (Helble *et al.*, 2020). It also has rich deposits of fluorspar, molybdenum, uranium, tin, tungsten and natural gas. The discovery of further significant deposits seems highly likely as about 70% of Mongolia's territory has yet to be explored (Mongolia EITI, 2021).

The structure of the small economy reflects this and is highly unusual. GDP is almost entirely dependent on mining (23.7%) and mining provides 26% of government revenues. Export concentrations (in products and market destination) are among the highest outside the Middle East, with minerals accounting for 90% of exports (Helble *et al.*, 2020, p. 3; Mongolia EITI, 2021).

In 2014, we remarked that mining was a 'hot topic' in Mongolia, driven largely by the mine at Oyu Tolgoi,[26] which at the time was predicted to be the main contributor to a tripling of national *per capita* GDP by 2018. It was a hot topic also, however, because of rumours concerning bribery of senior government officials, which was the cause of widespread popular resentment of the perceived unfairness to Mongolia of the agreements signed with foreign mining corporations. In particular, there was considerable public pressure to revisit the Oyu Tolgoi agreement in order to increase Mongolia's share of mining proceeds. Talk that elicited from mining interests,[27] the 'development community' and the corporate-sponsored media the familiar alarms of 'risks of capital flight' and 'threats to investor confidence' (Blunt, 2014, p. 384).

At the time of writing, Oyu Tolgoi remains in the headlines for all of the wrong reasons. For example, quoting leaked cables from the US embassy, Ahlers *et al.* (2020) point to shady deals between Rio Tinto and corrupt politicians who promised to be able to 'force' through parliament agreements that were disadvantageous to Mongolia. Kiezebrink *et al.* (2018) also provide substantial evidence of tax avoidance by Rio Tinto that involved channelling billions of dollars through a shell company in Luxembourg to set up a bogus loan facility itself. Rio Tinto thereby defrauded the Government of Mongolia (GOM) by self-financing the development and operation of the mine and charging the GOM Libor plus 6.5% interest for 'loans' that it claimed to have obtained from the market. In November 2019, the Mongolian parliament unanimously passed a resolution requiring that all Oyu Tolgoi agreements be reviewed. The power of mining corporations and co-opted officials to resist is demonstrated by the fact that the first investigation of transfer pricing by a foreign mining corporation (Rio Tinto) only began in December 2020 (production at Oyu Tolgoi commenced in 2013). Government had been forced to act by growing popular concern about poor returns from Oyu Tolgoi, where projections suggested that little in the way of corporate income taxes would be paid over the next 30 years (McClure, 2021).

The mining sector project that is the source of the empirical evidence on ownership that we discuss here was designed and implemented in this highly charged atmosphere.

Following Blunt (2014, pp. 383–384), our discussion explains how joint research involving the Ministry of Mines in the GOM and the Swiss Agency for Cooperation and Development (SDC) was developed, approved and implemented;

why the research in question was chosen; the nature of project ownership by the two parties; and the reaction of SDC to the findings of the research, which resulted in a complete embargo on them for reasons of perceived economic and political self-interest on the part of the donor.

The research topic agreed by SDC and the Ministry of Mines – that of community development agreements (CDAs) between mining corporations and government – was regarded by both parties to be 'safe' politically. CDAs do not entail any of the big questions surrounding mining, such as the shareholdings of the different entities involved or royalties or tax liabilities. The agreements are 'local' and the money involved is 'small change' when compared with corporate investment or turnover or even declared returns (typically minimised by transfer pricing and other means). However, these small investments are capable of yielding more or less immediate and substantial returns to corporate image, local stability and community acceptance,[28] and thereby uninterrupted exploitation of the resource. Considerable political benefit is also likely for both national and local governments, who can be seen to be safeguarding the interests of local communities, by insisting on recompense that comprises more a 'token kindergarten here or local clinic there'. In short, this seemed like safe ground for conventional development assistance and, in the words of the World Bank, to be a potential 'win-win' for all involved (Blunt, 2014, p. 384).

The research project proceeded on the basis of a formal agreement between SDC and the Ministry of Mines, which incorporated an undertaking of confidentiality on the part of SDC. This was required because the Ministry of Mines agreed to disclose documents that, though strictly in the public domain, were not normally released because the private corporations involved did not want them to be. This was a very unusual concession.

Some of the main questions addressed in the research and the answers to those questions that the evidence from Mongolia and other countries, and principles like equity and fairness, support were as follows (from Blunt, 2014, pp. 385–386):

a. Can mining, and does it usually, cause serious (local) social, economic, and environmental disruption and damage? Yes.

. . .

d. Do foreign mining corporations anywhere (in any developing country) engage voluntarily in well-considered and sustainable local development that is designed to make up for the environmental damage and social disruption caused and to ensure that community life can continue after mining has stopped, the resource has been fully exploited, and the miner has left? No.

. . .

g. Is existing Mongolian legislation demanding enough and clear and detailed enough to achieve (d) above? No.
h. Do existing agreements between the Mongolian state and mining corporations require of the miner sufficient contributions of the right kinds? No.

i. Would it be in Mongolia's interests to do something (retroactively) to rectify this (h)? Yes.

As 'background', the research report also made the following points:

n. Has Mongolia been subject to this [neoliberal] grand design? Yes.
o. Do these conditions predispose resource-rich developing countries towards a so-called 'resource curse' fate? Yes.
. . .
q. Is it likely that in these general conditions that mining companies left to their own devices will do the right thing? No.
r. Is it not reasonable that the citizen owners of the minerals that foreign companies wish to exploit should want to maximise their returns? Yes.
s. Have citizen owners been able to do this anywhere? With very few exceptions (such as Norway, Ecuador and Venezuela), No.

Before its release to the Ministry of Mines, the research report was read by the director and deputy director of the SDC office in the Mongolian capital, Ulaanbaatar (SDC management). As noted earlier, they immediately banned the report because they feared that if the Australians or Canadians got wind of it, they might complain to the Swiss ambassador in Beijing, which would be the cause of political embarrassment. SDC management did not explain any of this to the Mongolian counterpart institution (the Ministry of Mines) and behaved as if there was no need to do so (Blunt, 2014, p. 386).

The following points are noteworthy. First, the research report's recommendations were clearly in the development interests of Mongolia. Second, for the reasons given earlier, they were not necessarily counter to those of the foreign countries and corporations likely to be affected by them. Third, SDC had embarked (presumably) knowingly on the research in the first place. Fourth, SDC management was unmoved by any of this. Indeed, fifth, SDC management's intransigence resulted in the immediate unilateral cancellation of the research project. Sixth, the research 'partner' whose 'leadership' and 'ownership' of the project was violated – the Ministry of Mines – was neither consulted nor afforded the courtesy of any form of explanation (Blunt., 2014).

These actions by SDC management were based on their assessment of how they thought SDC, and the Swiss Federal Department of Foreign Affairs of which it is a part might react. There was clearly significant fear of retribution from superiors in Switzerland (bureaucratic structural violence), and this was the cause of considerable trepidation among SDC country managers, who, while they admitted to being sympathetic to many of the report's findings and recommendations, felt compelled nonetheless to behave as they did (Blunt, 2014, p. 386).

Clearly, there is nothing in any of the above to suggest that SDC management did not understand what ownership meant in practice or whose ownership was involved on the demand-side. Equally clearly, it is evident that SDC management was prepared to abrogate formal agreements as soon as it perceived there to be the slightest threat to its interests or those of other LDIs. This is further striking evidence of the vacuity and shallowness of development-speak and its claims of 'collaboration' and 'partnership', 'participative approaches', 'meaningful engagement', and to government 'ownership' and 'leadership' (Blunt, 2014, p. 386); but also a confirmation that 'capitalist growth requires an imperial arrangement' (Hickel, 2021). Switzerland's lack of an imperialist track record did not prevent it from taking advantage of the conditions for corporate predation created by the historical structural violence inflicted by others or from defending, expanding and refining those conditions or establishing new ones. It thereby emulated or even surpassed the bureaucratic structural violence of the development assistance provided by the other countries in our sample.

Afghanistan (2014–2016)

From the times of Alexander the Great and Genghis Khan to the present, the history of Afghanistan is strewn with monuments to the failures of foreign invaders. Arguably the most devastating and bloody invasions have been the most recent, those of the Soviet Union and, immediately thereafter, of the United States and its allies.

The US's ignominious defeat by the Taliban and its frenetic departure from the country in August 2021 marked the end of the latest unsuccessful attempt by a foreign invader to bend Afghanistan to its will. The most powerful nation in human history, with weaponry and hubris to match, had shown itself to be incapable of subduing a rag-tag army of guerrilla fighters armed only with conventional weapons. In the end, the most powerful nation in human history slunk away in humiliation in the dead of night from its major air base at Bagram. A triumph of US 'divine right'[29] and arrogance over good judgement and the clear lessons that even a cursory examination of Afghanistan's recent history would have revealed. Brute force and blind self-assurance alone have rarely been sufficient to subdue and defeat a committed resistance that has the support of the Indigenous population.[30]

Establishing and maintaining a coherent and effective sovereign state in Afghanistan has always been difficult and expensive. This is partly because of the importance of its geographical position to the geopolitical interests of world powers and neighbouring states, which has resulted in numerous invasions and protracted wars; and partly because of its huge area, mountainous terrain, and the bitter and chronic rivalries between its principal ethnic groups. Conquest *and* government of Afghanistan have been difficult for the same reasons. Indeed, according to Rubin (2002), until the turn of the century, for most Afghans, the idea, and reality, of a national government was irrelevant. Conditions that in some ways prevail to the present day (Blunt *et al.*, 2015).

Of course, as in Iraq and Vietnam and other nations that have been subjected to LDI imperialism, most of the enormous costs of Afghanistan's historical violence have been borne by the Afghan people, generations of whom have known nothing but war and foreign occupation and the untold miseries that accompany them. As in Iraq, tens of thousands of innocent Afghan civilians have lost their lives, and millions have been displaced internally or become refugees in foreign lands. About one-third of the population is malnourished (Crawford, 2021). Small gains in health, education and life expectancy – especially for women – are likely to be reversed under the Taliban.

On 15 August 2021, the desperation and bewilderment of a chronically traumatised Afghan population were conveyed dramatically on TV as hordes chased down the runway of Kabul airport in pursuit of a departing US Air Force plane (see *Afghanistan*, 2021). Some, who managed to gain a hold of the plane, later fell to their deaths.

These images of frantic, disorderly departure by the United States and its allies, of the most powerful armies in the world in full flight, embarrassed many who had worked alongside, and depended on, Afghans during the occupation and had promised them that they would not be left at the mercy of a vengeful and ruthless Taliban. Some made it out, but many did not and were left to fend for themselves. Understandably, Afghans abandoned in this way felt betrayed. Many of the foreign personnel who worked with them agreed.

Once again, in the light of this blundering US-led 20-year cataclysm, its inglorious end, and the abandonment of all responsibility by the vanquished, we would be surprised if our discussion of government ownership of LDI technical assistance to Afghanistan over the period 2014–2016 did not reveal complete donor unconcern for it.

As in some of the other cases discussed earlier, the project addressed questions of decentralisation and subnational governance (SNG), which were still in vogue at the time among donors for 'democracy promotion' reasons. Donor-held beliefs on the subject were just as impervious to counter-evidence and argument – as they had been years earlier in Cambodia, in Iraq and in Indonesia – largely because they were ideological, a matter of faith (Blunt *et al.*, 2015, p. 281).

The most striking example of donor 'democracy (and decentralisation) promotion come what may' in our Afghanistan data concerned technical assistance to SNG policy development by the Independent Directorate of Local Governance (IDLG) in the Government of Afghanistan (GOA).[31]

Blunt *et al.* (2017, p. 82) show that a very long and 'impenetrable' SNG 'policy' (415 pages!), which had been found by the few who had read it to be 'completely devoid' of 'policy direction', had been approved by cabinet in 2010 and has not been superseded since then. While this was found to be at least partly a result of widespread (mainly) supply-side technical incompetence, it was clear that all demand- and supply-side parties were willing participants in an elaborate make-believe that was designed to present an edifice of developmental governance behind which to conceal the realisation of vested interests. On the supply-side, the 'pantomime' entailed projects of development assistance that proclaimed to be in accordance with a 'policy' that none would have read and whose contents in any case did not contain any discernible policy direction to follow.

On the demand-side, the existence of a high-level 'policy' that was known to be a policy in name only and whose contents were worthless seemed to matter as little as it did on the supply-side, suggesting strongly that the whole business of SNG policy served other purposes. Both sides clearly expected that a 'policy' be produced (indeed, donors had demanded it)[32] and that 'stakeholders' should say that they were in compliance with it (which donor projects were at pains to do). But, just as clearly, neither the demand- nor the supply-side expected that the 'policy' would be put to any useful development purposes. Tacit collusive pretence, or pantomime, among all interested parties was the only plausible explanation.

A new, and much shorter and clearer, SNG policy developed by the Project was better in every respect than the long 'policy' but was rejected by the president for reasons that appeared to have nothing to do with its intrinsic technical merits and everything to do with political and personal considerations, the most significant one being the fall from grace of the policy's government sponsor, the former Director General of IDLG, Jelani Popal.

The lack of demand-side surprise or concern at this result supported the conclusion that factors other than the merits of the new policy were known to be at play. Most critically, it was understood and accepted that the main purpose of the new policy was to maintain appearances and to enable all affected parties to satisfy their respective vested interests. The short policy did this more convincingly than its long, opaque, and largely unread predecessor had (Blunt *et al.*, 2017).

For donors, the plasticity of the long 'policy' meant that it could be used to support anything that they felt like doing. The short, technically superior, successor policy was also put to donor purposes, as revealed in a donor email to the principal author, which admitted that donors were eager to use the new SNG Policy as a basis for planning and promoting donor reform agendas. Both sides were content to go along with the charade, and this is to be expected in demand-side governance settings where predatory patronage-based networks are in the ascendency and, on the supply-side, where donor investment and stakes are high. The result is the prolongation of human misery for the populations of affected countries (Blunt *et al.*, 2017).

As in most of the other cases that we have discussed to this point, the previous constitutes another clear example of government ownership of technical assistance for purposes that had little or nothing to do with the equitable development of the state. Indeed, the idea of decentralisation in a country where up to 70% of its territory at the time was not under the complete control of the central government was ludicrous. Yet, for the reasons set out previously, both donors and government engaged in an elaborate pantomime to support the development of SNG policy that enabled both the supply- and the demand-sides to do as they pleased.

Not a shred of evidence here either of donor misunderstanding of ownership or of which government agencies were responsible for exercising it.

Samoa (2016–2021)

Unlike the countries discussed earlier, Samoa's experience of externally imposed historical structural violence is relatively free of destructive conquest and deliberate mass slaughter. Its small size, long distance from the main markets, lack of natural resources and relative geostrategic insignificance explain why. For the LDIs, there have always been much bigger fish to fry. Since independence in 1962, left pretty much to its own devices, Samoa has therefore been a stable (meaning obedient) and peaceful state-capitalist society.

The country's first experience of colonisation was as a part of the German Empire, from 1900 to 1914. German colonial rule came to an end at the outbreak of the First World War. Its successor was New Zealand. Responding to a request from the United Kingdom for it to perform 'a great and urgent imperial service', in August 1914, a small New Zealand expeditionary force of about 1400 men landed in Samoa unopposed and seized control from the Germans. For the next half-century, Samoa was controlled by New Zealand (Boyd, 1968).

Undoubtedly the most traumatic and lethal consequence of Samoa's contact with the outside world was the influenza epidemic of 1918–1919. In September–December 1918, Samoa fell victim to the pandemic's most virulent wave, which had morbidity rates in excess of 90%. Samoa was the worst affected of the Pacific Islands, losing 22% of its population within a matter of weeks. Deaths were not evenly distributed: 30% of men, 22% of women and 10% of children died. Losses were even more disproportionate among political and family groups: 45% of *matai* (head or titled members of an extended family group) perished, while only six of the 30 *faipule* (councillors) survived.

Virtually overnight, the epidemic thereby devastated family and political structures. Social cohesion and colonial government services were stretched to the limit by the need to care for the sick and the dying and the large numbers of widows and orphans. The high levels of mortality also caused severe disruptions to agricultural production, which heightened chronic labour supply problems and exacerbated the always contentious question of Chinese labour (Tomkins, 1992).

The influenza epidemic of 1918 was a watershed in Samoa's relations with its colonisers and, together with the events of Black Saturday,[33] an important catalyst for the *Mau* independence movement. A trauma of such magnitude, and its mishandling by the colonial authorities, will have been etched in the national psyche, producing lasting effects on Samoan attitudes to outside interference more generally. Attitudes which, to the present day, are likely to simmer close beneath the surface of Samoan 'traditional courtesies of formal address and official interpretation' asserted by Boyd (1968, p. 158).

Such attitudes and resentment will have been stoked by colonial culpability regarding the influenza pandemic, which had a number of incriminating and grievance-worthy features. These convey the pronounced self-interest and deeply ingrained imperial (civilisational-ascendancy-type) attitudes and beliefs that have been such a distinctive feature of the historical structural violence inflicted on the other countries discussed to this point. Attitudes continue to find expression in New Zealand and Australia today (e.g. Thaker, 2021; Ramachandran, 2020) and are evident in the empirical evidence of donor behaviour from Samoa that we discuss here and in Chapter 4.

The first grievance-worthy feature of the colonial response had to do with the withholding of information about the pandemic. Long before it arrived in Samoa, the British Colonial Office in London became aware of the third wave's outbreak in Sierra Leone, in August 1918, and its extreme virulence, but failed to inform its other dependencies. The Colonial Office only reacted when the virus began to spread rapidly in Britain in November 1918. On 5 November 1918, it sent out (by regular mail) a circular to all colonies warning them of the disease. In most colonies, the virus arrived well before the circular. Government authorities in Auckland also knew about the nature of the epidemic before the ship that introduced it – the Talune – had anchored in Apia and its passengers had gone ashore. Yet, not even Logan, the New Zealand colonial administrator in Samoa, was informed. He learned about the epidemic from local newspaper reports after the Talune had berthed in Apia and Samoans had been infected (Tomkins, 1992).

Perhaps most grievance-worthy, however, were the ways in which the colonial authorities rationalised the failures of 'scientific European medicine'[34] – a 'progressive tool of empire' – to prevent or combat the pandemic. The first was to stress the coloniser's 'devotion', hard work and 'benevolence' during the epidemic regardless of its failures in other respects. The measure of success was not in deaths or suffering averted but rather the goodwill and 'moral virtues' of the European colonisers. The clear intention being to cultivate an image of a great and good European community 'selflessly united' to care for its 'stricken subjects' (Tomkins, 1992).

The second rationalisation employed by the colonial authorities resorted to the tried-and-tested blame-the-victim tactic. According to Tomkins (1992), the picture created was one of benevolent and tireless Europeans doing everything they could to deal with an intractable situation. Their best efforts constantly undermined and 'doomed to failure' not by the virus but by the 'ignorance and superstition' of the Indigenous population. Colonial administrators alleged that Samoans did not understand or cooperate with their benefactors. More than anything, for European observers, the epidemic revealed the moral weaknesses of Indigenous people. New Zealand's second Military Administrator of Western Samoa, Colonel Robert Tate, claimed that (Tomkins, 1992, pp. 189–190):

> Samoan leaders 'showed not the slightest interest in their people while the plague was raging and gave me not the slightest assistance in feeding the sick or burying the dead, that half the deaths were due, not to influenza, but to the neglect of their families by the Heads, and that they themselves are deeply to blame for failing to assist.' . . . In Samoa, 'it was only by our using strong language that the Samoans could be induced to bury their dead' and the Administrator was 'extremely disappointed with the Samoans, who showed such want of determination during the epidemic'.

These are some of the beginnings of New Zealand's proprietorial interests in Samoa. 'Often accused of being arrogant and domineering', Australia has long held similar attitudes towards what its Prime Minister, Scott Morrison, referred to as 'our patch' ("Australia is Battling China", 2019).

However, from the turn of the twenty-first century, the proprietorial complacency of Samoa's 'traditional partners' became increasingly rattled by 'bleak' geopolitical assessments, meaning the growing presence of China in the region and its alleged 'adventurism' (Townshend, 2021).[35] This provoked a surge of reluctant generosity and, following the lead of the United States, overt – coat-tail – belligerence. For example, in 2018, Australia established an AUD 2 billion fund for regional infrastructure and set up high commissions in the Cook Islands, French Polynesia, the Marshall Islands, Niue and Palau ("Australia is Battling China", 2019).

The AUKUS nuclear submarine deal of late 2021 was another sign of coat-tail belligerence (Clarke, 2021). Proprietorial interest, paternalism and entitlement are evident in the US's reactions to China's growing presence. Purportedly, 'echoing a familiar view', US Secretary of State Antony Blinken warned Pacific Island leaders of the dangers of 'economic coercion' and 'retribution'. Being 'small' and 'remote' apparently increased their vulnerability to 'strategic manipulation' by 'outside powers' (Wallis, 2021).

Indeed. But clearly, 'manipulation by outside powers' and 'economic coercion' are only problematic or 'dangerous' when you do not 'own' the 'patch' or are not a 'traditional partner'.

Like all of the Pacific islands, Samoa is heavily dependent on official development assistance (ODA). The region ranks first in terms of *per capita* ODA, and ten Pacific Island countries rank among the 25 most aid-dependent countries in the world. The region also has the highest proportion of technical assistance (Dornan & Pryke, 2017). In 2019, Australia provided 37% of ODA to the region, followed by New Zealand at 14% (OECD, 2019).

Following Blunt *et al.* (in press), the projects and case incidents discussed later were housed in a conventional bilateral technical assistance programme (the Programme) whose objectives, systems and procedures were formally recorded in a programme operations' manual (POM). Funded by the Government of Australia, the Programme's purpose was to work with government according to the standard template, that is, to develop and strengthen policies and institutions that enable sustainable and inclusive economic growth, especially private sector-led growth; and to improve economic governance by addressing issues that affect underlying public sector capability and performance.

The POM was clear and unequivocal about questions of good governance and ownership, proclaiming that the Programme's governance, structure and functioning would be consistent with important principles of aid management and effectiveness set out in the Paris Declaration (2005) and reaffirmed by the (2011) Fourth High Level Forum on Aid Effectiveness held in Busan, South Korea. Moreover, the POM stressed the importance of 'recipient government leadership and ownership' of development assistance; 'alignment' with recipient government plans and strategies; and 'harmonisation' with other projects and programmes of development assistance.

In addition, the POM declared that the Programme would be characterised by 'close working relations' between its members and by conventional principles of good governance such as accountability, transparency, effectiveness, merit-based decision-making and efficiency. The importance of what it called 'authenticity' was also stressed, which bound the Programme to 'taking pains to be seen' to observe the principles of good governance that it espoused.

The strategic management of the Programme and all decisions regarding the technical assistance provided were formally agreed to be the responsibility of a steering committee whose membership comprised three chief executive officers of central government agencies (one of whom was chair) and the donor's most senior representative in Samoa.

Blunt *et al.* (in press) provide a comprehensive account of the pre- and post-COVID-19-pandemic bureaucratic structural violence that characterised the Programme: three pre-pandemic project examples and three post-pandemic examples are given. In all six projects, the avowals of good governance and government ownership and leadership that had been formally agreed and were set out in the POM were contravened unilaterally by the donor.

Here, we discuss briefly one pre- and one post-onset example and general anti-ownership measures introduced by the donor after the onset of the COVID-19 pandemic.

Pre-Pandemic Case Incident: National Security Policy

Our brief discussion earlier of the geopolitics of the region and our accounts of historical structural violence in the preceding sections of this chapter are highly predictive of donor reactions to this case.

From the beginning, rising regional tensions meant that a national security project was bound to attract immediate and close attention from the donor. The Programme had been entrusted with such a politically charged high-level task because it had managed in the (40 or so) projects that it had delivered to that point to establish its credentials in the terms set out in the POM, but particularly with regard to 'integrity', integrity meaning, in particular, that technical assistance would be guided solely by the interests of the recipient. The Programme had been able to do this because none of the projects it had implemented to that point had raised any 'red flags' in the eyes of the responsible donor officials.

The first sign of donor discomfort regarding the national security project arose in relation to the selection of a consultant to carry out the work. The alarm bells began to sound when it became apparent to the donor that a foreign national (non-donor-country citizen) was the top-ranked candidate. The donor's immediate response was to issue a written order directing the Programme not to proceed with the selected consultant and to appoint, instead, an Australian national from a short list of candidates supplied by the donor.

This was done in full knowledge of the fact that the original selection abided by (Australian government) merit-based procurement rules set out in the POM, which the Programme was legally obliged to follow; and that agreement regarding the selection had also been reached with the principal government counterpart.

The donor followed up its written instruction with an oral command to the Programme that in future *all* projects would first have to be approved by the donor, and before being subjected to the formal approval processes set out in the POM.

The effects of these instances of bureaucratic structural violence were, first, by contravening the formal requirements of the POM, breaking its own procurement rules (and, technically putting the implementing contractor in breach of its contract), the donor violated unambiguously professed commitments to government 'ownership' and 'leadership' and clearly exposed the real intent underlying the 'soft-soap' and 'sugar-coating' of its development rhetoric. For the host government, the clear message was that 'we shall decide what's good for you' even if this contradicts a decision that you had made according to formal rules that had been 'set and agreed to jointly'. And it demonstrated emphatically the donor's view that the rules were 'for them to decide' and to adhere to or not at their discretion and for 'others to break at their peril'. This made a 'complete sham' the 'elaborate edifice' of the Programme's formal governance structure (Blunt *et al.*, in press).

Ownership under COVID-19

For all countries, the social and economic consequences of the pandemic had been severe, and unprecedented since at least the beginning of the twentieth century (e.g. Cantore *et al.*, 2020). The prevalence of unusually high levels of non-communicable diseases and of obesity in Samoa placed its population at much greater risk of developing severe or terminal illness if infected with SARS-CoV-2. In addition, Samoa's national health system was likely to be overwhelmed quickly by a local outbreak of COVID-19 (Blunt, 2021b). In these circumstances, the consequences for Samoa of donor-induced bureaucratic structural violence were significantly higher than they would otherwise have been.

The post-onset case and the general control measures instituted by the donor discussed in this section reveal whether any of this made any difference to donor behaviour.

Post-Pandemic Case Incident: Reserved and Restricted Lists (Areas of Foreign Investment)

Approved by the Programme in mid-2019, this project was suspended by the donor suddenly and unilaterally in July 2020. In the year between its approval and suspension, there had been no change to any substantive or 'risk' aspects of the project *per se*. The project's development context had changed significantly, however.

First, the declaration of the COVID-19 pandemic in mid-March 2020 magnified greatly the economic and social implications of foreign investment policy for the Government of Samoa. Second, from the donor's perspective, the overriding concern was the escalation of tensions in the region between the PRC and US-led interests (e.g. Walden & Choahan, 2020). This meant that a 'China' feature of the project became problematic, namely, community resentment caused by the presence of ethnic Chinese entrepreneurs in Samoa's small-scale retail sector. For the donor official in question, this carried enough risk of 'political complications' to warrant suspending the project immediately – revealing extreme sensitivity to the remotest possibility of sanction or displeasure from headquarters. The Programme was therefore directed to engage in 'appropriate' technical discourse with the government counterpart so as to rationalise the donor's 'peremptory and unilateral action' (Blunt *et al.*, in press).

Programme-Wide Measures Relevant to Government Ownership

At the same time, the donor instituted a number of programme-wide measures designed to tighten its control over programme activities. The first was a bi-weekly meeting between the donor supervising official and the Programme. These meetings preceded formal meetings of the Programme's steering committee and gave the donor the opportunity to veto unilaterally any project or activity that it did not like.[36] This clearly undermined the formal authority of the Programme governance structure. Further control came in the form of a donor 'stop/go' point in the project development critical path set out in the POM. These bitter pills were coated in platitudes of 'enhanced communication and consultation' between the Programme and the donor.

The donor's eagerness to achieve complete control was exposed further when, in late August 2020, the managing contractor was instructed to find a way of 'moving forward' with the programme team leader (PTL) to 'restore trust'. The clear message was that the donor would insist that the PTL be dismissed unless he acquiesced more completely to what the donor (rather than the host government) wanted the Programme to do (Blunt *et al.*, in press). This was a clear example of what Graeber (2015, p. 58) refers to as bureaucratic structural violence stemming from 'systematic inequalities ultimately backed up by the threat of force'.

The donor gave three reasons for its ultimatum. First, the donor regarded the PTL's performance under the new 'ways of working' recounted above to be lacking in 'enthusiasm and commitment'. Second, the donor said that it could not 'trust' the PTL to work in its interests – as opposed to government's – and that the PTL seemed to have an 'agenda' that was not aligned with the donor's. Third, in a manner reminiscent of a politburo, on the basis of some of his publications (e.g. Blunt, 2021a; Blunt *et al.*, 2011), the PTL was 'denounced' by the supervising donor official as being 'ideologically unsuitable and suspect' (Blunt *et al.*, in press).

Of course, none of these questions could be found in the PTL's job description, or in the selection criteria for his position, confirming the donor's unconcern for the letter and the spirit of formal employment relations when it 'suited its purposes'.[37] 'Alignment' was clearly a mandatory requirement for Programme staff and consultants, but it was alignment with donor interests rather than the development needs of the host government (Blunt *et al.*, in press).

The high point of donor alarm came in early October 2020 when it forbade altogether any project that had to do with foreign investment. This was announced as a *fait accompli* to a meeting of the steering committee, the pretext being a desire to minimise 'duplication' with agencies that had supposed 'comparative advantage', like the World Bank and the Asian Development Bank. Perhaps the most striking aspect of all of this was the donor's presumption that it would get its way (which it did). The meek reply from the three government members of the committee was that they felt that the Programme offered a 'valuable alternative perspective'. However, the government officials were sufficiently intimidated by the imbalance of power and Samoa's aid dependence not to resist. Once again, this series of events 'demonstrated unequivocally' the fiction of government 'leadership' and 'ownership' of the Programme and the travesty of its formal governance structure (Blunt *et al.*, in press).

In Samoa, and in the context of the pandemic, our evidence shows that donor officials were unmoved by the global emergency. Their strong predilections to 'control . . . in increasingly detailed and encompassing ways' (Escobar, 1995, p. 47) and for forms of 'technical discourse' that are designed to conceal 'hidden purposes of bureaucratic power or dominance' (Mosse, 2005, p. 2) were as (or more) pronounced under emergency as they had been before it (Blunt *et al.*, in press).

We return to these questions in Chapter 4, where we examine more fully the bureaucratic structural violence surrounding this case and others, as revealed at critical interfaces involving the main actors.

Conclusion

What general answers to the question 'whose ownership and for what purposes?' can we infer from the cases discussed earlier, and what do they tell us about donor claims regarding definitional and agency problems surrounding the notion of government ownership?

First, it is abundantly clear that claims of donor misunderstanding and uncertainty regarding the meaning of government ownership, and of agency, are hollow. In all of the cases discussed, it was impossible to find any evidence to suggest that either of these claims had any merit.

Second, cavalier and often flagrant disregard by LDIs for government ownership is shown to have been remarkably consistent across widely differing development settings, between LDIs, and over time. Frequently on the slightest pretext, the state sovereignty of the aid recipient was trampled at will or simply ignored altogether, as if the concept was irrelevant or did not exist. Consistently, donor 'strategy' appears to have been, 'we will say one thing, but, when it suits us, we will do the other'. This striking feature of donor behaviour was clearly a reflection of hypersensitivity to perceived transgressions of what they assumed to be *their* ownership 'rights' over the issues addressed by technical assistance, the advice that was given, and the findings that arose. But it was also a reflection of an assumption by donors of complete 'power over' the host country. This was most vividly expressed, and at its most extreme, in the case of Iraq. But, to varying degrees, it was evident in all of the countries in our sample. The cases leave no room for doubting who was really in charge and whose interests counted most.

Third, the findings from Cambodia, Afghanistan, Indonesia and, to a lesser degree, Timor-Leste show that largely non-developmental interests were served on both sides. Recipient governments satisfied 'ownership' standards, but in doing so achieved non-developmental ends that served their own special interests rather than those of the general publics they were meant to represent, a clear win-win for donor and recipient connivance, what Blunt *et al.* (2017, p. 70) refer to as a 'mutually beneficial stasis'. In these cases, both the supply-side and the demand-side could be said to have inflicted bureaucratic structural violence.

Notable as well are the clear and consistent lines of LDI behaviour that can be traced from the historical structural violence experienced by each country to the bureaucratic structural violence of the development assistance that followed and which prepared the ground for the continuation of LDI predation. In this regard, the historical structural violence inflicted on Cambodia, Timor-Leste, Indonesia, Iraq and Afghanistan is particularly revealing. It shows how, for LDIs like the United States and Australia, the meaning and depiction of 'bloodbaths', and LDI willingness to be associated with them directly or indirectly, was entirely a function of the extent to which LDI economic or geostrategic interests at the time were being served. As noted earlier, for LDIs, bloodbaths are not necessarily a bad thing. They may be 'unremarkable, benign, or positively meritorious' (Chomsky & Herman, 1973). Our sample of LDIs treated government or host country ownership in much the same way.

Our discussion also illustrates how proficiently LDIs metamorphosed their relationships with subject or target nations, from invader or oppressor or their accomplice to 'development partner'. For LDIs, these were seemingly 'natural' transformations, from moth to butterfly in the blink of an eye or, more aptly, from one type of predator into another.

The magnitude of LDI power, control, and self-interest evident in these cases and their persistence in the circumstances of the COVID-19 pandemic would appear to leave little room for constructive reformulation of LDI technical assistance. Nevertheless, in the crawl spaces that are left, we discern the following possibilities.

First, purely from the perspective of accountability to their own taxpayers for money well spent, there is considerable scope for improvement. Evidence from the countries where decentralisation was pursued tells us why. In these cases, donor pursuit via decentralisation of 'democracy promotion come what may' in circumstances where it was clearly unlikely to yield any benefit for the public good, or would have made things worse, was wasteful. It was also *wilfully* wasteful in that such ends were pursued relentlessly in the face of clear evidence that no good for the host country would come of them. Undoubtedly, by contributing to the trough of patronage predation, such projects helped to appease local elites and thereby to purchase the much-prized host country compliance. But we suggest that, even where donors cannot be persuaded to shift their attention from compliance, a less harmful and more efficient way of maintaining it would be to provide technical assistance that has a genuine prospect of achieving some measure of public good while acknowledging that a proportion of the resources might be used to fuel patronage predation. Donor integrity, and accountability scores to their own taxpayers and the citizens of recipient countries, would rise accordingly; and donor interests need not be threatened.

Second, it seems patently clear from the evidence that we have presented that few of the actors involved really believed the 'development-speak' and 'blather' (Blunt *et al.*, in press), that is, the rhetoric of the technical assistance that was on offer. For example, in Afghanistan, we showed how all of the actors in a policy development project were knowing participants in an elaborate pantomime, which enabled them to achieve their respective, largely non-developmental, ends. The behaviour of supply- and demand-side actors in Indonesia in principle was very similar. The more intelligent and developmental adjustment to donor behaviour that we suggest in the preceding paragraph would entail its withdrawal from such charades. We believe that the authenticity and integrity credits that would flow from this would benefit donors and the public good.

In Samoa, where there was relatively little evidence of patronage predation, we have demonstrated how donor disregard for formal programme governance structures elicited little opposition and no surprise from senior executives of the host government. Lack of trust and disrespect for donor behaviour on the part of the host government seems probable in such circumstances. Moreover, the damage to donor reputation is likely to be much greater than it would be in post-conflict settings like, say, Afghanistan and Iraq, or Cambodia and Indonesia, where patronage is systemic. It is so, we suggest, because the substantive bureaucratic structural violence inflicted by the unilateral cancellation of a developmental project, or the prohibition of a whole field of activity like foreign investment, was made substantially worse by the blatant and public disregard for formal, agreed procedure. This openly flouted and scorned the agreements that had been made, but it did the same to 'the traditional courtesies of formal address and official interpretation' referred to above, which carry considerable social significance in Samoa.

Piling insult upon injury in this way established unequivocally the master–servant aspect of bureaucratic structural violence referred to by Graeber (2015). It was also eerily reminiscent of colonial rationalisations surrounding the influenza epidemic of 1918, where clear substantive injury was followed by demeaning insult. Denying any culpability for the introduction of the disease to Samoa, the New Zealand colonial administration then blamed its failure to deal with the consequences on the immorality and fecklessness of a Samoan population, which it said was guilty of 'neglect', a 'lack of interest' and a 'want of determination' to minister to its own sick and dying. A combination of immense physical injury, falsehood and insult.

We consider such behaviour to be not only undesirable but also unnecessary and counter-productive to the donor's own interests. Much better to dispense altogether with the pretence and pantomime by stating up-front how the donor will act to protect its interests and spelling this out in a programme's formal documents and procedures. The credits to donor authenticity and integrity would far outweigh any costs. And there would be no need to threaten supplicants or to force them to choose between principle and collusion.

The authentic transformation of duplicitous, self-centred 'masters' or oppressors is clearly not a straightforward task, but it is one that the unprecedentedly urgent and terminal threats now facing humanity demand.

In the next chapter, we pursue these reform possibilities in greater detail by examining the most critical interfaces of bureaucratic structural violence as they are reflected in the interactions between 'masters', 'messengers' and 'minions'.

Notes

1 It is also legitimate to ask whether civil society – as the purported ultimate beneficiary of development assistance – would be a more valid 'owner' than government (Martinez-Alvarez, 2018).
2 In 2019, together, our subset of LDIs accounted for almost 37% of contributions to the OECD. See OECD (n.d.).
3 What we refer to as the commonsensical notion of government ownership implies that outside assistance should address questions of development that host governments want it to in ways that they are comfortable with. That is, it assumes that *all* governments have the right, and are able, to decide their own development goals and the strategies for achieving them and that donors do not interfere in this (Brolin, 2017). Some analysts suggest that donor interest in the question of ownership arose initially because aid effectiveness was seen to be crucially influenced by a country's commitment to development and that 'ownership' was intended as an assessment of this. This view decries departures from this normative stance because, it is claimed, it has been wrongly assumed that, since the aid effectiveness declarations signed in Paris and Accra, most countries already have genuinely development-oriented political leaderships (Booth, 2012). As if to say that, on the other hand, *all* donors have *their* hearts and minds in the right place. The evidence that we present in this book contradicts this supposition, suggesting that, so long as their own interests are satisfied, LDIs do not always really care whether government ownership is developmental or not. It also shows that non-developmental interests are not confined to recipient governments. Donors are just as, or more, susceptible. Non-developmental interests are not just a victim problem.
4 Or with frequently alleged lack of 'capacity', 'political will' or 'development commitment' in the recipient country (whether government or civil society), that is, a patient that is so debilitated that she is incapable of managing the 'treatments' meted out as donor benevolence.
5 There is purposeful widespread 'historical amnesia' regarding such violence among its perpetrators, which, according to Chomsky (2016), is dangerous because it erodes 'moral and intellectual integrity' and sets the stage for more of the same, or worse, to come. Farmer (2004) regards the erasing of such history as necessary for the construction of alternative accounts that are more generous to the hegemonic or imperialist perpetrator.
6 From 4 October 1965 to 15 August 1973, the United States dropped almost three million tonnes of bombs on Cambodia. More than 10% of this bombing was indiscriminate.

The massive cost of civilian dead and wounded enraged the Cambodian people and 'drove [them] into the arms of an insurgency' that had little popular support before the bombing began (Owen, 2006).

7 In Cambodia, knowledge and interpretation of the freshly minted PD and its statements regarding ownership and harmonisation and the like varied widely among the 10 bilateral donors studied by Blunt and Samneang (2005).

8 Here, and in the other countries in our sample where democracy promotion was an imperative, 'democracy' in the neoliberal era means state capitalism or a system of state governance in which government and business interests collude to develop state policy and practice that are used to ensure that national wealth is held almost exclusively by corporate and political elites and their cronies – or 'plutonomies' (Chomsky, 2010) – creating ever-widening inequality between the rich and the poor (Blunt & Lindroth, 2012).

9 In Khmer Sanskrit, 'seila' stands for 'foundation stone'. The programme was launched in 1996 to alleviate poverty in rural areas.

10 For example, in 2004, the principal author sent a 'note on outstanding policy issues' to the donor programme manager. Among many others, the note argued that the context of decentralisation and deconcentration in Cambodia suggested that policy on these matters should endorse continued incrementalism at a measured pace, that is, commensurate with the strengthening of central government, the availability of resources, willingness by the centre to relinquish control and appropriate staffing and other resource levels for commune councils. It argued, further, that such policy should make clear what government understood the terms 'decentralisation' and 'deconcentration' to mean in practice. This would have required policies to specify the degree of autonomy of decision-makers at different territorial levels in the ministries and the authorities of the provincial governors and district chiefs. More importantly for the commune councils, the policies would have had to define the links and division of authority between the commune councils, the Ministry of Interior and the line ministries. Attempts to direct the programme's attention to matters that would have had a significant positive effect on the lives of ordinary Cambodians were also largely ignored. An example was a social concessions scheme that entailed the allocation *gratis* of unoccupied state-owned land ('state private land') to poor and disadvantaged groups. It was pointed out that the role of the commune council could have been to identify such groups within their communes, to vouch for the authenticity of their qualification according to the laid-down criteria and their needs, and to represent their interests in decision-making forums. This function had clear and direct implications for poverty reduction because it targeted the most disadvantaged groups in the commune and provided them with a crucial asset for their survival. The administrative load imposed on commune councils would have been low as was the potential for producing additional administrative burden in the decentralisation superstructure. However, the direct benefits for attaining ultimate objectives were substantial (Blunt, 2004b).

11 Donor-instigated decentralisation had been set in motion in February 2002 with the support of the Seila programme (which had been working on local government since 1996) and the multi-donor Partnership for Local Governance.

12 Blunt and Turner (2005) noted that civil servant salaries were below subsistence levels, making it likely that 'rent seeking' would be systemic.

13 Australia's eyes had always been firmly fixed on the oil and gas resources in the Timor Sea, backing whichever 'partner' it felt would yield the best access to them. Declassified documents have revealed that Australia's interests had to do with rights to these oil and gas deposits, which it felt were best served by supporting the Indonesian occupation of Timor-Leste (Davidson, 2018). When East Timor became independent in 2002, it seemed likely that its maritime boundaries would be drawn to incorporate the prized oil and gas reserves. Australia quickly shifted its attention and 'support' to Timor-Leste

(Davidson, 2018). The commercial pay-off was substantial. A deal was struck that enabled the countries to share about $65 billion in revenues from the Greater Sunrise gas fields in the Timor Sea (Gloystein & Paul, 2018). Soon after, an under-sea gas pipeline was built, linking the Timor-Leste Bayu-Undan Field (situated in the Joint Petroleum Development Area between Timor-Leste and Australia) to the liquefied natural gas plant near Darwin in the Northern Territory of Australia (ConocoPhillips Australia, 2019).

14 A less generous but no less plausible interpretation, which in many ways is more consistent with the other cases discussed in this book, is that most of the projects designed, promoted and implemented by the Programme did not pose any significant direct threat to the donor's goal of gaining control over the country's natural resource wealth.

15 This was because to this point the trust's funds had been 'submerged' in support of a major existing programme – the Kecamatan Development Program – which did not afford the principal donor sufficient distinctive 'visibility'.

16 Indonesia is consistently ranked among the top five borrowers by the World Bank. See World Bank Group (2016).

17 Germany was a vocal non-financial member of the DSF.

18 Kim and Nam (1998) and Blunt and Jones (1997) explain the significance of 'face' in Asia.

19 Tyson (2015) reports that a former vice president of the World Bank viewed 'a culture of arrogance' within the organisation as being a 'problem'. A much earlier report of the same phenomenon by Rowen (1992) suggests that the problem is chronic and ingrained.

20 The principal author was told as much by the principal donor on more than one occasion.

21 As Roy (2003b) made clear at the time: 'Today, we know that every argument that is being used to escalate the war against Iraq is a lie. The most ludicrous of them being the United States government's deep commitment to bring democracy to Iraq'.

22 Corporate control of Western media and the power of the corporate military-industrial complex have meant that the citizens of the countries who caused these things to happen have little knowledge of the lethal and tragic consequences for the Iraqi people. Such wilful or manufactured ignorance and amnesia help to explain nationalistic responses to the COVID-19 pandemic and the extent to which, when it came to the distribution of vaccines, corporate profits have outweighed the public good in the political calculations of the rich governments of the West in particular. Demonstrating the degree of global inequality, to 27 February 2022, COVID-19 vaccine doses (initial protocol doses and booster doses) administered per 100 people, by income group (all doses, including boosters, are counted individually: as the same person may receive more than one dose, the number of doses per 100 people can be higher than 100) were as follows: high income, 189.39; upper middle income, 189.30; lower middle income, 106.74; low income, 17 (Ritchie *et al.*, 2020).

23 As in Cambodia, the technical assistance was in support of a decentralisation programme.

24 In Klein's (2007) view, Iraq is a prime example of the 'shock doctrine' whereby state capitalist powers induce – through invasion and occupation and other means of 'shock therapy' – a catatonic condition and *tabula rasa* for the imposition of 'free market fundamentalism' or 'the privatisation of Iraq', and capitalist predation. Stiglitz (2007) has observed that the general case against free market policies and assumptions is 'even stronger' than the one made by Klein.

25 The contract was awarded to the US-based contractor, Research Triangle Institute.

26 The gold and copper mine at Oyu Tolgoi is jointly owned by the Government of Mongolia (34%), the Rio Tinto Group (Australia) and Turquoise Hill Resources (Canada) and is being developed as a joint venture by the same entities. Oyu Tolgoi will become the world's second largest operating copper mine once the underground phase II expansion is in full operation (Mongolia EITI, 2021).

27 These included 'stern warnings' from the country CEO and director of Rio Tinto to local politicians 'agitating' for better returns from the country's natural resources, saying that Mongolia's economic 'transformation' could be brought to a standstill by 'legislative uncertainty' ("OT CEO Warns Politicians", 2011). The tone and presumptuousness of these remarks is telling, about who is, and who should be, 'in charge'.

28 Such 'acceptance' should be set against the likelihood that local communities are not always able to assess accurately the likely high negative effects of mining operations on their own livelihoods in the longer term, on the environment and on community health, or the relatively minor costs to the miner of community development projects.

29 Which, as with the US-led invasion of Iraq, underlay the US-led occupation of Afghanistan: 'Perhaps this belief in its own divinity also explains why the U.S. government has conferred upon itself the right and freedom to murder and exterminate people for their own good . . . imperial democracy delivered to your doorstep with a daisy-cutter' (Roy, 2003a, p. 323).

30 Even so, though politically increasingly difficult, the most powerful nation in human history could have elected to fight on. According to Chomsky and Prashad (2021), the US withdrawal is conditional. It allows the Taliban to assume power on two conditions. First, that the United States maintains its presence (most likely in the form of private contractors), and second, that China and Russia have no role in Afghanistan.

31 Another example from Afghanistan can be found in Blunt and Khamoosh (2016).

32 It is alleged that the 'policy' was pushed through cabinet because of donor insistence (personal communication to the second author of Blunt *et al.* (2017) from the then director general of IDLG).

33 On Saturday 28 December 1929, a Mau parade along Apia's waterfront to welcome home two members who had been exiled in New Zealand was fired upon by the police culminating in the deaths of at least eight people, among them the prominent Samoan leader Tupua Tamasese Lealofi III (NZ Ministry for Culture and Heritage, 2020. See also Field, 1991).

34 As opposed to implied or understood 'savage or primitive superstition'.

35 China's 'adventurism' abroad comprises a single military base in Djibouti on the horn of Africa, that is, 799 fewer than the United States has (Chomsky, 2021; Robinson & Chomsky, 2022).

36 The donor also insisted on being able to vet the draft agendas for programme steering committee meetings before the Programme team leader (who was secretary to that committee) had discussed them with the chair of the committee (a senior government official).

37 One of the allegations was that 'there must be something wrong' because the donor had heard nothing but praise for the Programme from government, presumably meaning that this could only have been achieved if it was government's rather than the donor's interests that were being served.

References

Afghanistan: Striking Image Captures Kabul Exodus. (2021, August 17). BBC News. https://www.bbc.com/news/world-asia-58242733

Ahlers, R., Kiezebrink, V., & Dugersuren, S. (2020, February). *Undermining Mongolia: Corporate Hold Over Development Trajectory*. Centre for Research on Multinational Corporations & Oyu Tolgoi Watch. www.somo.nl/wp-content/uploads/2020/02/Undermining-Mongolia-EN.pdf

Ariunzaya, A., Bayanchimeg, Ch., Uochi, I., & Amarbal, A. (Eds.). (2020). *Mongolia Poverty Update 2018. Main Report of 'Household Socio-Economic Survey 2018'*. National Statistics Office of Mongolia & World Bank. http://1212.mn/BookLibraryDownload.ashx?url=Poverty_report_2018_ENG.pdf&ln=En

Australia is Battling China for Influence in the Pacific. (2019, January 19). *The Economist*. www.economist.com/asia/2019/01/19/australia-is-battling-china-for-influence-in-the-pacific

Batatu, H. (1978). *The Old Social Classes and the Revolutionary Movements of Iraq: A Study of Iraq's Old Landed and Commercial Classes and of Its Communists, Ba'thists, and Free Officers (Princeton Studies on the Near East)*. Princeton University Press.

Blakemore, E. (2019, February 19). *What Is Colonialism? The History of Colonialism Is One of Brutal Subjugation of Indigenous Peoples*. National Geographic. www.nationalgeographic.com/culture/article/colonialism

Blunt, P. (2004a, February). *Explanatory Note on Decentralisation and Deconcentration* [Briefing Note]. Commune Council Development Project, Cambodia. Retrieved February 24, 2022, from www.researchgate.net/publication/354597887_Explanatory_Note_on_Decentralisation_and_Deconcentration

Blunt, P. (2004b, March 15). *Cambodia Decentralisation and Deconcentration: Note on Outstanding Policy Issues, and Policy Proposals* [Policy Brief]. Commune Council Development Project, Cambodia. Retrieved February 25, 2022, from: www.researchgate.net/publication/316391562_CAMBODIA_DECENTRALISATION_AND_DECONCENTRATION_NOTE_ON_OUTSTANDING_POLICY_ISSUES_AND_POLICY_PROPOSALS

Blunt, P. (2009). The Political Economy of Accountability in Timor-Leste: Implications for Public Policy. *Public Administration and Development, 29*(2), 89–100. https://doi.org/10.1002/pad.522

Blunt, P. (2012). Toxic Technical Assistance in Conditions of State Fragility: Field Notes From Iraq. *Progress in Development Studies, 12*(4), 337–352. https://doi.org/10.1177/146499341201200405

Blunt, P. (2014). Whose Resources Are They Anyway? 'Development Assistance' and Community Development Agreements in the Mongolian Mining Sector. *Progress in Development Studies, 14*(4), 383–399. https://doi.org/10.1177/1464993414521491

Blunt, P. (2021a). Development Undone: Weber, Kafka, and the Organisation of Supply-Side Vested Interests. *Journal of Interdisciplinary Economics, 33*(1), 74–102. https://doi.org/10.1177/0260107919896879

Blunt, P. (2021b). *Fateful Synergies: Climate Change and Non-Communicable Diseases in the Pacific Island Countries* [Discussion Paper]. Retrieved February 25, 2022, from www.researchgate.net/publication/354597783_Fateful_Synergies_Climate_Change_and_Noncommunicable_Diseases_in_the_Pacific_Island_Countries_1

Blunt, P., Escobar, C., & Missos, V. (in press). Emergency Responses Under COVID-19: Development Assistance, 'Structural Violence', and 'Interpretive Labour' in Samoa. *Journal of Interdisciplinary Economics*.

Blunt, P., & Jones, M. (1997). Exploring the Limits of Western Leadership Theory in East Asia and Africa. *Personnel Review, 26*(1/2), 6–23. https://doi.org/10.1108/00483489710157760

Blunt, P., & Khamoosh, S. (2016). Vexatious Voice: The Politics of Downward Accountability and Subnational Governance Reform in Afghanistan. *Progress in Development Studies, 16*(1), 81–100. https://doi.org/10.1177/1464993415608085

Blunt, P., & Lindroth, H. (2012). Development's Denial of Social Justice. *International Journal of Public Administration, 35*(7), 471–481. https://doi.org/10.1080/01900692.2012.655357

Blunt, P., Mamundzay, F., & Nasary, M. (2017). The Long and the Short of Policy Pantomime in Afghanistan. *Progress in Development Studies, 17*(1), 67–88. https://doi.org/10.1177/1464993416674303

Blunt, P., Mamundzay, F., Yama, N., & Afghan, H. (2015). Policy Paradigms, Subnational Governance and the State Sovereignty Gap in Afghanistan. *Progress in Development Studies, 15*(3), 270–285. https://doi.org/10.1177/1464993415578981

Blunt, P., & Samneang, M. (2005, October). *Aid Effectiveness and Aid Coordination in Cambodia: Stakeholder Perceptions*. The Asia Foundation. Retrieved February 24, 2022, from http://webarchive.nationalarchives.gov.uk/+/www.dfid.gov.uk/mdg/aid-effectiveness/newsletters/cambodia-report.pdf

Blunt, P., & Turner, M. (2005). Decentralisation, Democracy and Development in a Post-Conflict Society: Commune Councils in Cambodia. *Public Administration and Development*, *25*(1), 75–87. https://doi.org/10.1002/pad.349

Blunt, P., Turner, M., & Hertz, J. (2011). The Meaning of Development Assistance. *Public Administration and Development*, *31*(3), 172–187. https://doi.org/10.1002/pad.592

Blunt, P., Turner, M., & Lindroth, H. (2012a). Patronage's Progress in Post-Soeharto Indonesia. *Public Administration and Development*, *32*(1), 64–81. https://doi.org/10.1002/pad.617

Blunt, P., Turner, M., & Lindroth, H. (2012b). Patronage, Service Delivery and Social Justice in Indonesia. *International Journal of Public Administration*, *35*(3), 214–220. https://doi.org/10.1080/01900692.2011.641050

Booth, D. (2012). Aid Effectiveness: Bringing Country Ownership (and Politics) Back In. *Conflict, Security & Development*, *12*(5), 537–558. https://doi.org/10.1080/14678802.2012.744184

Boyd, M. (1968). The Military Administration of Western Samoa, 1914–1919. *The New Zealand Journal of History*, *2*(2), 148–164. www.nzjh.auckland.ac.nz/docs/1968/NZJH_02_2_04.pdf

Brolin, T. (2017). Ownership and Results in Swedish General Budget Support to Mozambique. *Forum for Development Studies*, *44*(3), 377–399. https://doi.org/10.1080/08039410.2017.1388279

Cantore, N., Hartwich, F., Lavopa, A., Haverkamp, K., Laplane, A., & Rodousakis, N. (2020, July 10). *Coronavirus: The Economic Impact – 10 July 2020. A Health Pandemic or a Pandemic for the Economy?* Policy, Research and Statistics Department, United Nations Industrial Development Organization. www.unido.org/stories/coronavirus-economic-impact-10-july-2020#story-start

Carothers, T. (2015). The Deeper Struggle Over Country Ownership. In OECD. *A Governance Practitioner's Notebook: Alternative Ideas and Approaches* (pp. 249–255). www.oecd.org/dac/accountable-effective-institutions/Governance%20Notebook%203.2%20Carothers.pdf

Chomsky, N. (1999, October). East Timor, Horror and Amnesia. *Le Monde diplomatique*. https://mondediplo.com/1999/10/02chomsky

Chomsky, N. (2010). *Hopes and Prospects*. Penguin eBooks.

Chomsky, N. (2016). *Who Rules the World? (The American Empire Project)*. Metropolitan Books.

Chomsky, N. (2021, September 24). The Future of American Power: Noam Chomsky on The Cruelty of American Imperialism. *The Economist*. www.economist.com/by-invitation/2021/09/24/noam-chomsky-on-the-cruelty-of-american-imperialism

Chomsky, N., & Herman, E. S. (1973). *Counter-Revolutionary Violence: Bloodbaths in Fact and Propaganda* (Module 57, pp. 1–46). Warner Modular Publications. http://web.archive.org/web/20040611022032/mass-multi-media.com/CRV/#sec4

Chomsky, N., & Prashad, V. (2021, May 7). *Chomsky and Prashad: The Reality Behind the US 'Withdrawal' From Afghanistan*. AlterNet. www.alternet.org/2021/05/us-afghan-troop-withdrawal/

Clarke, M. (2021, September 22). The AUKUS Nuclear Submarine Deal: Unanswered Questions for Australia. *The Diplomat*. https://thediplomat.com/2021/09/the-aukus-nuclear-submarine-deal-unanswered-questions-for-australia/

ConocoPhillips Australia. (2019, March). *Bayu-Undan Gas Export Pipeline Production Cessation* [Environmental Plan – Notice of Consultation]. https://static.conocophillips.com/files/resources/bayu-undan-gas-export-pipeline-production-cessatio.pdf

Crawford, N. C. (2021, September 1). Calculating the Costs of the Afghanistan War in Lives, Dollars and Years. *The Conversation*. https://theconversation.com/calculating-the-costs-of-the-afghanistan-war-in-lives-dollars-and-years-164588

Davidson, H. (2018, May 7). Oil and Gas Had Hidden Role in Australia's Response to Indonesian Invasion of Timor-Leste. *The Guardian*. www.theguardian.com/australia-news/2018/may/07/oil-and-gas-had-hidden-role-in-australias-response-to-indonesian-invasion-of-timor-leste

Decentralisation Support Facility. (2010). *Decentralisation Support Facility Annual Report 2010*. Retrieved February 28, 2022, from www.researchgate.net/publication/354710846_DECENTRALIZATION_SUPPORT_FACILITY_ANNUAL_REPORT_2010

Dornan, M., & Pryke, J. (2017). Foreign Aid to the Pacific: Trends and Developments in the Twenty-First Century. *Asia & the Pacific Policy Studies*, *4*(3), 386–404. https://doi.org/10.1002/app5.185

Escobar, A. (1995). *Encountering Development: The Making and Unmaking of the Third World* [1st printing]. Princeton University Press.

Evans, G. (2011, November 3). East Timor and Me: A Response to Noam Chomsky. *The Interpreter*. https://archive.lowyinstitute.org/the-interpreter/east-timor-and-me-response-noam-chomsky

Falcone, D. (2017, October 30). *Noam Chomsky on Our Wonderful Indonesian Moderates*. teleSUR. www.telesurenglish.net/opinion/Noam-Chomsky-on-Our-Wonderful-Indonesian-Moderates-20171030-0013.html

Farmer, P. (2004). An Anthropology of Structural Violence. *Current Anthropology*, *45*(3), 305–325. https://doi.org/10.1086/382250

Farouk-Sluglett, M., & Sluglett, P. (2001). *Iraq Since 1958: From Revolution to Dictatorship* (Revised ed.). I.B. Tauris.

Field, M. J. (1991). *Mau: Samoa's Struggle for Freedom*. Polynesian Press.

Gloystein, H., & Paul, S. (2018, March 7). *How Australia-East Timor Treaty Unlocks $65 Billion Gas Fields*. Reuters. www.reuters.com/article/us-timor-australia-lng-idUSKCN1GJ0L8

Gottesman, E. (2002). *Cambodia After the Khmer Rouge: Inside the Politics of Nation Building*. Yale University Press.

Graeber, D. (2015). *The Utopia of Rules: On Technology, Stupidity, and the Secret Joys of Bureaucracy*. Melville House.

Helble, M., Hill, H., & Magee, D. (Eds.). (2020, June). *Mongolia's Economic Prospects: Resource-Rich and Landlocked Between Two Giants (Country Diagnostic Studies)*. Asian Development Bank. http://dx.doi.org/10.22617/SGP200172-2

Hickel, J. (2021, December 5). The Age of Imperialism Is Not Over—But We Can End It. *Current Affairs*. https://www.currentaffairs.org/2021/12/the-age-of-imperialism-is-not-over-but-we-can-end-it

Kamm, H. (1998). *Cambodia: Report From a Stricken Land*. Arcade Publishing.

Kathem, M. (2020). New Imperialism in Iraq: How the US Occupation Helped Establish But Then Cannibalised the Sadr City District Council. *Peacebuilding*, *8*(3), 363–378. https://doi.org/10.1080/21647259.2019.1621074

Kiezebrink, V., Ahlers, R., & Dugersuren, S. (2018, January). *Mining Taxes: The Case of Oyu Tolgoi and Profitable Tax Avoidance by Rio Tinto in Mongolia*. Centre for Research on Multinational Corporations & Oyu Tolgoi Watch. www.somo.nl/wp-content/uploads/2018/01/Mining_taxes_V_1.2.pdf

Kim, J. Y., & Nam, S. H. (1998). The Concept and Dynamics of Face: Implications for Organizational Behaviour in Asia. *Organization Science*, *9*(4), 522–534. https://doi.org/10.1287/orsc.9.4.522

Klein, K. (2007). *The Shock Doctrine: The Rise of Disaster Capitalism*. Metropolitan Books.

Lundsgaarde, E., & Engberg-Pedersen, L. (2019, July 11). *Revisiting the Aid Effectiveness Agenda: Has the Paris Declaration Disappeared?* [Policy Brief]. Danish Institute for International Studies. https://pure.diis.dk/ws/files/2914827/Erik_og_Lars_Paris_Agenda_disappeared WEBFINAL1207.pdf

Martinez-Alvarez, M. (2018). Ownership in Name, But not Necessarily in Action; Comment on "It's About the Idea Hitting the Bull's Eye": How Aid Effectiveness Can Catalyse the Scale-Up of Health Innovations. *International Journal of Health Policy and Management*, 7(11), 1053–1055. https://doi.org/10.15171/ijhpm.2018.72

McClure, J. H. (2021, March 23). *Mongolia's First Transfer Pricing Assessment – What Could Be the Issues?* MNE Tax. https://mnetax.com/mongolias-first-transfer-pricing-assessment-what-could-be-the-issues-43088

Minasny, B. (2020, July 2). The Dark History of Slavery and Racism in Indonesia During the Dutch Colonial Period. *The Conversation*. https://theconversation.com/the-dark-history-of-slavery-and-racism-in-indonesia-during-the-dutch-colonial-period-141457

Mongolia Extractive Industries Transparency Initiative. (2021, December). *Mongolia Fifteen EITI Reconciliation Report 2020*. https://eiti.org/files/documents/mongolia_eiti_2020_report_in_eng.pdf

Mosse, D. (2005). *Cultivating Development: An Ethnography of Aid Policy and Practice*. Pluto Press.

Mourer, J-L. (2021, March 22). Indonesia in '3D': Development, Dictatorship and Democracy. *The Newsletter*, (88), 10–11. www.iias.asia/sites/default/files/nwl_article/2021-03/IIAS_NL88_1011.pdf

New Zealand Ministry for Culture and Heritage. (2020, September 2). *Black Saturday*. New Zealand History. https://nzhistory.govt.nz/politics/samoa/black-saturday

Organisation for Economic Co-operation and Development. (2011). *The Evaluation of the Paris Declaration. Country Ownership of Development: Political Correctness or a Practical Key to Better Aid?* (Policy Brief No. 4). www.oecd.org/dac/evaluation/dcdndep/48704765.pdf

Organisation for Economic Co-operation and Development. (2019). *Development Aid at a Glance. Statistics by Region: Oceania*. www.oecd.org/dac/financing-sustainable-development/development-finance-data/Oceania-Development-Aid-at-a-Glance-2019.pdf

Organisation for Economic Co-operation and Development. (n.d.). *Member Countries' Budget Contributions for 2019*. www.oecd.org/about/budget/member-countries-budget-contributions.htm

OT CEO Warns Politicians not to Change Agreement. (2011, October 20). *Mongolian Mining Journal*. www.mongolianminingjournal.com/a/15713

Owen, T. (2006, October 12). Bombs over Cambodia. *The Walrus*. https://thewalrus.ca/2006-10-history/

Peou, S. (2019). Cambodia's Hegemonic-Party System: How and Why the CPP Became Dominant. *Asian Journal of Comparative Politics*, *4*(1), 42–60. https://doi.org/10.1177/2057891118788199

Polychroniou, C. J. (2022, August 4). 21st-Century US Foreign Policy Is Shaped by Fears of China's Rise, Chomsky Says. *Truthout*. https://truthout.org/articles/21st-century-us-foreign-policy-is-shaped-by-fears-of-chinas-rise-chomsky-says/

Porter, R. A. (2009). *Realpolitik* in Mongolia-US Relations. *Ritsumeikan Journal of Asia Pacific Studies, 26*, 49–63. https://en.apu.ac.jp/rcaps/uploads/fckeditor/publications/journal/RJAPS_V26_PorterR.pdf

Prashad, V. (2018, March 1). *In the Ruins of the Present*. Tricontinental Working Document No. 1. https://thetricontinental.org/working-document-1/

Ramachandran, V. (2020, September 22). *What Happened to the 'Asian Century'? COVID-19 in Australia and New Zealand?* COMPAS. www.compas.ox.ac.uk/2020/what-happened-to-the-asian-century-covid-19-in-australia-and-new-zealand/

Ritchie, H., Mathieu, E., Rodés-Guirao, L., Appel, C., Giattino, C., Ortiz-Ospina, E., Hasell, J., Macdonald, B., Beltekian, D., & Roser, M. (2020). *Coronavirus (COVID-19) Vaccinations* [Data set]. Our World in Data. Retrieved February 28, 2022, from https://ourworldindata.org/explorers/coronavirus-data-explorer?zoomToSelection=true&facet=none&uniformYAxis=0&pickerSort=asc&pickerMetric=location&Interval=7-day+rolling+average&Relative+to+Population=true&Color+by+test+positivity=false&country=Low+income~High+income~Upper+middle+income~Lower+middle+income&Metric=Vaccine+doses+%28by+type%29

Roberts, M. (2022, May 20). Australia: Turning for the Worse. *Michael Roberts Blog*. https://thenextrecession.wordpress.com/2022/05/20/australia-turning-for-the-worse/

Robinson, G. (2011). East Timor Ten Years On: Legacies of Violence. *The Journal of Asian Studies*, *70*(4), 1007–1021. http://doi.org/10.1017/S0021911811001586

Robinson, N. J., & Chomsky, N. (2022, August 15). If We Want Humanity to Survive, We Must Cooperate With China. *Current Affairs*. https://www.currentaffairs.org/2022/08/if-we-want-humanity-to-survive-we-must-cooperate-with-china

Rourke, A. (2019, August 29). East Timor: Indonesia's Invasion and the Long Road to Independence. *The Guardian*. www.theguardian.com/world/2019/aug/30/east-timor-indonesias-invasion-and-the-long-road-to-independence

Rowen, H. (1992, May 24). Lewis Preston Aims to Ax World Bank's Arrogance. *The Washington Post*. www.washingtonpost.com/archive/business/1992/05/24/lewis-preston-aims-to-ax-world-banks-arrogance/487293e4-4c5a-4619-a1bb-785ba97ea814/

Roy, A. (2003a). Noam Chomsky, Neoliberalism, and the New War on Iraq. *Contemporary Justice Review*, *6*(4), 321–327. https://doi.org/10.1080/1028258032000144767

Roy, A. (2003b, January 27). Confronting Empire [Speech audio recording, print edition February 14, 2003]. *Frontline*. https://frontline.thehindu.com/world-affairs/article30215627.ece

Roy, A. (2004). *The Ordinary Person's Guide to Empire*. HarperCollins Publishers.

Rubin, B. (2002, June 25). *The Fragmentation of Afghanistan: State Formation and Collapse in the International System* [Transcript of the talk delivered to the Carnegie Council]. Carnegie Council. www.carnegiecouncil.org/studio/multimedia/20020625-the-fragmentation-of-afghanistan-state-formation-and-collapse-in-the-international-system

Shaw, M. (2016, June 23–25). *Imposed Culture and Mongolia's Democratic Transition* [Paper presentation]. CEEISA-ISA 2016 Joint International Conference, Ljubljana, Slovenia. http://web.isanet.org/Web/Conferences/CEEISA-ISA-LBJ2016/Archive/87a681fa-fdda-4467-b4bd-1531d632b94e.pdf

Simons, G. (2002, December). The Making of Iraq. *The Link*, *35*(5), 1–13. www.ameu.org/getattachment/ad156cbf-3b68-4454-8c01-87c114c55f2e/The-Making-of-Iraq.aspx

Stiglitz, J. E. (2007, September 30). Bleakonomics. *The New York Times*. www.nytimes.com/2007/09/30/books/review/Stiglitz-t.html

Tasevski, O. (2020, August 10). The Dutch are Uncomfortable with Being History's Villains, Not Victims. *Foreign Policy*. https://foreignpolicy.com/2020/08/10/dutch-colonial-history-indonesia-villains-victims/

Thaker, J. (2021, May 18). A Year After New Zealand's First COVID-19 Lockdown, Discrimination and Racism are on the Rise. *The Conversation*. https://theconversation.com/a-year-after-new-zealands-first-covid-19-lockdown-discrimination-and-racism-are-on-the-rise-160858

Tirman, J. (n.d.). *Iraq: The Human Cost*. MIT Centre for International Studies. Retrieved February 28, 2022, from https://web.mit.edu/humancostiraq/

Tomkins, S. M. (1992). The Influenza Epidemic of 1918–19 in Western Samoa. *The Journal of Pacific History*, *27*(2), 181–197. www.jstor.org/stable/25169127

Townshend, A. (2021). Australia's New Regional Security Posture. In The International Institute for Strategic Studies (Ed.). *Asia-Pacific Regional Security Assessment 2021: Key Developments and Trends*. Routledge.

Tyson, J. (2015, January 16). *Former VP: 'Culture of Arrogance' is a Problem at the World Bank*. Devex. www.devex.com/news/former-vp-culture-of-arrogance-is-a-problem-at-the-world-bank-85258

Visser, R. (2011a). Policing a Messy Federation: The Role of the Iraqi Federal Supreme Court, 2005–2010. *Orient*, *52*(2), 12–18.

Visser, R. (2011b, December 28). The Arbil Agreement Versus Daawa Authoritarianism. *Iraq and Gulf Analysis*. https://gulfanalysis.wordpress.com/2011/12/28/the-arbil-agreement-versus-daawa-authoritarianism/

Walden, M., & Choahan, N. (2020, July 27). China Is Pushing Its South China Sea Claims During the Coronavirus Pandemic – This Is What the Tensions Are About. *ABC News*. www.abc.net.au/news/2020-07-27/south-china-sea-what-tensions-with-us-australia-are-about/12492432

Wallis, J. (2021, June 21). The Risks of Escalating Strategic Competition in the Pacific Islands. *The Interpreter*. www.lowyinstitute.org/the-interpreter/risks-escalating-strategic-competition-pacific-islands

World Bank Group. (2016). Top 10 Countries IBDR Statement of Loans – Latest Available Snapshot [Data set]. Retrieved February 28, 2022, from https://finances.worldbank.org/Loans-and-Credits/Top-10-countries/5xqk-t59j

4 Critical Interfaces of Bureaucratic Structural Violence

Masters, Messengers and Minions

Introduction

This chapter examines the bureaucratic structural violence inflicted by individuals holding positions of power at critical interfaces of technical assistance in the field. In Chapter 3, we showed how such violence is situated within, and reflects, or in some sense is a continuation of, historical structural violence, what Farmer (2004) calls the 'social machinery of oppression'. This view regards the power of the state and of major corporations and concentrations of wealth, often exacerbated by race and gender, as forces that shape societies and the beliefs and behaviour of individuals and groups within them (Foucault, 1975/1977).

We categorise the principal actors involved in the dynamics of bureaucratic structural violence associated with technical assistance in the field as being 'masters', 'messengers' or 'minions'. Masters occupy those positions that possess the greatest power over the design, approval and implementation of technical assistance programmes and projects. As demonstrated in Chapter 3, most often, the responsible donor official in the field sits at the pinnacle of control over such matters. We say 'most often' because there are rare instances when the donor delegates its power, and the role of master, to the managing contractor, as shall be seen in the Iraq case.

Typically, however, the contractor occupies the second tier of control, immediately beneath the donor, who has complete discretion over the appointment, reward and removal of the contractor. This more or less guarantees that contractors are obedient and unquestioning appendages of the donor, or 'docile subjects' (Foucault, 1975/1977). We therefore depict them and the supervising managers or directors that they appoint to oversee programmes or projects of technical assistance as 'messengers'.

Minions are underlings or supplicants, who are the subjects of the bureaucratic structural violence inflicted by masters and messengers. To cope, they must engage constantly in interpretive labour. We categorise as 'minions' programme managers or team leaders employed by the contractor, government members of programme steering committees, and government principal counterparts for projects.

DOI: 10.4324/9781003284352-4

This chapter is structured as follows. First, we define the different forms of power that we employ in our discussion of the relationships between the principal actors. Second, we analyse the relationships between masters and minions, while taking into account the intermediary role of messengers, and we consider how the bureaucratic structural violence inflicted by masters and messengers is expressed, the effects of this and the factors that influence it. Finally, third, we briefly discuss relations between minions and their several and joint attempts to cope with the bureaucratic structural violence inflicted on them.

Forms and Sources of Power

We accommodate power as individual agency and power as a reflection of historical and bureaucratic structural violence by utilising the concepts of 'power over' and 'power to' proposed by Kashwan *et al.* (2019) and the classical notions of referent, expert, legitimate, reward and coercive power identified by French and Raven (1959).

'Power over' is a function of both historical *and* institutional or systemic forces. It is manifested at the lower reaches of technical assistance bureaucracies as some combination of the 'legitimate' power, and 'reward' and 'coercive' power, of the supervising donor official. It can also incorporate 'referent' power, where minions identify with the master or messenger by supposing: 'I am like, or want to be like, the master and therefore I shall comply with the master's wishes and adopt her beliefs' (see also Marcuse, 1936/1972); and 'expert' power, where minions accept that the master or messenger possesses authentic, superior skills or abilities, or knowledge.

The level of coercive and reward power associated with a master's position and the degree of control that can be imposed is a function of the magnitude of rewards or punishments that can be meted out: to minions by masters or messengers and to messengers by masters. Legitimate power stems from internalised values that accept that the master has the right to control or influence the messenger or minion and that the messenger or minion is obliged to accept this control (French & Raven, 1959). Such values and legitimacy are likely to be the product of long-term conditioning regarding the master's possession of more or less complete material control over the life-giving circumstances of the minion.

On the other hand, 'power to' can be used to protect the *status quo* or to change it (Kashwan *et al.*, 2019). Later, we are particularly concerned with the ability of minions to resist bureaucratic structural violence through the ingenuity of their interpretive labour.[1]

Master–Minion Relations

Being completely subservient to the master's reward, coercive and legitimate power, we recognise that in important ways contractors as messengers are simply higher order minions. But we conceive of them as more master than minion because, first, they identify with masters; and, second, because of the reward and coercive power that they hold over programme personnel, who are their employees, hence our designation of them as messengers. They are willing messengers and identify with the master, because business survival and profit depend on their absolute compliance with the master's wishes, which they regard as legitimate.

Contractor subservience makes them highly sensitive to any hint of donor displeasure. In particular, the donor supervising official (who decides annual contractor bonuses and has an important influence on contract extensions and renewals), at all costs, must be pampered, humoured and protected, particularly from 'bad' news. For contractors, the ultimate measure of programme performance is therefore donor 'happiness' (as opposed to genuinely developmental technical assistance), which their behaviour seeks to maximise: by advancing and constantly reinforcing the interests of the master; by amplifying master directives and making sure that they are implemented; by portraying the master in the best possible light at every opportunity; by insulating the master from reputational risk and any dirty work that needs to be done; by filtering and, if necessary, doctoring project/programme information that the master receives; by acting as a hypersensitive barometer or weathervane of the master's every wish or desire and mood; by keeping minions over whom they have control firmly in line; and by reprimanding and punishing transgressors on behalf of the master.

The principal interface between masters and minions and between messengers and minions is with or through the programme team leader (PTL) in the field.

In the previous circumstances, and particularly in so far as projects that the donor would regard as 'red-flag' are concerned, the ability for minions to exercise 'power to' – that is, to do development work that is in the interests of the host country – is highly constrained. The exercise by minions of expert and other forms of power is limited to projects that do not register a donor red flag. Otherwise, as we shall see, technical expertise or expert power carries no weight and is unable to provide any effective counter to donor-induced bureaucratic structural violence.

Of course, minions like PTLs and principal government counterparts or steering committee members also possess varying levels of legitimate, reward, coercive and, in some cases, referent power regarding their own organisations or work units: teams of consultants, government departments or agencies, and so on. But such power has little or no bearing on the behaviour of masters or messengers regarding the technical assistance that we discuss later.

In general terms, the evidence that we presented in Chapter 3 – on 'democracy promotion come what may' in Cambodia, Indonesia, Iraq and Afghanistan, the protection of foreign corporate interests in mining in Mongolia, and 'red-flag' projects in Samoa – demonstrates this.

In what follows, we dig a little more deeply into the dynamics of the relationships surrounding the bureaucratic structural violence associated with our country cases and the personalities of, in particular, the masters and messengers involved.

Cambodia (2003–2006)

In Cambodia, master control was vested in two positions, a foreign donor official (M) from the responsible multilateral agency (ADB) and a deputy who was a locally appointed Cambodia national (DM).[2] DM was stationed in Phnom Penh for the full 3 years of the Programme. M was based at ADB headquarters in Manila and made short visits to Phnom Penh several times a year. Neither M nor DM possessed any technical expertise that was relevant to the Programme's work. Yet, as indicated earlier, their power over the principal messenger (the implementing contractor) (MES) and the principal minion (the PTL) was absolute.[3]

This had three main consequences. First, it meant that M's and DM's attention was focused on the *letter* of programme documents and contracts, and micromanagement. A central feature of this was the pursuit of decentralisation as democracy promotion, as explained in Chapter 3. Other examples included the form and frequency of reporting, and the alignment of their substance with the democracy promotion agenda; the number and timing of 'coordination' meetings, with a view to shepherding other donors in the 'right' direction (see later); and the maintenance of harmonious relations with the principal government counterparts irrespective of the attainment of developmental ends for the public good. The critical part of relations with the principal counterpart was the expectation that the PTL would influence government to take the 'right direction', meaning decentralisation for democracy promotion.

Second, it meant that there was little or no prospect of meaningful discussions taking place between M or DM and the PTL about the substance of programme aims and activities unless it was about the extent to which they conformed to democracy promotion ends. Third, the absolute power of M meant that she had no interest in the points of view of significant others (lack of empathy) – unless such views detracted from democracy promotion and, as we anticipate in Chapter 2, that she was inclined to suppress creativity and critical thinking in general unless it was in support of democracy promotion via decentralisation. Important also – perhaps crucial – was the fact that the part of the Programme that was devoted to the construction of commune council office buildings had been financed by an ADB loan to the Government of Cambodia. Indeed, it seems likely that the technical assistance parts of the Programme had been developed around a loan-financed 'concrete core' of building construction, meaning that the commitment to decentralisation had vital institutional and ideological components.

As suggested in Chapters 1 and 2, personality variables were also important. M's personality seemed to relish and thrive on the power that she possessed, which was reinforced by her interactions with DM and MES and with government. This left little room for critical debate or dissent. From the point of view of the PTL, the atmosphere was one of 'perpetual tension' and largely suppressed discord, which gave rise to a number of the dysfunctions of organisational culture identified by Bate (1984) and Blunt (1988), and elements of the 'fragmented (negative) cultures' discussed by Blunt (1991). For example:

Unemotionality – Where the expression of views about organisational issues is avoided. Problems therefore tend to be internalised and to smoulder for long periods of time. If problems are brought into the open, they are dealt with at arm's length. Wherever possible, face-to-face confrontation is avoided. People tend to be overcautious and inflexible. Collaborative problem solving and decision-making rarely occur, and people's concerns focus on coping with the *status quo* rather than attempting to change it.

Antipathy – Where it is assumed that most other people will oppose you and that no one can be trusted. Competing interest groups and alliances are the norms. Relations are antagonistic. All issues are seen as win–lose. Even relatively minor issues are bitterly contested.

Clearly, from the point of view of developmental technical assistance, the jobs of M and DM were bullshit-like, in that their disappearance would not have had any adverse effects on programme performance and, indeed, might have improved it. Equally clearly, however, the systemic legitimacy of such jobs[4] and the necessity of some of their administrative functions mean that they are unlikely to disappear. Technical assistance will continue to have to contend with them. In Chapter 5, we address the necessary evil of these jobs by asking how they might be made less oppressive, repressive and counter-productive.

Representatives of the financial donors to the Programme – from the Netherlands and Sweden – were based in their home countries. The principal author and PTL had no contact with the Netherlands representative. He met the Swedish representative briefly over coffee or lunch on his annual visits to Phnom Penh. In the latter case, the PTL explained his views regarding the demerits of decentralisation in Cambodia, but if these were conveyed to M, they had no discernible effect. *De facto*, the Netherlands representative was content to defer to M, the ADB donor official. Both donor positions were consistent with the conventional view regarding the merit of causal links between decentralisation and democratisation.

The implementing contractor was an Australian firm whose responsible director – MES – was based in Australia and did not visit Cambodia during the life of the Programme. MES was a non-confrontational 'nice guy' whose behaviour corresponded closely with the general account of messenger behaviour that we set out earlier in the introduction to this section. In short, he was deferential to M, and compliant, and was intent on 'not rocking the boat'. He had no knowledge or expertise that was relevant to the Programme.

The principal government counterpart for the Programme was the Director of the Department of Local Administration in the Ministry of Interior. Day-to-day contact with the Programme was delegated by him to an assistant. As noted in Chapter 3, demand-side interests had mainly to do with the consolidation of the political power of the CPP. So long as decentralisation did not entail any significant devolution of power from the centre and was concerned mostly with capacity building of local government officials (both of which were the case), the principal government counterpart showed little interest in discussing anything other than the administrative aspects of programme implementation.

The principal author (as PTL) was the main interface between the Programme and M/DM and MES. He was based in Phnom Penh for 6 months in 2003, the whole of 2004, 6 months in 2005, and 2 months in 2006.

The PTL's critical orientation towards rich country, mainly Western, forms of intellectual and cultural hegemony (e.g. Blunt & Jones, 1997) and his growing awareness of the severe limitations of neoliberalism and predatory development assistance (e.g. Blunt & Rondinelli, 1997) were always likely to have made for an uneasy relationship with M. Soon after his appointment, different forms of role conflict began to manifest themselves. In particular, first, it quickly became apparent that there was considerable *intersender conflict*, where role expectations from one member of the role set[5] oppose those from one or more of its other members (such as the different views of decentralisation held by the PTL and M); and second, *person-role conflict*, where role expectations[6] clash with the values or orientations of the focal person (in this case, M). Managing these tensions and conflicts demanded considerable interpretive labour on the part of the PTL and was chronically stressful. Stress made worse by the fact that the PTL recognised that M and MES had coercive and reward power over him that was legitimate, but that it might not always be used legitimately, as in the Samoan examples given in Chapter 3, where, in order to keep his job, the PTL was compelled to collude in activities that were not legitimate according to the terms of reference for his position, the donor's own rules, or according to procedures agreed formally with the host government.

In these circumstances, the PTL's expert power in the broad fields of development management and decentralisation was largely worthless to developmental ends. For M, its principal virtue was that it enabled the Programme's activities to be cast in technical terms that conveyed an informed view of decentralisation as democracy promotion, that is, its value as 'rationalising technical discourse' behind which to pursue the self-interests of 'bureaucratic power or dominance' (Mosse, 2013).

As can be seen, all avenues for the pursuit by the PTL of programme activities that might have had more developmental results were closed off. M was ideologically committed to 'democracy promotion come what may' and unwilling to consider counter-arguments. DM followed along obediently. MES deferred completely to M and would not countenance any suggestion that might elicit M's displeasure. In any case, discussions with MES about the substance of the Programme were not possible because MES lacked relevant expertise. And the host government acceded to the appearance of democracy promotion because it enabled them to consolidate the position of the ruling party, the CPP.

From the standpoint of developmental technical assistance, the organisational culture that resulted was dysfunctional in the ways set out earlier.

The question that arises, and that we address in Chapter 5, is whether a more developmental programme could have been made to satisfy donor interests *and* achieve sufficient government ownership for it to be able to implement activities that were in the public interest.

Timor-Leste (2006–2008)

In Chapter 3, we remarked on the unusually constructive organisational culture surrounding the relationship between M and programme minions in Timor-Leste, particularly the PTL – one that was 'exemplary', the most important ingredients being those of mutual respect and trust combined with healthy and undefensive critical debate of high quality concerning the development and management of issues confronting the Programme.

In the cases that we discuss in this book, these conditions were unique. How did they come about? M's intelligence, personality, management style and development orientation were crucial. A graduate with first-class honours in philosophy, politics and economics from the University of Oxford, he was clearly capable intellectually. But he combined this with what appeared to be a genuine interest in achieving developmental results for the new government of Timor-Leste and a management style that was refreshingly micromanagement-free and encouraged the PTL to make full use of his technical expertise.[7]

The culture that evolved around the relationship between M and the Programme and PTL had many of the qualities of the 'synergistic cultures' discussed by Blunt (1991), namely, agreement about values and attitudes, shared purpose and commitment to the organisation's mission and ways of working. These were the hallmarks of Mintzberg's (1989) 'missionary organisation'.

This enabled the Programme to do the best that it could in the difficult circumstances of Timor-Leste at the time to achieve developmental results for the country. The Programme was able to operate with complete integrity and to conform to the rules and procedures that had been agreed with the host government regarding the design, approval and implementation of projects. Unlike in Samoa or Mongolia (see later), no pressure was put on the Programme to do otherwise so as to protect donor interests. On the contrary, in this case, M seemed implicitly to have adopted a strategy that allowed the Programme to do work that was in the best interests of the host country on the assumption that this was the most effective way of producing the kind of goodwill and mutual respect that would facilitate the achievement of the donor's interests, namely, access to the significant oil and gas resources of the Timor Sea (referred to in Chapter 3).

This strategy meant that, so long as the donor and the Programme were seen to be doing their best, that is, to be doing what they agreed to do and behaving authentically and honourably that this would carry more weight with the host country than whether the technical assistance was effective or not, which would be regarded as a bonus. It would also have the considerable advantage of being easier to evaluate. As we demonstrate more fully in the Mongolian and Samoan cases later, it is more or less immediately apparent to all involved when M is being hypocritical or deceitful or dishonourable or patronising. On the other hand, apart from programme activities, the multitude and complexity of independent variables or causal factors (the most important of which technical assistance has no ability to influence) make the business of programme or project evaluation, at best, semi-educated guesswork.

The contrast between the relationship depicted earlier – between M and the Programme and PTL – and the relationship between the PTL and the MES, the Australian managing contractor was stark. Unlike the Cambodian case discussed earlier, in this instance, the MES was a frequent visitor to the capital, Dili, and used his coercive and reward power to pressure the Programme to take steps that provided maximum protection to the MES's commercial interests. File notes made by the PTL at the time refer to the following qualities of the contractor and MES: the knowing appointment of consultants to positions for which they were clearly not qualified; attempts to exercise undue influence over selection decisions in the field and special pleading for candidates with whom they were personally connected or people known or thought to be AusAID-friendly; 'slime-ball management by stealth', the appointment of 'moles' and the cultivation of the 'wailing-wall' phenomenon – in relation to programme staff;[8] a 'good old boy' culture based on drinking and personal connections rather than capability or performance; ignorance of basic principles of management combined with excessive authoritarianism and arrogance; insufficient consultation, indeed zero consultation; insufficient knowledge of fundamental questions of development; editing of technical reports by people who were not qualified to do so – that is, who knew nothing about development. Censorship of reports and reporting to AusAID based on judgements made by unqualified and inexperienced people about what AusAID would 'like' and what would present (MES) in a good light; an almost complete absence of policy and therefore no consistency in decision-making; and a philosophy of please AusAID at all costs and absence of principle.

The high turnover of management staff in the contractor headquarters in Australia – for example, six so-called programme senior managers in less than 1 year – was evidence of the validity of these criticisms.

The 'hostility' and 'unemotionality' that was said earlier to characterise the relations between M and the PTL/Programme in the Cambodian case were evident in Timor-Leste in the relationship between the PTL and the MES. MES had no relevant technical expertise, little management experience or capability and, as with M in the Cambodian case, this was combined with a personality that seemed to relish the 'power over' that went with his position. The result was the types of bureaucratic structural violence referred to in the PTL's file notes.

The contrast between these two cultures – PTL/M versus PTL/MES – was remarkable for another reason. One might have expected that the 'keep the donor happy at all costs' principle, which is uppermost in the minds of all MESs, would have meant that the excellent relations that had been established between the PTL and M would have lessened the MES's perceived need to interfere with programme activities. The fact that it did not point again to the importance of personality at the critical interfaces of the delivery of technical assistance. The lack of relevant policy and bad selection by the contractor combined with youth and inexperience and authoritarianism in the MES made for the worst of all possible outcomes.

Clearly, in this case, for the Programme and the PTL, the main source of bureaucratic structural violence was the contractor and the MES. As the PTL's file notes suggest, the vast majority of the PTL's interpretive labour was therefore directed at mitigating the effects of this structural violence and trying to prevent or avoid continuing outbreaks of it.

Indonesia (2008–2011)

As noted in Chapter 3, in this case, the principal author's role was that of manager of a large multi-donor trust fund administered by the World Bank (the Bank) that supported the Decentralisation Support Facility (DSF). He was brought in to turnaround the DSF, which was on the point of collapse because the principal LDI donor had threatened to withdraw funding.

As in the Cambodian case (where an ADB project supervising staff member was designated as a master), under normal circumstances, the principal author's position as a staff member of a leading multilateral development agency would also be designated as master. However, in this case, we treat the position differently. We do so because, in the highly charged atmosphere surrounding the DSF that we described in Chapter 3, 'power over' was almost entirely in the hands of the principal financial donor, who was threatening to withdraw its support, and the other financial donors, who were threatening to do the same.

In these circumstances, the role of the Bank was more akin to that of an implementing contractor.[9] But it was not a typical implementing contractor. Unlike conventional contractors, nearly all Bank staff were highly qualified technically and capable. It was also apparent that, by comparison, they regarded LDI donor staff to be 'light-weight' intellectually, so referent power or expert power (of donor staff) were not considerations. And while, in this case, the principal donor in particular had considerable reward power over the Bank, this was acknowledged reluctantly by the Bank, and resented. The DSF seemed to be regarded as a major irritant by the Bank because it posed a threat to the Bank's reputation and because it gave LDI donors cause to be 'uppity' and disrespectful. It was a problem that the Bank wanted to go away so it could get on with its core business of lending.

This helps to explain the puzzle of the principal author's employment by the Bank in the first place. Any doubts that the Bank might have had about the principal author's political correctness or ideological suitability were outweighed by its desperation to find someone credible, quickly to fix the DSF problem. An internal appointment to the position was made unlikely by the 'poisoned-chalice' features of the job and the high risks it posed to career progress within the Bank.

Accordingly, in this case, we designate the principal donor (DfID) as M, and the other financial donors as DMs. We designate the Bank as a reluctant, but still powerful, messenger (MES), and the PTL and government counterparts as minions.

The PTL's main upward interactions were with the responsible head of department within the Bank (MES1) and with the head-of-office of the principal donor (M) in Jakarta. The frequency and intensity of these interactions dropped precipitously as soon as it became clear that the DSF's implosion had been averted. With the MES1, the lack of interaction and responsiveness became so dysfunctional that the PTL made a written complaint up the line to the head of the World Bank office in Jakarta. It is worth reproducing this email – written in August 2009 – *verbatim* as it conveys a great deal about the general work cultures that prevailed between the DSF and MES1 and within the DSF itself:

> Dear . . .
>
> Since joining the Bank in August last year, I have been doing the job of Programme Manager of the DSF in Jakarta. As you know, the DSF was in considerable disarray when I joined and at risk of being shut down. It is in much better shape now, and we have just been granted a no-cost extension by our principal financial donor (DfID) through to September 2011. But the turnaround has been hard going, and will continue to be, partly because of the mixed-bag of professional staff on DSF's books and because of the time that it takes to replace people who leave, to fill new positions, and to build morale and productivity among those who remain.
>
> My reason for telling you all of this is that for pretty much all of my time here I have found it very difficult to extract responses (decisions) from the person to whom I report . . . This makes an already difficult job unnecessarily much more so. The delays and lacunae are most pernicious when they impede my ability to employ people as quickly as (slow) Bank systems will allow. More often than not my requests for clearance or feedback are greeted with prolonged silences, which are impervious to repeated polite (fawning?) written and oral reminders. Prompt, reasonable decision-making and communication are clearly the meat and drink of good management. And I would not expect or hope for any more than the conventional in this respect, that is, if a request that I make does not meet some Bank procedural requirement, or is lacking in other ways, that I be told as quickly as possible so that the deficiency can be rectified and business can proceed. If the request is OK, then I should be given the green light, expeditiously. When neither of these things happens – or they happen infrequently – then something is clearly amiss.
>
> Naturally, I hope that I am not being studiously ignored, and that the explanation for the above is along the lines of the more prosaic and conventional 'bottleneck' or 'overload'. I do not know enough about Bank culture to be able to gauge whether trust funds are regarded as being peripheral to the Bank's core business and to people's careers and therefore to be less deserving of attention. I must say though that the way in which things have played out does suggest to me some kind of conscious or semi-deliberate style of 'management by neglect' on the part of . . . If valid, this might have broader implications.

> Whatever the case may be, I do hope that something can be done about it. Having said that, I am acutely aware of the 'damned if you do', 'damned if you don't' quality of complaints of this type and of the jeopardies involved. As you will be aware, in such matters, the dilemma is nearly always: on the one hand, "if I complain and something is said to my boss by his/her boss, no matter how delicately put, my boss will be annoyed and this will make things even worse;" and on the other, "if I do nothing about it, the business will flounder or fail and I will shoulder most of the blame."
>
> I should make clear that there is nothing personal in any of this. My relations with . . . have all of the surface cordiality that one would normally expect of such things. I also realise that . . . is about to retire; whereas I have just agreed to stay on for a further two years immediately upon my retirement in February next year. Perhaps in the circumstances – if I may suggest – the low-risk strategy (and my preference) would be to try to build-in improvements around the succession? From my side, I am happy to do whatever needs to be done to make things better, at the very least to discuss the general question with whoever takes over.
>
> I am sorry to make the 'wailing-wall' feature of your job the basis for our first exchange, but with the transition imminent I thought this would be the time to do it. Let me make clear also that I am very glad to be working for the Bank and simply want to do everything I can to make my time here as fruitful and productive as possible.
>
> I am taking leave for a few weeks from tomorrow, but I would be pleased to discuss any of this on my return should you deem it necessary or desirable.
>
> Best wishes,

There was no subsequent discernible change to the behaviour of MES1. Neglect by MES1 was followed, after her retirement, by the reverse. Her successor – MES2 – was a much younger, more ambitious and upwardly mobile individual who clearly felt that he had to put his stamp on the DSF. Benign neglect was replaced by much less benign, and frequent, interference by someone who, while extremely capable in his field (economics), had little knowledge or experience of development (he had come to the Bank 2 or 3 years before from an academic position), knew little about decentralisation and had no experience or knowledge of management. 'Antipathy' soon became the defining feature of the MES2/PTL relationship.

For MES2, the DSF stakes had been raised by a complaint received from a minister in the Government of Indonesia (GOI) about concerns expressed by the DSF regarding the GOI's procurement of a local contractor to implement a project funded by the DSF.[10] The PTL's/DSF's interest was to optimise development benefit and to minimise patronage predation, which was endemic in Indonesia (Blunt *et al.*, 2012a, 2012b). MES2, on the other hand, did not want a disturbance to World Bank/GOI relations more broadly to occur on his watch, which was implicit in the minister's written complaint, and MES2's clear preference was for the DSF to turn a blind eye. His close attention to DSF activities seemed as much to prevent 'excessive' good governance vigilance by DSF – and another complaint from the GOI – as it was anything else, thereby reducing or eliminating the DSF as a source of threat to the Bank's broader relations with the GOI.

Once again, this case reminds us of the critical importance of individual differences to bureaucratic structural violence. The systemic features of structural violence – its DNA – can be made considerably better or worse by individual differences and the reactions of the agents of structural violence to the environments in which they are operating. The absence of relevant policy facilitates this.

Iraq (2011–2012)

Among those discussed in this chapter, this project – flimsily disguised as development assistance – was perhaps the most striking instance of the purposeful violation of national sovereignty inflicted on an already devastated country 'by the same hand that had created the crisis in the first place' (Blunt, 2012, p. 347).

The critical interfaces between master and minions in this case involved the principal contractor as a proxy for the donor (USAID) and project staff. The donor *per se* did not interact directly with project staff. As the donor surrogate, the principal contractor (MES) managed all programme activities in the field and was a constant physical presence at the project premises in Baghdad. The principal author and a number of other project staff were employed by a subcontractor – MES(b) – that played no part in project management.

The MES representative in the field was an unusually abrasive and domineering character who knew little about the technical aspects of the Project's substantive business. As demonstrated later, his coercive and reward power were employed harshly to achieve complete control and to inflict substantial bureaucratic structural violence on project staff, on the project's activities, and on any prospect of developmental outcomes for the people of Iraq.

Project staff were not permitted to have any direct interactions with representatives of the Government of Iraq.

The general culture of MES relations with project staff and the principal author and intra-project relations are conveyed by the second half of the attachment to the principal author's letter of resignation (the first half of which was discussed in Chapter 3), which is reproduced *verbatim* hereafter.[11]

Weak Project Management

Virtually every aspect of the project's strategic, general, and human resource management was deficient, in some cases seriously so.

Strategic Management

In relation to strategic management, problems were exemplified by, for example, frequent changes of project scope, with little or no underlying rationale and no consultation with government about what they might want; political naiveté; and weak understanding of the project's core business. Here are just a few of the more serious examples.

1. **Poor understanding in project management of the project's core business, such as the meaning of 'governance'** either in theory or in practice (in a project entitled, the 'Governance Strengthening Project'), and therefore little or no understanding of its main features and their implications for project design and implementation. Such understanding is not something that is acquired overnight or easily compensated for by good advice from someone who knows better, the problem being that the decision-makers do not have a sound basis upon which to make judgements about the advice that they are receiving.
2. **Weak understanding of decentralization** in developing countries and little or no knowledge of comparative experience or of the recent research literature concerning it or any acknowledgement of the importance of this. It was [as] if the prime contractor (PC) and project management were concerned solely with shovelling out of the door as quickly as possible as much training and development and 'institution building' as could be managed.
3. **Target agencies at the provincial level**. First, we were to be addressing issues of capacity and oversight in all government agencies at the provincial level (central and local government officials, and elected representatives); then we were to be dealing with all units except the deconcentrated units of central government; then we were to be dealing with the elected provincial legislators and part of the governor's office and administration; and all within the space of about one month.
4. **Target provinces.** One day the initial number of target provinces would be 4 to 6, the next day it would be 15, a few days later, 4 to 6, and so on.
5. **Project visibility.** One day we were told by USAID to 'keep our heads down' because there was significant opposition in central government to decentralization, which seemed like a sensible thing to do. A few days later we were told to commence work in 15 provinces (!).
6. **Political 'strategy' or lack of it.** As mentioned above, there seemed to be little interest in the crucial aspects of the political governance aspects of Iraq and their implications for the project, particularly on the part of the PC. This contributed to the haphazard approach to questions of government ownership, but there were other effects too. For example, project management scheduled a visit to the provincial government in Erbil in what was known to be a highly charged political context (including strong criticism in the media of Biden's fascination with the Kurdistan Regional Governate – KRG – and his visits there),

and against my advice and the advice of others on the project, and without first obtaining the approval of either the relevant authorities in government or of USAID. The timing was inopportune for other reasons, some of which are evident from the observations made below.

7. **Unsafe assumptions.** Another example was the apparent disregard of the fact that the 15 provinces outside of KRG were extremely heterogeneous politically and therefore likely to be viewed quite differently by key central government agencies (most importantly, the Prime Minister's Office – PMO). It seemed highly unlikely that the PMO would view at all favourably a USAID project blundering around the provinces marketing a strong brand of decentralisation at a time when the PMO and other key agencies at the centre were trying to resist centrifugal pressures and to manage the delicate balancing act of keeping all of the heterogeneous interested parties from each other's throats.
8. **Operational confusion and 'frantic', rather than considered, response.** The clear result of the above was one of strategic and operational confusion on the part of the main players associated with the project and the creation of a general sense of frantic, rather than considered, response. All of this was clearly taking place in an environment that cried out for the opposite, namely, clear thinking and careful and consistent action. It created the impression of a clumsy and ham-fisted management with no sense of political or strategic compass.
9. **Little or no consultation**. There were numerous examples of this, including a more or less complete lack of consultation concerning important personnel selection decisions and other matters of strategic significance concerning my own and other senior professional colleagues' responsibilities.
10. **Over-reporting and low-quality reporting and, in some cases, misleading reporting.**

General Management

General management of the project was weak and project organisation poor or non-existent. Examples included:

11. **Poorly thought-through roles and functions, and reporting relationships**, resulting in considerable role conflict and role ambiguity among staff.
12. **Culture of personal lobbying rather than open and fair management**. This was encouraged by the above, resulting in private deals being struck by individual staff – and currying of favour – with project management, contributing to a culture of secrecy and lack of trust.
13. **Little or no scope for the exercise of professional judgment or influence by staff because of the generally top-down nature of**

the project management from the chief of party (COP) and deputy chief of party (DCOP), a tone that was set emphatically by the PC. There was a strong sense in the project that position in the hierarchy counted above all else, despite wide gulfs of understanding and experience and accomplishment between those in 'management' positions and in the PC and some of those beneath them in the hierarchy.

14. **Poor basic management skills,** as evidenced by an inability to set priorities and to follow-through on them; and an inability to recognize, and an unwillingness to tackle, the serious problems of role conflict and role ambiguity arising from poor organizational design (mentioned earlier). And a lack of staff meetings, which, when they were held, were poorly managed. Rarely were agendas supplied; minutes were never taken; discussion was poorly managed; and there was no allocation of task responsibility, or follow-up.
15. **No notes or minutes kept of important meetings between the PC and key stakeholders (USAID, government)**, so that a clear and unambiguous project view of direction and strategy could be built.
16. **Little or no follow-up on meetings with USAID or government**.
17. **Repeated moving of goal posts.** Important examples of this are given throughout this document – for example, 3, 4 and 5 above. But this practice extended to 'agreements' made with me and other professional staff about work to be undertaken, the timing of that work, and the conditions under which it was to be undertaken.

Signs of Distress

Floundering and out of their depth. The above are clearly serious indictments of the quality of project leadership and management, suggesting a COP that, while a nice person, was floundering and out of his depth professionally, a condition that was widely perceived to be the case by project staff. The influence of the DCOP had become disproportionate as a result of this and out of keeping with her position on the organisation chart. She was viewed by many to be just as dysfunctional as the COP, although for different reasons.

Evidence of mounting distress included:

18. **Escapism or avoidance behaviour**. In conditions where there was little that was going right and a great deal that was going wrong, there were – particularly on the part of the COP – frequent episodes of what can only be described as escapist or avoidance behaviour, involving, for example: excessive amounts of time spent and interest devoted to **cooking** (despite the presence of a highly competent full-time cook), and over-elaborate farewells to any PC staff departure, no matter how junior (including elaborate colour 'Photoshop' portraits presented to every departee that had been produced by the COP).

19. **Inappropriate, and sometimes aggressive and discourteous forms of engagement with senior staff of the project,** as evidenced by authoritarian control and a general lack of consultation thereby demonstrating a poor grasp of the fundamentals of people management in a professional setting.

Ineffective Prime Contractor

The PC could have been construed to have been the source or instigator of some of the problems referred to above, and to have exacerbated some of them or added others, as set out below.

20. **Seeming unwillingness to engage in analysis of any kind** – or to allow others, much better qualified than they, to do so – of the fast-changing governance environment, resulting in a first-year planning and other documents that were purely technocratic, unrepresentative of the views of its senior technical project staff and in some ways unrealistic, and that paid no heed to the crucial political governance aspects of the operating environment. These aspects of the operating environment, which had been discussed clearly in an early draft of the document, were removed unilaterally from the planning document and with no explanation by the PC. It was as if the planning document was to be used in a political vacuum. To any informed and intelligent observer, at best, this would have been seen as naïve, at worst, irresponsible.
21. **Seeming naiveté concerning the political volatility of the subject of decentralisation** – see above and also below.
22. **Unintelligent engagement**. Intelligent, commonsensical and detailed consideration of the structure and functioning of provincial government, as a basis for making judgments about oversight roles, was seen as excessive and described as 'academic' (this message was conveyed to me by my supervisor at MES(b), having been told to him by his counterpart at the PC).
23. **Staffing.** As of the end of December, appointments to a number of important positions had still not been made.
24. **Excessive delays in obtaining the necessary formal (written) approvals from central government to allow the project to operate legally** and muddled thinking and action in relation to this (also highly attributable to PC project management on the ground) and resentment and defensiveness in relation to any comments from staff concerning this unsatisfactory state of affairs. Note that by 31 December 2011, this had still not been obtained. Indeed, the first meeting on the subject was not held with government until the third week of December, more than three months after the PC established a physical presence on the ground in Iraq.

25. **Seeming reluctance to acknowledge the vital importance of government ownership** of the project, meaning that government should have the final say on its aims and objectives and methods of operation and the provinces in which it would operate. There was some acceptance by the COP of my suggestion concerning the benefits of a joint government/donor steering or management committee or governing body for the project, but no concerted attempt to make this happen or to bring up the possibility with USAID, despite repeated suggestions to do so.
26. **Excessive delays in obtaining formal registration of a legal entity** (company) in Iraq that would serve as a legal host for the project combined with general defensiveness and lack of transparency about lack of progress in relation to this.
27. **Excessive delays in establishing the physical and logistical conditions for effective and efficient project operation** – office space; satisfactory living accommodation for staff; essential equipment and supplies, and so on, and misleading conduct in relation to this – to staff and to USAID. When staff raised some of these matters (and the crucial question of registration) with the visiting PC senior VP, they were dismissed by him as unreasonable 'whining' and that we should 'stop sitting around on our butts and get on with it'. He said that he had expected us to be living in containers. As at the end of December 2011, the formal contract with the security provider, who was responsible for providing living and office accommodation, had still not been signed. Temporary and unsatisfactory offices were still in use at that time, three months after project commencement.
28. **Excessive micro-management and control** and interference in the project on the ground, including in relation to substantive matters of governance and decentralization.
29. **Peremptory dismissal of professional staff without consultation with the immediate supervisor and without due process or natural justice for the employee** – as in the case of the short-term consultant, KK. There were no discernible grounds for performance-based warning or dismissal in this case. The whole matter was handled without transparency or fairness and gave the distinct impression of a personal vendetta. Needless to say, the effect on staff was to make them feel that any one of them could be subject to the same mistreatment without warning and at any time. This created a culture of subservience, compliance and fear among some staff and resentment among many of them. The incident made a complete mockery of PC statements and documents proclaiming 'living our values' and of a two-day team (and trust!) building exercise conducted at the time that the dismissal was in train. This was a particularly corrosive incident and one that was emblematic of the general style and conduct of the PC.

30. **Inconsistent or (possibly) misleading advice to national staff,** many of whom complained that the terms and conditions of their employment or, in some cases, their roles, were not those that they had been promised, sometimes in writing. This resulted in at least one resignation shortly after employment.
31. **Lack of transparency and openness and merit-based decision-making in relation to recruitment of national staff:** this was a particularly disturbing practice that I commented on soon after my arrival and was told that good practice would take too long (which it did not). At the cost of some friction with PC managers and the COP, I nevertheless insisted that there would be open and transparent competitive selection of staff for all MES(b) positions under my jurisdiction. MES(b) management was highly supportive of this. This was in sharp contrast with what took place for PC appointments, where word of mouth and personal contact as a basis for selection decision-making was the norm, often with no consultation with those on the project that the person would report to. In at least some cases, the practice as applied (for example, by the DCOP) could have been construed to be nepotistic. It goes without saying that this sets a poor standard in a project that purports to 'teach' others about 'good governance' and to be eager to apply 'international best practice' in relation to governance. In my view the condoning of such practices on any grounds is irreparably damaging to the integrity of the project, its management, and the PC, creating an impression among national staff of a cavalier project given to opportunism that is excused on much the same grounds as would be used by the patronage systems that the project is supposed to be helping to combat. The allocation of jobs on the basis of nepotism and other non-merit-based criteria is the cornerstone of patronage, which is likely to be endemic in Iraq. Several national staff volunteered comments to me to this effect.
32. **Over-reliance on young and under-qualified and inexperienced staff.** In 'professional bureaucracies' (in Mintzberg's sense of the term) like the Governance Support Programme, the selection of professional staff at any level is one of the most crucial responsibilities of management. It is not a job that should be left to 25-year-old PC employees in their first jobs, who haven't had the benefit of any education in management, let alone any experience of it. Numbers are no substitute for quality and experience. Not just anyone should do.
33. **Impression management for USAID at all costs and above all else**. The PC placed this above everything, and expected staff to toe the line, whatever the reality might be. The aim appeared to be one of creating a façade of progress, when there was little or none, in the hope no doubt that the reality might eventually catch up with some of the fictitious accounts that were being presented. Attempts by me to present a more accurate account – even of seemingly innocuous events – were

edited out of reports to present them in 'a more positive light' because 'that is what USAID wants to see'. My writing style was described as 'inappropriate' for USAID, implying that it had to be 'dumbed-down' for their consumption, which I found to be extraordinary, and unacceptable.

34. **In spite of all of the above, attribution of blame by the PC** to non-management project staff and to sub-contractors on the ground for the lack of project progress. Remember that no project work could begin without 24, 25 and 26 and, to some extent, 29 above. National staff made it clear – and it should have been known – that some provincial governments would not speak to them unless they had a formal letter of authorisation from central government. Others would be very reluctant to do so. This, of course, would be the case in most sovereign countries.

Safety Management

The approach to staff safety by the PC could have been construed to place commercial considerations above its duty of care to staff, as exemplified by:

35. **Clear conflicts of interest** between the commercial interests of the PC and the safety of its staff, resulting in heavy pressure to remain in country until the last possible minute.
36. **Clear conflicts of interest** between the (admitted) financial needs of the PC security officer on the ground in Iraq and the security and safety of staff, resulting in advice to staff and the PC that would always see the security 'glass' as being 'half full' – in cases where this could be construed to be a minority, and commercially-driven, view.
37. **Seeming disregard for the possible illegality of staff presence in the country** – this arose as a consequence of the fact (known well in advance – mid-November) that the government's policy on immigration and visas was to change on 31 December 2011 and that all immigration permits or visas could cease to be legal on that date. My employer, MES(b), chose early on to adopt a policy that would protect its staff against the possible consequences of this. They informed the PC of this who was said to be 'unhappy' at what amounted to MES(b)'s breaking ranks. I was nevertheless allowed to leave on 30 December 2011 and to take leave without pay.
38. **Disagreement not allowed**. An unwillingness or marked reluctance on the part of the PC security officer and PC senior management (to VP level) to countenance any discussion or challenge on questions of security no matter how reasonably expressed or politely put. It was [as] if the security situation could only be as officially described by the PC and its agents and any other account amounted to unacceptable dissent or 'uppityness'. It is challenges of this sort that are thought to underlie

or to have contributed to the unfair dismissal of the professional member of staff mentioned under 29 above.

39. **Hostility and censure** towards any dissent from the view that 'everything was under control', when it patently was not and, by definition, could not have been.
40. **A clear dislike of any discussion of the political and security situation**, and a regard for any who might do so as being alarmist or as being provocateurs or 'divisive'.
41. **Unfair accusations**. An unwillingness to accept that security conditions are in a state of constant flux and that commitments made by staff on appointment were always subject to review by the individuals concerned and/or by their sub-contractor employer. Arising from this, implicit false accusations of disloyalty or breach of contract against those individuals who sought to obtain leave for security reasons as a result of the deteriorating security environment, and statements to the effect that 'unfortunate' precedents would be set where sub-contractors had a policy that was at variance with that of the PC.
42. **A tendency to pass-off escalating risk and violence in the country as 'nothing to worry about'**.

In short, MES–minion relations in this project constituted an extreme case of dysfunctional organisational cultures and of learned helplessness (Blunt, 2012).

Mongolia (2012–2013)

As in the Indonesian example, in this case the principal author was employed as a contract member of staff by a development agency, namely, the bilateral LDI donor agency, the Swiss Agency for Development and Cooperation (SDC). His position of governance programme manager (GPM) entailed management of the governance and decentralisation programme in Mongolia; policy research and development; and the provision of advice on governance and development to SDC in Mongolia and in other countries such as Bhutan.

The main protagonists in this case were the head and deputy head of the SDC office in Ulaanbaatar (masters), the GPM (minion) and Government of Mongolia project counterparts (minions).

Master relations with the GPM were dominated by two prominent features of the GPM's work. The first concerned his investigation of issues surrounding community development agreements (CDAs) between mining corporations and the communities affected by their operations, whose implications for government ownership we discussed in Chapter 3. The second concerned his analysis of SDC's support of fiscal decentralisation (Blunt, 2013).

Here, to portray the expression of bureaucratic structural violence by the head and deputy head, we explain how the fiscal decentralisation case became a source of contention in master–minion relations and we revisit the CDA case.

Fiscal Decentralisation

The January 2013 Integrated Budget Law (IBL) devolved authority over substantial local development fund (LDF) grants to *aimag* and *soum* local governments (LGs) and to LGs in the Capital, Ulaanbaatar. Discretionary spending by LGs thereby increased by up to a hundred-fold. At the time, the per capita amount of LDF was among the highest – if not the highest – in developing countries. The introduction of the IBL therefore entailed both opportunity and risk for local development in Mongolia. It was clearly important to find out whether the increased funding was being put to good use and what the major impediments might be, which were the subjects addressed by Blunt (2013).

Two of the main findings from this work evoked master displeasure. For reasons clearly set out in Blunt (2013), the first finding suggested that LG beneficiaries of LDFs were not making optimal use of the LDF grants. It was found that the same projects 'cropped up again and again' irrespective of the size or development profile of the LG. Favourites included street lighting,[12] garbage collection and disposal, kindergartens, and public bath houses. This was not to say that such projects had no value but simply that from a development perspective they may not have been the most needed or cost-effective. It was not to say either that projects concerned with public enjoyment or leisure were not worthy of funding, but that judgements about which projects to fund should have been made according to what constituted the most important and urgent development needs and the most cost-effective ways for dealing with them (Blunt, 2013, p. 3).

As a test of the extent to which LGs were identifying development-effective projects, every LG in Blunt's (2013) sample was asked whether it had a clean water supply and whether the supply was connected to the clinic and school. About half of the LGs answered 'no' to one or both of these questions, making it unlikely that less obviously development-effective projects would have been included on LDF project lists (Blunt, 2013, p. 3).

Why was this arms-length finding unpalatable to SDC masters? The only plausible explanation was that, from the beginning, SDC had been a staunch supporter of fiscal decentralisation for democracy promotion reasons. Before the appointment of the GPM (the principal author), SDC had provided substantial technical support to the design and implementation of Mongolia's fiscal decentralisation programme. Revealing so soon after its implementation fundamental flaws in an enterprise that SDC and SDC masters had invested so heavily in seemed to be regarded as almost subversive.

The second finding that evoked master displeasure had to do with the procurement processes followed by LGs in their utilisation of LDFs, where safeguards designed and supported by SDC had been introduced. These (procurement) certifications of bid evaluation committee members were mandatory, and allowed for participation of civil society organisation (CSO) representatives in bid evaluation committees (BECs) and for the possibility of assigning responsibility for monitoring project implementation performance to CSOs. All of these measures had 'surface appeal' as (technocratic) ways of providing for 'clean' procurement and limiting patronage predation and other forms of corruption (Blunt, 2013).

The analysis acknowledged that while awareness and understanding of the rules was clearly a necessary condition for compliance with them, the commitment to 'saturation' certification of BEC members implied that when procurement rules were not followed, it was mainly because BEC members were ill-informed about the rules or did not have a good understanding of them. That is, the assumption was that the 'procurement problem' was primarily one of capacity, a problem that could be fixed by ensuring that all BEC members were formally certified. The report (Blunt, 2013) referred to the considerable comparative research evidence to suggest that such an assumption was unsafe where patronage networks were well established, which seemed highly likely in LGs in Mongolia. In such conditions, informal influences are rarely outmanoeuvred by technocratic ones, by themselves; they cannot guarantee 'clean' procurement.

A similar problem underlay the possible inclusion of CSO members on BECs, which assumed that by definition CSO people were more virtuous than anyone else and that this would reduce the likelihood of corruption. It ignored the fact that in small, close-knit communities, CSO members were no less susceptible than anyone else to informal pressures. The paper concluded that the possibility of CSO involvement as members of BECs and in the project monitoring should be qualified accordingly (Blunt, 2013, pp. 9–10).

Again, the strong implication of master reactions to these findings was that, at best, the GPM was being unhelpful, at worst, subversive.[13] For the reasons given earlier, the SDC masters paid no heed to the findings and in the end actively suppressed them.

Community Development Agreements

The CDA work discussed in Chapter 3 and in Blunt (2014a) and Blunt and Sainkhuu (2015) was carried out after the assessment of the fiscal decentralisation project. As we shall see later, the mounting opprobrium of the GPM in the masters' eyes and their growing dissatisfaction with what they saw to be his recalcitrance were soon to reach fever pitch.

For the GPM, the climax of bureaucratic structural violence came in mid-November 2013, 15 months into his 3-year contract, when he was suddenly and peremptorily dismissed because of 'irreconcilable' differences of opinion regarding the 'strategic direction' of the SDC Governance and Decentralisation Programme that he managed (Blunt & Sainkhuu, 2015, p. 378). The precipitating events surrounding his dismissal, which are set out in Blunt and Sainkhuu (2015), were all forms of resistance that went beyond interpretive labour by the GPM because they were designed to make known to sympathetic parties in government the findings of the CDA report that had been banned by SDC and the suppressed fiscal decentralisation report (Blunt, 2014a). It could be said that, in taking this calculated risk, the structural violence of the GPM's dismissal had been knowingly self-inflicted. The GPM knew that his defiance[14] would strain SDC's narrow band of tolerance to the limit and, at breaking point, it would result in the ultimate sanction of dismissal.

Several features of the dismissal, the events leading up to it, the personalities involved, and its implications are noteworthy. First, in 'provoking this kind of unconstrained, spontaneous rage' the GPM's interpretive labour exposed 'the instincts of some of these normally cautious, supposedly "neutral" people, the pillars of democracy – judges, planners, academics' (Roy, 2016, p. 190), and development officials. When thwarted or challenged, or when the masters' layers of deceit are peeled back by intellectual enquiry, retribution can be swift and uncompromising (Chomsky, 2011; Chomsky & Barsamian, 2013; Hedges, 2011). It can produce what Roy (2016, p. 190) refers to as 'a bilious rush of abuse, intimidation, and blind anger': in short, 'the intellectual equivalent of a police baton charge'. Either you do and say the things that are required of you in your 'service to power' or you suffer the consequences (Chomsky & Barsamian, 2007).

Second, the 'dense cloud' of SDC and SDC-orchestrated bureaucratic structural violence depicted later, and by Blunt and Sainkhuu (2015, p. 281), proved 'impossible to evade and difficult to counteract'. This 'theatre' of donor-led control and bureaucratic structural violence was a 'choreographed' combination of corporate and donor-supplied material inducement directed at co-opted local officials; and real or imagined institutional demands regarding the behaviour of masters from within SDC; all bound together by the ruling ideology of neoliberalism. 'Accordingly, without conscious arrangement between them, such – bullied, bought or merely indoctrinated – "prisoners of the paradigm" can mount attacks from different angles either in concert or opportunistically, thereby weakening challenge significantly or extinguishing it altogether' (Blunt & Sainkhuu, 2015, p. 281).

While the strength, sophistication and vindictiveness of LDI and LDI-induced 'baton-charges' will vary according to a country's natural resource profile and other local circumstances (including the personalities involved – see later), such bureaucratic structural violence seems inevitable in all resource-rich developing countries. LDI vigilance and nastiness will be a function of the magnitude of the self-interests at stake, meaning that – as in resource-rich Mongolia – the slightest hint of real or imagined threat is unlikely to escape notice or avoid retribution.

Third, following his dismissal by SDC, further bureaucratic structural violence directed at the GPM and his Mongolian SDC-employed colleagues included the immediate cancellation of the GPM's work visa, which gave him 2 weeks to leave the country or to make other arrangements; and, a few days later, the interrogation of a national colleague by SDC management about matters connected with the banned CDA document, the report produced by the SDC Governance Team on fiscal decentralisation (outlined earlier), and a documentary film depicting the involvement of the Swiss-based Glencore corporation in the exploitation of Zambian copper – referred to in Blunt

(2014a).[15] Regarding the latter, the national staff member had (after hours and *pro bono*) written Mongolian sub-titles for the documentary so that it could be broadcast on Mongolian TV. She had done so in response to a request from the Mongolian Minister of Mining, who had seen the video and thought that its account of such matters as transfer pricing and fraudulent investment inflation and collusion between corrupt mining executives and government officials should be broadcast to the general public.[16] Despite the fact that the video was in the public domain, the Mongolian SDC staff member was 'grilled' by SDC management about her actions and motivation, the implicit threat being one of dismissal. She was also interrogated about the translation and distribution to local government officers at a meeting in Ulaanbaatar in late October 2013 of the fiscal decentralisation paper. This was done despite the fact that the paper indicated clearly that it was an 'SDC/GDP Discussion Paper'.[17] 'Neither SDC's proclivity for doublespeak nor its cavalier disregard for freedoms of information was diminished by its contemporaneous promotion of "horizontal learning"' (Blunt & Sainkhuu, 2015, p. 379).

Fourth, a few weeks before the GPM's dismissal, the SDC country director in Mongolia had been replaced by someone whose reputation as an SDC 'hardman' had preceded him. During the contract termination meeting with the GPM, the new director asserted that had he been in charge when the banned CDA document referred to above had been produced, he would have 'brought things to an end then' (Blunt & Sainkhuu, 2015). Where his predecessor, with the same information at his disposal, had demurred, the new director acted without hesitation. Personality was clearly a critical causative variable in the timing, scope and severity of the bureaucratic structural violence that ensued.

Fifth, as with the Cambodian and Indonesian cases discussed earlier, the culture of the relationship between the GPM and the SDC director and deputy director was dysfunctional and stressful, with significant intersender and person-role conflict and, simmering close beneath the surface of polite conversation, considerable tension and antipathy. The new SDC director quickly dispensed with the formal niceties and brought matters to a head by dismissing the GPM.

Sixth, while the drama of the peremptory dismissal of a senior member of SDC's staff (the GPM) will have been the feature headline of SDC office politics at the time, the most grievous national development injuries caused by SDC's bureaucratic structural violence clearly arose from its banning of the CDA report and its suppression of the fiscal decentralisation report. At least for the CDA case, the consequences were also perverse from the point of view of SDC, as they served 'to eradicate or weaken policy that [was] in the corporate interest as well as for the general good' (Blunt & Sainkhuu, 2015, p. 380). By comparison, though SDC's interrogation of SDC professional staff was reprehensible, and the manner of the dismissal of the GPM was unnecessarily vindictive, the bureaucratic structural violence that was inflicted was localised and relatively short-lived. Similarly, the reputational damage done to SDC by its own conduct will have been negligible, limited by the fact that all of the mining interests involved and at least some of the relevant government agencies and officials could have been tarred with the same brush.

In all of this, the views of the Mongolian people, more than 85% of whom were (and remain) resource nationalists and believed that Mongolia should own at least 51% of its strategic mineral deposits (Sant Maral Foundation, 2014), counted for nothing.

Afghanistan (2014–2016)

The main actors in the pantomime of technical assistance to the Independent Directorate of Local Governance (IDLG) in Afghanistan that we discussed in Chapter 3 were the responsible (DfID) donor official in the field, as master; the contractor's programme manager, as messenger; and, as minions, the programme team leader (PTL – the principal author) and government counterparts in IDLG.

All of the supply-side's principal actors were based in Kabul. As in Iraq, the messenger was a constant presence, indeed lived in the same large house as the PTL. Although, as we shall show, the likeness between the projects in Iraq and Afghanistan ended there, the outcomes of the bureaucratic structural violence for the countries were much the same.

The PTL was stationed in IDLG and, unless a security threat prevented it, spent all day in his office there, or interacting with senior government counterparts including the deputy minister of IDLG and directors of IDLG divisions, with all of whom he built very good working relations. These officials afforded the PTL formal and informal insights into the workings of government that would have been impossible for him to obtain otherwise, and which added considerable validity to his analyses and recommendations. The closeness of these ties is reflected in the co-authorships of the publications on Afghanistan referred to in this book (Blunt *et al.*, 2015; Blunt & Khamoosh, 2016; Blunt *et al.*, 2017).[18]

The implementing contractor was unusual in that it prided itself on appointing young, bright graduates (many of them Oxbridge alumni) as programme managers (messengers) in the field. For most of the 2-year duration of this project, the contractor's project manager in the field was a young Oxford graduate who had done a tour of duty in Helmand Province as a commissioned officer in the British Army.

Here, we examine the dynamics of the master–minion and messenger–minion relationships surrounding the SNG policy development case discussed in Chapter 3 and those surrounding an attempt by President Ghani, ostensibly, to curb corruption in the provinces by removing provincial councils' oversight authority over the award of contracts, which is the subject of Blunt and Khamoosh (2016).

Donor masters in this case, of which there were only two during the life of the project, while not expert in any of the relevant fields, were intelligent and considered. Their refreshingly frank assessments of some of the matters surrounding the SNG policy case are illustrative of this. For example, referring to the long SNG policy, one of them remarked that: 'This policy is a complete load of bollocks (newly-appointed donor official, Kabul, November, 2015)' (Blunt *et al.*, 2017, p. 71); and, regarding donor behaviour in relation to SNG, the other noted (*verbatim* excerpt from email of 14 February 2016, quoted in Blunt *et al.*, 2017, p. 81):

> For info, the US-hosted lunch on SNG last Thursday was interesting. I had no idea that there was so little donor coordination on SNG – the level of conversation I confess was a bit shocking to me. Everyone bemoaned the lack of any strategic coordination or oversight of the big money programmes. . . . They were keen on using the SNG Policy as a basis for planning and driving donor efforts to support [their] reform agenda (not exactly its purpose!).

However, such perspicacity did not prevent them from toeing the line on 'decentralisation for democracy promotion', as in their response to the president's attempts to remove or dilute provincial council oversight authority, which 'were causes of disappointment and regret and typically were seen as regressive – as "democracy" taking a backward step'; and in donor support for the establishment of district councils because of the concrete evidence of ('democratic') 'progress' this would constitute (Blunt & Khamoosh, 2016, pp. 93–94). All of this in circumstances where provincial councils were widely known to be corrupt, where up to two-thirds of the country could be said not to be under the complete control of central government in Kabul (Blunt *et al.*, 2017), and where alternative and more feasible and developmental evidence-based courses of action had been clearly spelled out (e.g. Blunt, 2015).[19]

Donor masters were just as immovable on the politically charged question of civilian casualties resulting from friendly fire, which analysis by the Project had found unsurprisingly was the source of 'pervasive community antipathy and alienation', which was likely to persist for generations, and would undermine the legitimacy of the state and the whole business of 'good governance' reform and the credibility of both its foreign and national purveyors. This was presented to the donor in the form of a concept note, urging that action should be taken as soon as possible to address legitimate civilian grievances, and stressing that there was no 'better or quicker or more cost-effective' way for government to establish its legitimacy in the eyes of the people (Blunt, 2014b, pp. 2–4). Nothing was done.

Messenger–minion relations, between the contractor supervising manager in the field and the PTL, were also congenial and conducive to intelligent discussion. Importantly, and unusually, the stringent and oppressive 'gate-keeping' function played by messengers in the other cases discussed to this point, which was at its most extreme in Iraq, in this case, was replaced by one that left the gate open for well-conceived and well-argued cases to be presented to the donor. While he may not have known much about the literature on subnational governance, the messenger's combat experience in Helmand will have informed his view about the wisdom (or not) of – for example – decentralisation and the establishment of district councils and the importance to harmonious community relations and state and donor legitimacy of the neglect of civilian casualties caused by friendly fire. This meant that project concept notes and briefing papers on these and other subjects were allowed through without redaction (e.g. Blunt, 2014b, 2015).

Master and messenger interactions with government counterparts in IDLG almost entirely were conducted indirectly through the PTL who, as noted earlier, had established close daily working relations with the uppermost tier of officials in the agency. These officials were all savvy and well-connected operators in a governance system where survival and progress depended much more on tribal affiliation, patronage network membership, personal connections with the president and so on, than they did on technocratic performance on the job. The latter was important partly because it provided what the president wanted to see, and to be seen by others, but mostly because it was convenient technocratic window dressing for the much less-savoury activities that it was designed to conceal. Like masters and messengers, and everyone in government around them, government minions in IDLG were undoubtedly 'knowing participants' in a process of 'counterfeit developmental governance' whose real purposes were to serve vested interests (Blunt *et al.*, 2017, p. 81).

The generally cordial relations that prevailed between all concerned in this case were welcome relief in a war-torn country where the threat of physical violence from resistance fighters was a constant, anxiety-provoking presence. But they did little to ameliorate the profound bureaucratic structural violence that was inflicted by masters, as summarised by Blunt (2021a, p. 82):

> [A]bove all, the behaviour of supply-side agencies was designed to maintain outward appearances and to serve donor and personal vested interests: by doing what would be accepted as developmental and supportive of the spread of 'democracy' (mainly via the appearance of political and administrative decentralisation) even if it was not; by pursuing standard means of technocratic reform subsumed under the general heading of 'capacity building' in circumstances where they had little chance of doing any good; by accepting at face value documents that claimed to be policies that clearly were not; and by refusing to acknowledge the significance to government legitimacy of civilian causalities caused by 'friendly fire', and the importance of being seen to address them, because this might entail implied or explicit admission of wrongdoing.

Samoa (2016–2021)

The Samoan programme is noteworthy for a number of reasons. Most notable of all, perhaps, was the fact that the relatively benign and peaceful development circumstances of Samoa, its light-weight (though growing 'China-flavoured') geostrategic significance, its lack of natural resources, and its small size and remoteness did not have an appreciable effect on the expression of donor-induced bureaucratic structural violence, which seemed to have very much the character of donor behaviour in places where there was clearly much more at stake and where historical structural violence had prepared the ground much more thoroughly. Our discussion in Chapter 3 demonstrates this by showing how the donor's disregard for formal agreements with the Government of Samoa, and for authentic government ownership, was triggered by the slightest suggestion of threat to what the responsible donor official perceived to be the donor's national interest.

Noteworthy also from our discussion in Chapter 3 was the fact that post-COVID-19-pandemic-onset behaviour by the donor showed no signs of letting up in these respects and, in some ways, worsened.

In this chapter, we analyse whether the four very different donor personalities that held the position of donor supervising official and master during the 5-year life of the programme made any difference to what transpired. And, as in the other cases discussed earlier, we do the same for messenger–minion relations.

As noted in Chapter 3, the first 2 years of the Programme were devoted to establishing its technical credibility and authenticity, assessing the level and type of demand from government, and developing with government programme governance systems and procedures. During this period, the supervising donor official (M1) was content to be 'hands-off' and to maintain a congenial and permissive, almost *laissez-faire*, background presence. Meetings with the PTL were only held, when necessary, in a friendly and constructive atmosphere. M1's personality, which we would classify as a 'Type B' (Blunt & Jones, 1992), was conducive to this.[20] More by good fortune than design, these were ideal conditions for building firm foundations for the Programme.

M1's successor, M2, was deputy head of mission and would not normally have been the Programme's supervising donor official. However, the strong reputation of the Programme and a delay in the appointment of M1's replacement constituted 'appropriate' circumstances for someone of her status to assume direct control of the Programme. Like M1, we would classify M2 as having been a Type B personality, with very much the same approach to programme supervision. Once again, the personality luck-of-the-draw had been favourable to developmental technical assistance.

There was, however, to be a (thankfully) short and sharp interlude, following the arrival of M1's replacement, M3. In Chapter 3, we recount the donor's (M3's) (mis)handling of the national security case and his unilateral abrogation of formal agreements, rules and procedures, and government ownership, to achieve what he considered to be an acceptable level of control. Again, there seemed to be a strong correlation between these actions and personality.[21] However, the expression of his aggression and underdeveloped 'interpersonal skills' was not confined to the Programme and soon began to be felt by his work colleagues in the donor office, whose objections to it led to M3's 'transfer-out' after a relatively short stay of a few months.[22]

Soon after, M2's posting came to an end. Following the appointment of her successor, M4, it started to become apparent that the halcyon days of programme operations under M1 and M2 were to be an increasingly fondly remembered thing of the past. While day-to-day interactions between M4 and the PTL were always polite and correspondence signed-off with 'warm regards', close beneath the surface of the interpersonal niceties was a very different reality. This manifested itself in the bureaucratic structural violence surrounding the 'reserved and restricted list' project and the 'programme-wide measures' discussed in Chapter 3 and the 'economic policy advice', 'citizenship investment scheme' and 'tertiary referral centre' projects recounted in Blunt *et al.* (in press). M4's objections to the latter two projects, and their designation as 'red-flag', seemed to rest on the assumption that the Government of Samoa would get into trouble because it didn't have the capability to make sensible decisions, regarding the citizenship scheme, because passports might be sold to 'dubious characters'; and, regarding the tertiary referral centre, because government might over-reach or be too ambitious. M4's principal concern appeared to be that, if either of these things happened, the donor might get some of the blame if it had been involved in providing advice to either project. The heavy undertones of paternalism evident in the donor's position 'went unremarked, perhaps unnoticed. But, equally, a genuine "development partner" might have wanted to help ameliorate such risks rather than distancing itself from [them]' (Blunt *et al.*, in press).

The cases from Samoa discussed in this book, and in Blunt *et al.* (in press), reveal how the expression of donor bureaucratic structural violence seemed at least partly to be a function of personality. Some of the most destructive violence was inflicted by personalities at whose core was a strong desire to dominate and control, whether expressed openly, directly and crudely, or more indirectly and behind the scenes and with more guile.[23] Sometimes this meant that donor misbehaviour was carried out 'without hesitation or any apparent sense of mischief or wrong-doing' and that their abrogation of formally agreed decision-making systems and conventional principles of good governance were 'plain for all to see', as if their behaviour was 'conventional' and 'to be expected' and that recipients would acquiesce.

Remarkable also was the fact that these were responses that the responsible donor officials were not obliged to give.[24] Such choices were justified on the basis of master perceptions of how the matter in question *might* have been viewed by superiors in Canberra. The default position was to play it safe. The guiding principle seemed to be: 'better to break a rule – even one of our own – than to risk the displeasure of superiors'. The development costs to the recipient seemed to count for nothing.

As with many of the other cases discussed in this chapter, the Samoan examples demonstrate that no matter how considered, deferential, informed and inventive minion (PTL in particular) interpretive labour might have been, it could do little to prevent or assuage the damaging consequences of master bureaucratic structural violence. At best, such labour postponed, helped to explain (to recipients) and occasionally ameliorated such violence. But it was tacitly understood by all parties where the real power lay, poorly concealed 'behind the *bonhomie* of formal meetings and face-to-face interactions . . . and the "warm regards" of written correspondence' (Blunt *et al.*, in press).

The evidence that we present in this book and in Blunt *et al.* (in press) demonstrates that while master relations with government minions were always superficially cordial, when donor interests were seen to be at stake, their actions could be dismissive, patronising and damaging. In most cases, government counterparts had little choice but to accede.

The implementing contractor's[25] role in all of this was surprisingly reasonable, and as even-handed as its commercial dependence on the donor would allow. The contractor's programme director for the final 3 years of the Programme, who was based in Canberra, and who only visited Samoa once a year, set the tone of messenger–minion (PTL) relations. His main point of contact in the Programme was the PTL. Interactions were frequent, cordial and constructive. There were few direct interactions between the messenger and government counterparts.

As in Afghanistan, in this case the messenger (MES) was intelligent, considered and open to argument. His hands-off approach to relations with the PTL and the Programme was based on his assessment that the Programme and the PTL had won the respect and trust of government, evidence of which was to be found in the highly politically sensitive and nationally significant projects that had been entrusted to its care. Again, as in Afghanistan, this meant that discussion papers written by the PTL on issues that were critical to Samoa's short- and medium-term development prospects – such as NCDs, the fiscal risks of climate change (Blunt, 2021b), and the establishment in Samoa of a tertiary referral centre (see Blunt, 2019; Blunt *et al.*, in press) – were let through uncensored by the MES, after he had read and commented on them.

This did not mean that the MES was unconcerned about the commercial interests of the implementing contractor and, therefore, donor sensitivities. But, without saying so explicitly, he seemed to understand the obvious, namely, that authentic, worthwhile partnerships are built on mutual respect and trust. He took the view that the strength of government–Programme relations in these respects could only be of benefit to the donor, and that the donor would see this.

He was therefore taken aback when the thinly veiled threat of (PTL) dismissal came up, instigated by M4 who, as noted in Chapter 3, behind the scenes, had denounced the PTL as having an 'agenda' and as being 'ideologically unsuitable' or subversive.[26] The PTL's 'agenda' could only have been that he paid too much attention to what government, as opposed to the donor, wanted; and that this often entailed a critical assessment of neoliberal standard practice by consultants employed because they were capable of supplying theoretically and empirically sound alternatives.[27] This was presented to MES as conclusive evidence of the PTL's subversiveness, as were some of his publications.

At this point, many messengers might have taken fright and volunteered to do what the donor seemed to want, that is, fire the PTL. The fact that MES did not and that he let some of his surprise at being expected to do so show resulted in a compromise that, while in some ways convenient to both the contractor and donor, was unusual in the circumstances. On the other hand, for the PTL, the storm clouds of bureaucratic structural violence were gathering. While he was not dismissed, the threat of dismissal was left 'hanging in the air', meaning that, for what was left of his contract, his work as PTL would be performed on very 'thin ice'.

News of the threat to fire the PTL of course leaked-out, so that before long it was widely known at the most senior levels of government. The underlying pretexts were also widely understood. It is not difficult to see whose credibility will have suffered the most as a result.[28]

The consequences for master–minion relations and for the Programme's organisational culture were just as predictable, with barely suppressed antipathy and unemotionality to the fore. Following the neutralisation of the PTL, M4 screwed the Programme lid on even more tightly with the introduction of the programme-wide measures discussed in Chapter 3, some of which were contrary to formal agreements with government.

One of the more egregious and blatant examples of this involved the minutes of meetings of the Programme steering committee, which were doctored according to the wishes of donor observers who were not formal members of the committee. Such illicit redactions were proposed – and, tacitly, insisted upon – despite the fact that the chair of the committee and all government members had already approved as accurate records drafts that had been circulated by the committee's secretary (the PTL). The minutes of the final meeting of the steering committee are graphically revealing. In the normal way, these had been circulated in draft to all members of the committee, asking for comments before a specified deadline. The government chair of the four-person committee and the other two government members all responded within the allotted time saying that they regarded the minutes to be an accurate record of the meeting. The day after the deadline had passed, M4, who was not a member of the committee (his boss, the head of mission was the fourth member), responded that 'our' comments on the minutes are attached. The PTL replied to M4, explaining politely that the deadline had passed and that, in accordance with normal practice, he would have to ask the chair if he was prepared to consider the suggested changes. One of the suggested changes concerned a statement made by the chair in his closing remarks. The statement praised the work done by the Programme during its life and attributed its success to the leadership of the PTL, which it said was a '*sine qua non*' of such success. Note again that these were the words of the chair of the committee, which he and his government colleagues had all confirmed as an accurate account of what had been said. M4, and the unnamed others who constituted the 'our' referred to in his email, wanted the statement about the PTL – which they knew fully well to have been confirmed as accurate by the government members of the committee – to be removed. The PTL reiterated to the chair of the committee that, in his view, the changes requested were not representative of what had been said at the meeting and that they added nothing of value to the minutes. He also pointed out that it was possible that the suggested edits were the work of observers who had no formal role in the committee and, therefore, were not authorised to comment on the minutes. Moreover, he stressed the obvious, namely, that the chair was the best judge of the accuracy of any statements attributed to him. The PTL observed that these considerations, together with the fact that three of the four members of a supposedly government-led committee had approved the minutes, meant that he (the chair) could leave the minutes as they were.[29] Indeed, he was advised that this would be the correct thing to do. He chose not to follow the PTL's advice and acceded to all of the changes requested by M4.

The most extreme bureaucratic structural violence in this case – the 'collateral damage' – was clearly that inflicted on three of the most senior and influential members of government: the chair of the committee, who was the CEO of the Ministry of Finance, the CEO of the Ministry of the Prime Minister and Cabinet, and the Chair of the Public Service Commission. The suggested edits to the minutes openly contradicted and discounted the legitimate, formal views of the government members of the committee and forced them into a humiliating back-down. Plainly a striking illustration of how far the donor master was prepared to stoop in its petty eagerness to admonish the PTL – to keep him firmly in his place – and how unconcerned it was about the brazen and churlish violation of agreed procedure and host government 'face' that this would entail, unconcern stemming from the master's dominance and complete lack of empathy.

How can such behaviour on the part of the donor be explained other than by recourse to something like, 'we own you because you are dependent on our financial assistance, because you are in "our patch", and because, generally, we do not consider you to be capable of managing your own affairs, that is, we have the right to do these things, and to rub your noses in it, or not as we may see fit'?

Either way, we doubt very much that the donor's geopolitical and economic interests in the region will have been well served by the types of bureaucratic structural violence presented here and in Chapter 3. We say this because Samoans value as much as anyone else their sovereignty and relationships that are built on authentic mutual respect that allows both sides to maintain their dignity and sense of self-worth. This is unaffected by their aid dependence and geopolitical insignificance. And although their development options outside of their 'traditional partners' are few, gratuitous structural violence of the sort described earlier will be bound to increase the likelihood that alternatives will be seriously considered. Alternatives that may be no less self-serving, but which display 'greater cultural empathy and integrity' and have 'less domineering inclinations' (Blunt *et al.*, in press). Developments of this kind seem more likely in the light of the security pact signed between China and the Solomon Islands in April 2022. A move that provoked 'deep disappointment' in the Government of Australia, suggestions by the main opposition Labour party that it would increase aid to the Pacific if elected, and set the alarm bells ringing in the United States (Birtles *et al.*, 2022).[30]

Minion–Minion Relations

In Cambodia, minion–minion interactions, between the Project and its principal government counterparts, were formal and perfunctory, a reflection of government's interest in technical assistance as a means to achieving the party-political interests of the CPP. Combined with the donor's interest in misguided ideologically based reform directed at 'democracy' promotion, this left little room for constructive discussion of developmental technical assistance between the Project and government. Surface appearances were nearly always cordial and 'coolly' harmonious, but there was little or no trust or shared interest in genuinely developmental activities.

The unusually permissive nature of master–minion relations in Timor-Leste was conducive to the design and implementation of developmental technical assistance activities. Government weakness and need following the devastation of Indonesian invasion and occupation, by necessity, dictated that minion–minion (Project–government) relations were constructive. But they were largely driven by the supply-side (the Project). Despite MES interference and ineptitude, the genuinely developmental interests of the Project meant that its work constituted the best that could be done in the very difficult circumstances of the country at the time.

The neopatrimonial, patronage-based, system of governance in Indonesia,[31] and its long experience of dealing with outside interests, made for minion–minion relations that satisfied all of the niceties of technical assistance rhetoric, but concealed demand-side interests that had little to do with the public good, that is, a state in which coalitions of government and business elites were adept at reflecting back the standard features of the 'decentralisation leads to democracy' school of thought so as to maintain the flow of (aid) investment, 'at least partly for factional predation and consolidation' (Blunt *et al.*, 2012a, p. 65). Middle levels of government, who were responsible for project implementation, were just as skilfully contrived, masking their real intentions in the orthodox language of good governance and aid effectiveness in order to maintain 'politically correct outward appearances'. Technical assistance was no match for this and was 'easily reconstituted and neutralised', allowing patronage networks more or less unrestricted access to the opportunities for predation provided by development assistance (Blunt *et al.*, 2012a, pp. 74–75).

These were clearly not conditions for minion–minion relations in the interests of developmental technical assistance.

The situation of the Iraq project forbade any formal interaction between project personnel and government officials. During his brief period of tenure in Iraq, the principal author therefore had no formal or informal contact whatsoever with representatives of the Government of Iraq. Largely to blame for this was the LDI's conviction that it could do as it pleased in Iraq and that interactions with government were therefore superfluous, coupled with project management that, in its infliction of the bureaucratic structural violence depicted earlier in this chapter, violated all of the somewhat idealised qualities of effective organisation envisaged by Blunt (1990, p. 309), namely:

> mutual trust and confidence; openness to constructive criticism and change; work for everyone at a level consistent with individual capabilities, values and interests; opportunities for everyone to progress as a function of their ability within existing constraints; fair and just treatment for everyone; clear articulation of accountability and role relationships; opportunities for work which allows for individual growth; and, where appropriate, for participation in strategy formulation; and finally, the clear articulation of long-term goals, a sense of purpose, mission, and above all, vision concerning future opportunities and constraints.

Relations between the GPM and government counterparts in Mongolia were dictated partly by SDC reactions to the CDA and fiscal decentralisation reports discussed in the relevant section of this chapter, partly by government interest to maintain good relations with an important donor, and partly by the GPM's introduction to a member of the Mongolian national assembly who was a committed and vocal resource nationalist.

Following the banning by SDC of the CDA report, relations between the GPM and government counterparts in the Ministry of Mines were terminated unilaterally and suddenly by SDC. The GPM was forbidden from having any further contact with Ministry officials and was not even permitted to offer them the courtesy of an explanation. The findings of the SDC discussion paper on fiscal decentralisation were more difficult to suppress because discussion with some local government officials had taken place soon after the report's completion and because of their publication in a local journal (in Mongolian). Thereafter, however, the GPM was given strict instructions by SDC masters to cease all discussion of the paper's findings.

At the highest levels of SDC–government relations (with a senior Mongolian adviser in the Office of the President), formal interactions were maintained but were bound, for some, to have been coloured by the events mentioned earlier.

The GPM's discovery of a kindred spirit in parliament (the co-author of Blunt & Sainkhuu, 2015), and the subsequent acquisition by him of the findings of the CDA report, will have hastened his (the GPM's) dismissal by SDC masters. As explained in Blunt and Sainkhuu (2015), the resistance to (mining) legislative change by corporate and donor interests and co-opted government officials proved impossible to overcome.[32]

In Samoa, minion–minion relations were always conducted in the dark shadow of master control, particularly following the appointment of M4 (for the final 2 years of the Programme). Nevertheless, such relations were always exemplary. The already trusting and highly effective working relations that had been established between the Programme and government project counterparts and government members of the steering committee up to the date of the appointment of M4 were revalidated and, if anything, strengthened by the threat to dismiss the PTL; by the unilateral cancellation of projects – on technical pretexts – that had been designed and implemented with government; by forbidding the Programme from engaging in whole areas of support (such as foreign investment); by interpersonal style, evident in the red flags attached to projects on climate change and a tertiary referral centre, and by actions regarding the minutes of steering committee meetings; and by the willingness to tighten the screws of control in the emergency conditions of the COVID-19 pandemic. It is worth noting here also that on the few occasions when government counterparts were reported to have shown (in meetings) some concern about the donor's unilateral actions, the donor conveyed to the PTL its 'surprise' and 'disappointment', as if to say that the 'restless natives' could only have acted in this 'uppity' way with the provocation and connivance of the PTL.

Conclusion

In one way or another, in all of the programmes and projects in our sample, irrespective of country circumstances, largely non-developmental LDI donor self-interests were served. With one exception, the vice-like grip of donor control and bureaucratic structural violence exerted either directly from masters to minions or indirectly via messengers, served to bring this about. Notably, in the one case where master–minion relations were more permissive – in Timor-Leste and, to some extent, in the early stages of the Samoa programme, under M1 and M2 – there were no adverse effects on the realisation of donor interests, but there were far greater prospects of achieving developmental results for recipient governments.

The expression of bureaucratic structural violence between masters and minions and messengers and minions was clearly at its most severe in Iraq, in Mongolia and – under M3 and M4 – in Samoa.

In Iraq, the decentralisation programme foisted on government, of which the project discussed in this chapter was a small part, seems highly unlikely to have yielded any benefits for the people of Iraq. On the contrary, it threatened to contribute to the fragmentation of the state, as part of a crude 'divide and rule' strategy by the donor. From a development standpoint, fortunately, the high levels of project dysfunctionality meant that the amount of additional damage that it could inflict was minimal. Perversely, this was a case in which the aggressive and domineering personality of the key messenger and the technical incompetence of the project team leader, which were among the main causes of project dysfunctionality, made for an ineffective project that could contribute little to the misguided decentralisation grand design of the LDI.

Master bureaucratic structural violence in Mongolia effectively extinguished any possibility of development benefit arising from the technical assistance reports on fiscal decentralisation and CDAs. The speed, severity and vindictiveness of master structural violence were influenced significantly by the master personalities involved. On the government side, reactions to master behaviour were mixed, ranging from small relatively isolated pockets of resistance around resource nationalists like MP Sainkhuu to collusive acceptance by co-opted government officials. The interpretive labour of resistance proved to be no match to the bureaucratic structural violence inflicted by the donor. SDC's suppression of the findings of the fiscal decentralisation report was likely to have found support from the implementing agents of SDC-funded projects and their staff whose income and jobs were threatened by some of the report's findings, and from government and corporate interests who stood to profit from the award of contracts under the huge increases in grant funding to local governments.

Likewise, in Samoa master personality was critical to the expression of bureaucratic structural violence. Arguably, those projects that stood to yield the greatest development benefit to the people of Samoa – on such critical topics, as global warming, foreign investment, economic policy in general and national security (health) – were the ones most adversely affected. The (donor) judgements regarding these projects appeared to be more a function of master idiosyncrasies than of formal donor policy. Neither the relative geostrategic and economic insignificance of Samoa nor the emergency conditions of the COVID-19 pandemic ameliorated the blatantness or severity of the bureaucratic structural violence perpetrated by donor masters.

By comparison, in Cambodia, Indonesia and Afghanistan, there was relatively little in the way of overt interpersonal bureaucratic structural violence between masters and messengers, on the one hand, and government minions on the other. In all of these cases, the supply- and demand-sides achieved a 'mutually beneficial stasis' (Blunt *et al.*, 2017, p. 70) that allowed them to achieve their respective largely non-developmental self-interests, while maintaining politically correct outward appearances.

Notes

1 As in all power relations, interpretive labour appears to be the only (or one of the few, safe) weapon(s) that the oppressed have at their disposal. They are compelled constantly to anticipate, analyse and attempt to fashion or influence the master's needs and wants, likes and dislikes. Throughout history, versatility, cunning and manipulative intelligence have been the only means of non-violent resistance for the weak (e.g., natives vs. colonisers, women vs. men, servants/slaves vs. masters, employees vs. employers). Such labour is not natural. It is socio-historically constructed and based on *need*. This is why the master is frequently oblivious to such labour (and to the life and mental processes of servants, or sometimes even who they are).

2 Strictly speaking, the role played by the ADB in this programme was that of messenger, as the technical assistance was financed by bilateral donors (the Netherlands and Sweden). Our designation here of ADB as a master is explained by the fact that the donors had chosen to relinquish all programme management authority to ADB and seemed content to have no say in the strategic management of the Programme.

3 Note also that in the cases where the master was assisted by a local national deputy – Cambodia, Timor-Leste, Mongolia and Samoa – invariably the master would select

someone whom they regarded to be a kindred spirit, that is, someone over whom they would be able to exercise referent power as well as coercive, reward and legitimate power. In some cases, this made the deputy a more extreme version of her boss.

4 As suggested in Chapter 2, such jobs are created deliberately to reinforce and maintain hierarchy and control.

5 A role set comprises a web of linked positions or offices that could include colleagues, bosses, subordinates and others within the organisation with whom the incumbent interacts (Blunt & Jones, 1992).

6 All the members of an individual's role set depend upon her behaviour in some way. Role set members therefore develop attitudes, or *role expectations,* about what the *focal person* should or should not do as part of her role. Such expectations are concerned with both form and content, that is, with what the focal person should do and how she should do it. Role expectations are also concerned with beliefs and values, as well as actions (Blunt & Jones, 1992).

7 Further evidence of this was the fact that M obtained formal approval for the PTL to provide the donor agency with advice regarding all of its programmes of technical assistance to Timor-Leste.

8 The 'wailing-wall' phenomenon encouraged programme staff to complain directly to the MES without going through the PTL.

9 Recall also that, in the Cambodian case, first, financial donors to the programme were passive and there were no threats to programme funding; and second, the ADB had employed a private firm from Australia as implementing contractor.

10 Government execution of jointly designed DSF-funded projects meant that the management of project funds, procurement of contractors and project implementation were the responsibility of government.

11 In these notes, the acronym for the principal author's employing sub-contractor has been changed to MES(b). The notes are transcribed in full because we felt it important to demonstrate how dysfunctional in almost every conceivable respect the project was. But we also want to show how little this seemed to matter to the donor. Or – as suggested earlier – how successful the implementing contractor was at preventing bad news from reaching the donor, even making allowance for the fact that what we (minions with genuinely developmental intent) might regard as 'bad' news (dysfunctional project behaviour) the master and the messenger might not.

12 In some instances, street lighting extended for hundreds of metres into the surrounding steppe, suggesting that its real purpose had little to do with shedding light.

13 As a small but significant aside, it is worth noting here that the wife of the deputy head of SDC was a senior staff member of the international NGO that had been appointed by SDC to implement the nationwide procurement certification capacity building for LGs in Mongolia. However, such blatant conflicts of interest were not tolerated as subjects of polite conversation, a rule that did not apply of course to the subjects of SDC's good governance initiatives.

14 That is, a conscious rejection of the necessity to constantly perform disproportionate amounts of interpretive labour.

15 See Guldbrandsen and Veileborg (2012) – a documentary film aptly named 'Stealing Africa'.

16 These features of the Zambian example seemed likely at the time to apply to Oyu Tolgoi and Rio Tinto, which, as we showed in Chapter 3, was a supposition that has since proved to be accurate.

17 GDP here referring to the Governance and Decentralisation Programme.

18 Farid Mamundzay was deputy minister of IDLG and, briefly, acting minister; in March 2021, he was appointed Afghan Ambassador to India. Nader Yama was a director in IDLG who went on to become deputy minister of IDLG and deputy head of mission, Afghan Embassy in Canada. Muqtader Nasary and Saeed Khamoosh were both directors in IDLG; and Hamidullah Afghan was an IDLG director who was later appointed as mayor of Afghanistan's second biggest city, Kandahar.

19 This view is endorsed by Brown (2017, p. 2), almost *verbatim*, when she says: 'As currently conceived in the context of 2018 elections, district councils would achieve few of these widely invoked objectives – greater local accountability, responsiveness, or effectiveness'. Using very similar language, she also corroborates the views expressed in Blunt *et al.* (2015, 2017) and Blunt and Khamoosh (2016) regarding the wide divergence between donor 'paper' reforms and ambitions and political realities: 'pushing for district council elections in 2018 risks perpetuating the long-standing fallacy in Afghan state-building: if subnational structures are built on paper, state legitimacy will follow. District councils would achieve some political decentralisation, but absent broader reform, the outcome will likely be yet another in a long pattern of missteps in the Afghan democratic project' (Brown, 2017, p. 5).

20 Type B personalities tend to be 'relaxed, speak slowly, make few tense gestures, move slowly and calmly, display no muscular tension or impatience, deny even moderate levels of drive or ambition, avoid deadlines, dislike competition, and feel no sense of urgency' (Blunt & Jones, 1992, p. 266).

21 In order of importance, the following Type A behaviours seemed most applicable to M3: a marked need to control his immediate environment, with lack of control evoking extreme hostility and aggression; hard driving and competitive and expressing hostility and/or irritation in response to challenge or threat; a persistent desire for recognition and advancement; and an intense, sustained drive to achieve self-selected but usually poorly defined goals (Blunt & Jones, 1992, pp. 265–267).

22 We learned subsequently that M3 had an established track record of short-lived appointments to development assistance postings.

23 Much of the Programme's micromanagement was delegated to locally employed assistants, at least some of whom seemed to have been selected with these qualities in mind.

24 This is consistent with Graeber (2015, p. 56): 'Violence's capacity to allow arbitrary decisions, and thus to avoid the kind of debate, clarification, and renegotiation typical of more egalitarian social relations, is obviously what allows its victims to see procedures created on the basis of violence as stupid or unreasonable'.

25 The same firm that had implemented the Afghanistan project.

26 Behind-the-scenes manoeuvring and procrastination are sometimes associated with passive aggression or the deliberate masking of covert feelings of anger and antipathy behind a surface appearance of passivity and friendliness. Conditions that are conducive to the development of 'hubris' or 'a grandiose sense of self, characterised by disrespectful attitudes toward others and a misperception of one's place in the world' (Asad & Sadler-Smith, 2020, p. 40) do not combine well with passive aggression. Hubris can be 'triggered by accession to a position of significant power, amplified by overestimations of one's abilities' (Asad & Sadler-Smith, 2020, p. 40) arising from a lack of constraints as to how the power should be exercised and from constant reinforcement from unquestioning supplicants or minions.

27 Suspicions were aroused initially because, following a fruitless search for consultant economists who were not simply neoliberal ideologues, the PTL disclosed that he had written to Yanis Varoufakis asking if he knew of any suitable candidates. Two of the economists he recommended were subsequently employed by the Programme (and are the co-authors of Blunt *et al.*, in press; and the collaborators on this book).

28 This incident shows that, under certain conditions, the (implicit or explicit) joining of forces of minions can ameliorate the structural violence displayed by the master. Donor personality and the stakes involved are the major determinants of what is possible. In Samoa, M4's perceptions of what was at stake (for the donor and personally) resulted in limited compromise. The opposite to the Mongolian case, where the immediate economic (and therefore personal) stakes were much higher and master personality was that of a dominant 'alpha male' as opposed to a more passive–aggressive type.

29 Also, the POM stated clearly that committee decisions would be taken by simple majority and that, in the event of a deadlock, the chair would have a casting vote.

30 The responses by Australia and its allies led Prime Minister Mannasseh Sogavare of the Solomon Islands to conclude, and declare in parliament, that his government was being undermined and that his country might be invaded (*Morrison Says*, 2022).

31 In 2010, according to survey data, Indonesia was perceived to be the most corrupt of 16 Asia-Pacific nations (Blunt *et al.*, 2012a).

32 In 2017, with *pro bono* support in the lead-up from the principal author (in-between missions to Afghanistan) and little or no financial backing, Ganbaatar Sainkhuu ran for president and was beaten (suspiciously) narrowly (by about 1,800 votes) into third place having garnered more than 30% of the popular vote.

References

Asad, S., & Sadler-Smith, E. (2020). Differentiating Leader Hubris and Narcissism on the Basis of Power. *Leadership, 16*(1), 39–61. https://doi.org/10.1177/1742715019885763

Bate, P. (1984). The Impact of Organizational Culture on Approaches to Organizational Problem-Solving. *Organizational Studies, 5*(1), 43–66. https://doi.org/10.1177/017084068400500103

Birtles, B., Dziedzic, S., & Wasuka, E. (2022, April 20). China and Solomon Islands Sign Security Pact, Beijing Says It Is 'Not Directed at Any Third Party' Amid Pacific Influence Fears. *ABC News*. www.abc.net.au/news/2022-04-19/china-and-solomon-islands-sign-security-pact-says-chinese-foreig/101000530

Blunt, P. (1988). Cultural Consequences for Organization Change in a Southeast Asian State: Brunei. *The Academy of Management Executive (1987–1989), 2*(3), 235–240. www.jstor.org/stable/4164834

Blunt, P. (1990). Strategies for Enhancing Organizational Effectiveness in the Third World. *Public Administration and Development, 10*(3), 299–313. https://doi.org/10.1002/pad.4230100306

Blunt, P. (1991). Organizational Culture and Development. *International Journal of Human Resource Management, 2*(1), 55–71. https://doi.org/10.1080/09585199100000051

Blunt, P. (2012). Toxic Technical Assistance in Conditions of State Fragility: Field Notes from Iraq. *Progress in Development Studies, 12*(4), 337–352. https://doi.org/10.1177/146499341201200405

Blunt, P. (2013, October). *Rural Mongolia's Early Experience With Local Development Fund Utilisation Under the Integrated Budget Law: Findings and Recommendations* (Discussion Paper 1/2013). SDC/GDP. Retrieved February, 24, 2022, from www.researchgate.net/publication/265300899_Rural_Mongolia%27s_Early_Experience_with_Local_Development_Fund_Utilisation_under_the_Integrated_Budget_Law_Findings_and_Recommendations

Blunt, P. (2014a). Whose Resources Are They Anyway? 'Development Assistance' and Community Development Agreements in the Mongolian Mining Sector. *Progress in Development Studies, 14*(4), 383–399. https://doi.org/10.1177/1464993414521491

Blunt, P. (2014b, October). *Civilian Casualties Caused by Military Operations and the Foundational Legitimacy of the State in Afghanistan* [Draft Project Concept Note]. Retrieved February 24, 2022, from www.researchgate.net/publication/329643190_CIVILIAN_CASUALTIES_CAUSED_BY_MILITARY_OPERATIONS_AND_THE_FOUNDATIONAL_LEGITIMACY_OF_THE_STATE_IN_AFGHANISTAN

Blunt, P. (2015, February). *Sub-National Governance in Afghanistan* [Briefing Paper]. Retrieved February 24, 2022, from www.researchgate.net/publication/355335535_SNG_Briefing_Paper

Blunt, P. (2019). *Public-Private Partnership for the Establishment in Samoa of a World-Class Tertiary Referral Centre* [Discussion Paper]. Samoa Governance Support Programme.

Blunt, P. (2021a). Development Undone: Weber, Kafka, and the Organisation of Supply-Side Vested Interests. *Journal of Interdisciplinary Economics, 33*(1), 74–102. https://doi.org/10.1177/0260107919896879

Blunt, P. (2021b). *Fateful Synergies: Climate Change and Non-communicable Diseases in the Pacific Island Countries* [Discussion Paper]. Retrieved February 25, 2022, from www.researchgate.net/publication/354597783_Fateful_Synergies_Climate_Change_and_Noncommunicable_Diseases_in_the_Pacific_Island_Countries_1

Blunt, P., Escobar, C., & Missos, V. (in press). Emergency Responses Under COVID-19: Development Assistance, 'Structural Violence', and 'Interpretive Labour' in Samoa. *Journal of Interdisciplinary Economics.*

Blunt, P., & Jones, M. (1992). *Managing Organisations in Africa.* Walter de Gruyter.

Blunt, P., & Jones, M. (1997). Exploring the Limits of Western Leadership Theory in East Asia and Africa. *Personnel Review, 26*(1/2), 6–23. https://doi.org/10.1108/00483489710157760

Blunt, P., & Khamoosh, S. (2016). Vexatious Voice: The Politics of Downward Accountability and Subnational Governance Reform in Afghanistan. *Progress in Development Studies, 16*(1), 81–100. https://doi.org/10.1177/1464993415608085

Blunt, P., Mamundzay, F., & Nasary, M. (2017). The Long and the Short of Policy Pantomime in Afghanistan. *Progress in Development Studies, 17*(1), 67–88. https://doi.org/10.1177/1464993416674303

Blunt, P., Mamundzay, F., Yama, N., & Afghan, H. (2015). Policy Paradigms, Subnational Governance and the State Sovereignty Gap in Afghanistan. *Progress in Development Studies, 15*(3), 270–285. https://doi.org/10.1177/1464993415578981

Blunt, P., & Rondinelli, D. (1997). *Reconceptualising Governance* (Discussion Paper DP(05)/D611/No. 2). Management Development and Governance Division, United Nations Development Programme. http://digitallibrary.un.org/record/268781

Blunt, P., & Sainkhuu, G. (2015). Serendipity and Stealth, Resistance and Retribution: Policy Development in the Mongolian Mining Sector. *Progress in Development Studies, 15*(4), 371–385. https://doi.org/10.1177/1464993415592763

Blunt, P., Turner, M., & Lindroth, H. (2012a). Patronage's Progress in Post-Soeharto Indonesia. *Public Administration and Development, 32*(1), 64–81. https://doi.org/10.1002/pad.617

Blunt, P., Turner, M., & Lindroth, H. (2012b). Patronage, Service Delivery and Social Justice in Indonesia. *International Journal of Public Administration, 35*(3), 214–220. https://doi.org/10.1080/01900692.2011.641050

Brown, F. Z. (2017, November 9). *Local Governance Reform in Afghanistan and the 2018 Elections* (Peace Brief 239). United States Institute for Peace. www.usip.org/sites/default/files/PB239-Local-Governance-Reform-in-Afghanistan-and-the-2018-Elections.pdf

Chomsky, N. (2011). *Power and Terror: Conflict, Hegemony, and the Rule of Force* (J. Junkerman & T. Masakazu, Eds., 2nd ed.). Pluto Press.

Chomsky, N., & Barsamian, D. (2007). *What We Say Goes: Conversations on US Power in a Changing World: Interviews With David Barsamian (The American Empire Project).* Metropolitan Books.

Chomsky, N., & Barsamian, D. (2013). *Power Systems: Conversations on Global Democratic Uprisings and the New Challenges to U.S. Empire. Interviews with David Barsamian (The American Empire Project).* Metropolitan Books.

Farmer, P. (2004). An Anthropology of Structural Violence. *Current Anthropology, 45*(3), 305–325. https://doi.org/10.1086/382250

Foucault, M. (1977). *Discipline and Punish: The Birth of the Prison* (A. Sheridan, Trans.). Pantheon Books (Original work published 1975).

French, J. R. P., Jr., & Raven, B. (1959). The Bases of Social Power. In D. Cartwright (Ed.), *Studies in Social Power* (pp. 150–167). Univer. Michigan.

Graeber, D. (2015). *The Utopia of Rules: On Technology, Stupidity, and the Secret Joys of Bureaucracy*. Melville House.

Guldbrandsen, C. (Filmmaker), & Veileborg, H. (Producer). (2012). *Stealing Africa (Why Poverty?)* [Film]. Guldbrandsen Film & The Why. www.thewhy.dk/films/stealing-africa

Hedges, C. (2011). Foreword. In N. Chomsky, *Power and Terror: Conflict, Hegemony, and the Rule of Force* (pp. 1–6). Pluto Press.

Kashwan, P., MacLean, L. M., & García-López, G. A. (2019). Rethinking Power and Institutions in the Shadows of Neoliberalism: (An Introduction to a Special Issue of World Development). *World Development, 120*, 133–146. https://doi.org/10.1016/j.worlddev.2018.05.026

Marcuse, H. (1972). *A Study on Authority* (J. De Bres, Trans.). New Left Books (Original work published 1936).

Mintzberg, H. (1989). *Mintzberg on Management: Inside Our Strange World of Organizations*. Free Press.

Morrison Says Australia Still Solomon Islands' First Option Despite 'Secret' Security Deal with China. (2022, May 5). *ABC News*. www.abc.net.au/news/2022-05-05/scott-morrison-responds-solomon-islands-prime-minister-tirade/101039816

Mosse, D. (2013). The Anthropology of International Development. *Annual Review of Anthropology, 42*(1), 227–246. https://doi.org/10.1146/annurev-anthro-092412-155553

Roy, A. (2016). *The End of Imagination*. Haymarket Books.

Sant Maral Foundation. (2014, March). *Politbarometer #13(47)* [Data set]. Retrieved March 14, 2022, from https://830a862d-3fe6-40e6-b731-5a65590fd0cf.filesusr.com/ugd/086765_c195abbdfdf3449584fdeb09ed5c210f.pdf

5 Development Implications and Aid Reformulations

Introduction

The implications of the climate crisis for global development are clear. Time is fast running out for preventive and unprecedented profound changes to important aspects of our political, economic and social systems to be made. The next 20 to 30 years may well be all that is left, placing the fate of humanity in the hands of the current generation (Chomsky *et al.*, 2020).

The evidence that we have presented in this book shows unequivocally that, under the blanket cover of neoliberalism, LDI bilateral technical assistance has been, and remains, a significant part of the problem.

None of the cases discussed in Chapters 3 and 4 could be said to have contributed significantly to the far-reaching changes that are needed to avert climate catastrophe or to have contributed significantly to the public good in other ways. Indeed, with the possible exception of parts of the Samoa programme, the technical assistance that was given was probably detrimental to global development. The net effects were negative. The tragic burlesques of the country cases of technical assistance illustrate vividly the extent to which LDI bilateral aid has helped to clear the way for our 'wild gallop towards the precipice'.

It has done so by reinforcing neoliberal-friendly policies and regimes, like the autocratic regime of Hun Sen in Cambodia, and by increasing the opportunities for patronage predation and the realisation of local and foreign elite self-interest in the neopatrimonial state of Indonesia. It has done the same by helping to soothe surface relations between Australia and the Government of Timor-Leste, so that Australia could fulfil its ambitions regarding the oil and gas riches of the Timor Sea.

No matter how clumsily, following a decade of sanctions, and the shock therapy of destructive invasion and occupation, the tragic burlesque of LDI technical assistance to Iraq sought to push an already comatose state towards geopolitical disintegration and chaos.

In Mongolia, the donor stubbornly and aggressively promoted and defended foreign corporate exploitation of the country's natural resources. Its blind aggression prevented it from seeing that the reforms suggested for mining

DOI: 10.4324/9781003284352-5

Table 5.1 Summary of Findings on Ownership and Critical Interfaces[1]

Programme Country – Donor	*Government Ownership*	*Donor Strategy and Self-Interest*	*Bureaucratic Structural Violence*	*Master–Minion and/or Messenger–Minion Relations*
Cambodia – the Netherlands, Sweden (via ADB)	Authentic ownership achieved but for largely non-developmental purposes	Largely non-developmental self-interests served on both supply- and demand-sides. No explicit donor strategy	Wilful misguided support to decentralisation served the interests of the ruling party much more than it did the people of Cambodia	Direct contact between master and minion (project). Considerable inter- and intra-sender conflict and person-role conflict. Principal features of culture: largely suppressed antipathy and unemotionality
Timor-Leste – Australia	Authentic ownership by a government 'on its knees' and with little choice	Conducive donor 'strategy' by default, stemming from master idiosyncrasies. Developmental support provided and donor self-interests satisfied	Inflicted entirely by messenger and largely confined to project staff	Direct contact between master and minion (project). Positive, permissive culture. Little or no role conflict. No antipathy
Indonesia – United Kingdom, Australia, Canada (via WB)	Authentic ownership achieved but for largely non-developmental purposes	No clear donor strategy. Largely non-developmental master, messenger and minion (government) self-interests satisfied	Support for decentralisation served interests of patronage predation and political party consolidation more than the general good	Messenger–minion relations largely dysfunctional. Negative organisational culture and barely suppressed antipathy between messenger and minion
Iraq – United States	No government ownership and no attempt made to secure it	Implicit donor strategy of complete domination, control and entitlement. Iraq treated as a vassal state. Donor self-interest achieved to the extent permitted by a dysfunctional project	Support for decentralisation contributed to the fragmentation of the state, likely designed to serve a 'divide and rule' interest on the part of the donor	Messenger–minion relations and project culture comprehensively dysfunctional

Mongolia – Switzerland	Any interest in government ownership abandoned as soon as there was the slightest threat to donor (and corporate) interests	Implicit donor strategy of complete domination, control and entitlement. Crude understanding of self-interest paramount	Principally, the defence of mining legislation that favoured foreign corporations; and the promotion of a flawed programme of fiscal decentralisation	Master–minion relations and project culture comprehensively dysfunctional
Afghanistan – United Kingdom	Authentic ownership achieved but for largely non-developmental purposes	No explicit donor strategy. Largely non-developmental master, messenger and minion (government) self-interests satisfied	Support for decentralisation in circumstances where everyone knew that it had little chance of succeeding. Denial of critical governance issues, such as civilian casualties from friendly fire	Master–minion and messenger–minion relations cordial. Intelligent discussion permitted, so long as it did not detract from the appearance of 'democracy promotion'
Samoa – Australia	For projects that were seen by the donor to threaten its ill-defined self-interests, government ownership, and formal agreements regarding it, were disregarded at will	No explicit donor strategy. Where the donor thought its (mainly geostrategic) interests were at stake, it acted quickly and decisively to protect them. Frequently, the ways in which this was done added significant, palpable insult to already damaging injury	Principally, the unilateral cancellation of developmental projects, and whole fields of support, approved by government that were seen not to align with Australian (neoliberal) policy or threatened Australian interests or 'sensitivities' in other ways	For the final 2 years of the programme, in particular, master–minion relations largely dysfunctional. Negative organisational culture and barely suppressed antipathy between master and minion concealed beneath a surface layer of cordiality

legislation could have been beneficial to its own interests as well as those of communities affected by mining operations. And it bought off or pandered to its co-conspirators in government by, among other things, supporting a clearly flawed programme of fiscal decentralisation and its opportunities for patronage predation. Government officials co-opted in this and other ways were essential to the pushing through of 'conducive investment climate' legislation and to the signing of lop-sided deals that favoured foreign mining corporations (e.g. Prima *et al.*, 2019).

The tragic burlesque of development aid in Afghanistan entailed the donor turning a blind eye to what it knew to be among the most critical issues of donor and government legitimacy (civilian casualties from friendly fire) because it might reflect badly on the donor. It also promoted a programme of decentralisation in circumstances where it had no chance of succeeding; and participated knowingly in an elaborate and meaningless pantomime of SNG policy development whereby, on the surface, both sides played by the rules, so long as this permitted each to achieve its respective, largely non-developmental, self-interests.

Though insignificant in terms of their global effects, the main features of the Samoan burlesque were no less tragic for the people of Samoa, and no less revealing of LDI motives and self-interests. Here, the standard hard line of donor bureaucratic structural violence entailed the imposition of neoliberal policies that were consistent with, or the same as, those of the Government of Australia. This stance was unaffected by the onset of the COVID-19 pandemic and its revelations regarding the severe shortcomings of neoliberalism and its well-known adverse effects on poverty and inequality.

From our discussion in Chapters 3 and 4, and the summary in Table 5.1, we can see no reason to suppose why these examples of bureaucratic structural violence would be unrepresentative of the general condition of much or most of LDI bilateral technical assistance in other places.

Where, we might ask, in this seven-act 'tragedy of development' is there any room for constructive reformulation? To begin to answer this question, our concern for global development that is in the best interests of the planet and all of its inhabitants requires that we address the contingencies that are most critical to the achievement of such a goal. We can do this by asking a series of subsidiary questions, and discussing them in terms of 'if not, what then'? All of the subsidiary questions should be read with the qualifying prefix, 'in the short time available'.

1. Is it likely that LDI countries, and the elites that control them, will forsake self-interest for the global good?
2. Is it likely that elites in developing countries will do the same?
3. If the answer to questions (1) and (2) is 'highly unlikely', is there any point in proceeding?
4. If the answer to question (3) is a qualified 'yes', because LDI technical assistance is not the most important variable of global development; and

because 'patients' in need of care should be administered to whatever the prognosis, what do our cases suggest can be done?

We therefore proceed with our proposals for the constructive reformulation of LDI technical assistance on the basis of the following assumptions. First, in the time available, neither the elites of LDI donor countries nor the elites of the countries they 'assist' will completely abandon self-interest in favour of the global public good. Second, while LDI technical assistance, as an enforcer (and, in some senses, a pimp) of neoliberalism, has been a significant contributing factor to the perilous state of the planet, the most important determinants have stemmed from the unbridled expressions of corporate power, greed and elite self-interest *within* the rich and industrialised countries. To avert climate catastrophe, it is there that the preventative and unprecedented profound changes to almost every aspect of economy and society will have to be made. Until that happens, LDI technical assistance is likely to 'bumble along obediently' in the 'political dust cloud' of neoliberalism's rear-guard action, doing as it is bid (Blunt *et al.*, in press). Third, within these narrow confines, it is nevertheless possible to discern possibilities for the constructive reformulation of LDI technical assistance that provides for a better fit between supply- and demand-side contingencies and the realisation of donor and host government self-interest and development good.

Reform Proposals

Based on the cases summarised in Table 5.1, our proposals for the constructive reformulation of LDI technical assistance are set out in the rest of this chapter. We acknowledge in advance that much of what we propose is already part of what LDI donors say, but our data have shown that they are all too rarely a part of what LDI donors actually do. We argue that LDI donors who are not in the habit of behaving honourably should start to do so, as much for their own interests as for the general good. In proposing this, are we thereby hoisted by our own petard, that is, by our own oxymoron? Are LDI donors so set in their ways, so blind to their own failings, so convinced of their technical superiority, and so complacent about their positions of power as to be beyond the reach of even modest reform? Can rational discourse influence an Empire that has assumed the right to go to war wherever and whenever it likes, and the right to save people from 'corrupting ideologies' and other social and economic malaises by the 'age-old, tried-and-tested practice of extermination' (Roy, 2003b) – a once 'glorious' Empire in retreat, yet still defiantly proclaiming the virtues of its discredited forms of democracy and state capitalism?

Against this forbidding background, our arguments for change dangle from two slim threads of hope. First, that our acceptance of, and appeal to, LDI donor self-interest will allow those arguments to be heard and acted upon. And second, that our arguments and evidence will build pressure for reform from below, that is, from government, civil society and other recipient-country

Table 5.2 Technical Assistance Organisational Arrangements

Programme Country – Donor	*Responsible Official in the Field*	*Principal Supply-Side Agents*	*Specialised LDI Donor Agency in the Field*	*Hands-on or Hands-off LDI Donor in the Field*
Cambodia (2003–2006) – the Netherlands, Sweden (via ADB)	Staff member of multilateral financial institution	Multilateral financial institution as agent for LDI donor; and implementing contractor (private firm)	No. Control exercised through multilateral agency	Hands-off, largely enabled by earmarked grant funding to a specific programme of decentralisation
Timor-Leste (2006–2008) – Australia	Donor official	LDI donor agency; and implementing contractor (private firm)	Yes. Specialised agency – AusAID – in operation at the time	Permissive, intelligent, hands-off
Indonesia (2008–2011) – United Kingdom, Australia, Canada (via WB)	Staff member of multilateral financial institution	Multilateral financial institution as agent for LDI donors; and LDI donor officials in the field	Yes. DfID (merged with the Foreign Office in 2020 to become the Foreign Commonwealth and Development Office – FCDO); and AusAID (absorbed by Department of Foreign Affairs and Trade, DFAT, in 2013)	Insistent principal donor strongly hands-on until programme strategic direction had been reset to its liking; thereafter, less hands-on but still vigilant
Iraq (2011–2012) – United States	No direct contact between project and donor. De facto control assumed by implementing contractor (private firm)	Implementing contractor (private firm)	Yes. USAID, but control mediated through implementing contractor (private firm)	Hands-on via domineering implementing contractor (private firm)

Mongolia (2012–2013) – Switzerland	Staff member of specialised LDI donor agency (SDC)	LDI donor agency; and implementing agents (NGOs and multilateral financial institutions)	Yes. SDC	Tight control of technical assistance delivered by SDC staff; less apparent concern for control of outside implementing agents
Afghanistan (2014–2016) – United Kingdom	Staff member of specialised LDI donor agency (DfID)	LDI donor agency; and implementing contractor (private firm)	Yes. DfID	Regular contact between project and donor, but otherwise hands-off. Intelligent implementing contractor.
Samoa (2016–2021) – Australia	Staff member of DFAT (diplomatic and aid responsibilities)	LDI donor agency; and implementing contractor (private firm)	No. DFAT (diplomatic and aid responsibilities)	Initially hands-off; last 2 years, tight hands-on. Intelligent implementing contractor

minions. In the best case, the proposals for change set out in this book will be a small but significant part of more fundamental and far-reaching reform of the main drivers of climate change and inequality. In the worst case, they will simply be a form of palliative care.

More mundanely, our proposals for reformulating LDI technical assistance also need to be set against the organisational arrangements for the delivery of the technical assistance in each of our cases by the LDIs and other agencies involved, which will set limits on what is feasible or likely. These arrangements are summarised in Table 5.2.

The organisational arrangements set out in Table 5.2 are clearly heterogenous between donors and within donors over time. Our data provide insights into four LDIs in particular: Australia in Timor-Leste, Indonesia and Samoa; the United Kingdom in Indonesia and Afghanistan; the United States in Iraq; Switzerland in Mongolia; and, to a much lesser extent, to a fifth, the Netherlands, in Cambodia. The data presented in Chapters 3 and 4 and the summary notes set out in Tables 5.1 and 5.2 are also relevant to the roles played by international financial institutions (ADB and WB) and corporate contractors in the delivery of LDI donor-funded technical assistance.

We acknowledge that the complexities of the organisational issues associated with the five LDI agencies and the two international financial institutions responsible for the delivery of technical assistance are likely to require much more detailed analysis than we can give them here. Nevertheless, on the basis of our extensive experience and a limited review of the relevant literature, we can make informed judgements about where our proposals for change would best fit and speculate about the chances of their acceptance.

Hereafter, we first set out our proposals for change and we then consider whether, and how, they might be accommodated by LDI donor institutional arrangements.

For Masters

1. LDI donor strategy should be based on the assumption that behaving empathetically, honourably, authentically and consistently in these respects, is always better than not. Adhere strictly to the good governance principles that you espouse. Respect the commonsensical notion of recipient-country (government and civil society) ownership defined in this book, and admit that your own non-developmental self-interests and track record of historical structural violence do not allow you to assume exclusive, or any, occupation of the moral high ground. From the beginning, be completely transparent about your 'red lines' and 'no go' or 'sensitive' areas. Do not allow such judgements to be solely dependent on the idiosyncrasies of LDI donor officials in the field. Where you can, develop clear policy. Do not patronise, or insult in other ways, the host government or its officials. Suppress, and preferably extinguish altogether, any sense of entitlement that you may have to do as you please. Observe local protocols of social exchange.

The limits of these proposals are most evident in the Iraq case, where LDI hard-line strategy regarding the fragmentation of what it assumed to be a vassal state seemed completely impervious to other possibilities. Amenability to such advice among LDI donors is likely to vary between them according to the strength of their hegemonic presumptions, or their beliefs in their (God-given) right to rule, according to the stakes involved, and according to their institutional arrangements. These limits do not detract from the logic of our argument; they simply point to the likelihood of its acceptance. But even for LDIs like the United States in Iraq, in these least fertile of grounds, we can see no reason why a donor whose ultimate purpose is to secure unfettered control of the oil and gas resources of the region (Chomsky, 2007) could not be persuaded by an argument along the lines that such an end would be easier to achieve in negotiation with a stable unified state where relations are built on some semblance of trust and mutual respect, rather than a fragmented and unstable one, where relations with government have neither respect nor trust and are characterised more by barely suppressed hostility. The difficulty of carrying this argument clearly lies in the many instances where LDIs have deliberately created political instability and social chaos because it suits their purposes better, that is, because in some instances they believe that it is easier, and more advantageous to them, to fish in troubled waters.

2. Assume that what is in the best interests of the host country (and of the planet), in the end, will be in your best interests too. Provide the best pragmatic technical assistance towards these ends rather than ideological or doctrinaire (neoliberal) prescription. Eschew completely the replication of your home country policies in the recipient country, unless these are clearly best for the recipient country too.

   Again, the limits to such a proposal are most evident in the Iraq case. There would appear to be little likelihood of converting the world's most powerful and hegemonic state to this way of thinking. And, as the self-professed leader of the so-called free world – of the 'bullied and bought' (Roy, 2003a) – the United States will set the tone for 'coat-tail' LDIs like Australia and the United Kingdom. This may be so even in places like Samoa, which until the rise of China's so-called adventurism in the region, was tucked away in the backwaters of the US's global domain. But China's rise, as an alternative source of development assistance everywhere, should provoke studied reconsideration, and a willingness to reform, and not just alarm and defensiveness on the part of LDIs (see Robinson & Chomsky, 2022).[2]

3. On the basis of (1) and (2), the responsible LDI donor agency will negotiate with the recipient government the broad structure and coverage of its aid to the country and the form and scope of the technical assistance and other programmes and projects that comprise it.
4. The responsible LDI donor agency will then assign responsibility and authority for the detail of technical assistance programme/project design

and implementation to an 'intelligent' contractor (e.g. Samoa and Afghanistan cases) that reports directly to the host government. All project and activity approvals will therefore be made by, for example, a host government steering committee whose membership includes the contractor's programme director and the project/programme team leader, who will also be secretary to the committee. The donor will have no representation on this committee. This also has the advantage of distancing the LDI donor from possible violations of (1) and (2). The reputational 'fall-guy' will always be the implementing contractor. The difficulty of the contractor's job will be a function of the extent to which the host government can be said to be neopatrimonial or characterised by systemic patronage, and its ability to hold its side of sometimes complex technical discussions. Nevertheless, carefully negotiated trade-offs that to some extent satisfy all interests should still be possible.

For example, in Cambodia, Indonesia and Afghanistan, support for measured deconcentration as opposed to all out decentralisation would still have allowed supply- and demand-side self-interests to be satisfied, though perhaps to a lesser degree. In Cambodia, effective deconcentration would still have contributed to CPP consolidation, but benefits for the public good would have been more likely. Likewise, in Indonesia and Afghanistan, support for deconcentration would still have presented opportunities for patronage predation, but with greater prospects for improvements to service delivery. Supply-side interest in 'stability' (state compliance) and measurable results would have been just as, or more, likely to be achieved with support to measured deconcentration, but with considerably less waste.

5. Make it incumbent on the contractor to appoint a programme director and select a programme or project team leader who have the analytical capability and technical knowledge to help host governments design projects that do not simply entail the application of standard neoliberal formulae, and have the potential to deliver benefits for the public good. These positions will best be housed in a form of organisation that combines elements of Mintzberg's 'professional bureaucracy' and 'adhocracy', where the principal forms of coordination and management are the standardisation of skills (heavy emphasis on recruitment and selection) and 'mutual adjustment'. These methods 'rule out direct supervision. . . . Coordination must rest with the people who have the knowledge and expertise, the professionals themselves' (Blunt & Jones, 1992, p. 157). We elaborate on this structure among our proposals for messengers later.
6. Specify clearly the contractor ground rules and stick to them, particularly regarding (1) and (2). These ground rules should be disclosed to the host government.
7. Regard mutual trust and respect, and credibility, as the bedrock of the relationship between the LDI technical assistance and the host government. Aim to build organisational cultures like the 'synergistic culture' outlined

by Blunt (1991) and those that were achieved between the programme and government in the case of Samoa. Reward government (by extending and/or increasing the size of the programme), contractors and programme team leaders accordingly.

8. Reward contractors for projects that contribute to the public/global good without infringing on donor and host government interests. Unless problems arise in this regard, rely solely on annual and bi-annual project/programme reports.
9. Make the primary purpose of independent evaluations of programme/project performance the assessment of the extent to which the implementing contractor has managed to establish the conditions for doing developmental work that enables all interests to be satisfied to some degree (as earlier, and later under 'messengers'). It should be assumed that developmental results will flow naturally from the establishment of such conditions. Dispense with project/programme evaluations that attempt to establish causality between project/programme activities and 'development outcomes' in circumstances where most of the critical independent variables are beyond the control of the project/programme. Use the substantial savings from this for improving project design and for hiring the best consultants that the market has to offer.
10. Encourage intelligent, well-researched, evidence-based discussions of critical development problems affecting the country in question. Indeed, require it.
11. Eliminate LDI donor (master) bullshit jobs (which points 3, 4 and 5 will allow), and assign to LDI donor masters in the field the kind of non-hands-on, background, permissive role exhibited by M1 and M2 in Samoa and M in Timor-Leste.[3] Wherever possible, select-out from such jobs any personalities that show signs of passive aggression or hubris.
12. Write clear and concise policies on the matters referred to in these notes and disclose them to all interested parties.
13. Incorporate (1) and (2) prominently in the education and development of donor masters in the field, and in their job descriptions.

For Messengers

1. The two most critical positions in our proposals for change are those of the contractor's programme director and the contractor-appointed programme/project team leader. To reiterate, above all, these positions should be filled by people who are able to help host governments design genuinely developmental projects that do not simply entail the application of standard neoliberal formulae, and that serve the donor's and host government's interests. Depending on the development circumstances of the country, donor and host government interests are likely to have developmental and non-developmental elements. Clearly, under these circumstances, project design will be crucial and difficult. The programme/project team leader

will shoulder most of the responsibility for designing such projects with government. The breadth and depth of experience, intellectual calibre, and beliefs and values – consistent with (1) and (2) under 'For Masters' – that will be needed to do these jobs well will be difficult to find. The same will be true for the contractor's programme director.

2. As noted earlier, the structure of the organisation that these two positions sit at the head of, which comprises the technical assistance programme or project, should combine elements of the professional bureaucracy and adhocracy. Following Mintzberg (1979, 1983), the principal features of the professional bureaucracy are, first, an operating core that houses educated technical specialists (in this case, consultants), which is the key part of the organisation; second, reliance on the standardisation of skills as the principal means of management, with an emphasis on careful selection, which brings with it in-built standards of performance and commitment among those employed; and, third, horizontal job specialisation combined with high levels of vertical and horizontal decentralisation of authority. This would be augmented by elements of the adhocracy, which is the structural configuration most suited to sophisticated innovation. Innovation implies a search for new ways of doing things, or a breaking away from established patterns. There tends to be little formalisation of behaviour, and less importance is attached to tight planning and control systems. More than anything else, the adhocracy must remain flexible. Interactions between members of the operating core of such a hybrid organisation should therefore rely principally on mutual adjustment (Blunt & Jones, 1992).[4]
3. Establish a programme governance structure comprising a programme steering committee (PSC) responsible for the strategic management of the programme and a programme management group responsible for operations. A primary responsibility of the PSC will be to approve projects for implementation under the programme that do not trespass on donor 'no-go' areas, which will have been disclosed in advance and agreed with government as part of the bilateral negotiations to proceed with the support in the first place. It will be the job of the contractor's programme director (CPD), as a member of the PSC, with the PTL, to negotiate and monitor the development and approval of projects that do not cross donor red lines or raise donor red flags. Where uncertainties or disagreements arise in this regard, the CPD will be responsible for raising the matter with the responsible donor representative in the donor head office.[5] All such discussions should be transparent. This will enable all sides to behave honourably and to be seen to be doing so.
4. The culture within the structure of the programme, and that established between the programme and government, should strive to achieve the main elements of the synergistic culture outlined by Blunt (1991) and Blunt and Jones (1992). In terms of Hofstede's well-known dimensions of organisational culture, such cultures should be low on 'power-distance',

low on 'uncertainty avoidance', low to medium on 'individualism' and low on 'masculinity/femininity'.[6]

5. Like the programme/project team leader, the consultants selected to do the work of the programme/project should also be non-doctrinaire experts in their respective fields who can demonstrate commitment to the beliefs and values set out earlier under 'For Masters' (1) and (2). Management by the standardisation of skills puts heavy emphasis on making good selection decisions, as – by definition – direct supervision or control of a wide variety of complex specialisms with indeterminate ways of working and uncertain outcomes is untenable. The onus for screening and shortlisting candidates for consultant positions will fall almost entirely on the programme/project team leader. He/she will also be responsible for arguing, and explaining, the case for a non-doctrinaire approach to problem analysis and project design to government. In Samoa, all of the above was critical to the very good relations that were established between government and the Programme.
6. It is vital also that the programme/project be seen to be its own harshest critic and the first to detect, and admit, problems in its own performance, particularly regarding the selection and performance of consultants. Too frequently managing or implementing contractors are seen by government, and act, primarily as agents of cover-up, that is, as apologists for failure who are bent on deflecting criticism or denying responsibility for poor performance, as demonstrated at the extreme by the Iraq case. Good selection should make such occurrences rare, however, as was the case in Samoa. In the supervision of the work that is done, programmes and projects should be perceived by government to be sitting on its side of the table.

Clearly, our proposal to relieve LDI donor officials in the field of any responsibility for the management of programmes or projects of technical assistance is likely to be the main sticking point, simply because it entails the most significant departure from conventional practice and because it seems to threaten or dilute control by donors who traditionally have assumed it to be their right. We reiterate that such fears are unfounded. Implemented well, we believe that, without jeopardising donor control, our proposals will have the following benefits. First, they will provide for greater donor consistency because donor actions regarding 'no-go' projects – which will have been clearly specified in advance – will be less subject to the individual differences of the responsible donor official in the field. Second, strict adherence to good governance principles of transparency and integrity, which will be required of the CPD and the PTL, will significantly reduce the likelihood of, or eliminate altogether, instances of deceit and subterfuge, which were such strikingly consistent features of the cases discussed in this book. Third, bureaucratic structural violence associated with micromanagement and the unilateral abrogation of formal agreements by the responsible donor in the field will be eliminated. Fourth, it will be easier to select suitable expertise,[7] intellect and personality in the CPD and the PTL than in, say, responsible donors in the field. The latter would always be likely to have broader responsibilities, making the possession of relevant technical capability by them virtually impossible to achieve because of the wide variability of programmes and projects. Fifth, this should have significant benefits for LDI donor/government relations; it would insulate the donor against reputational risk; and it should provide for better-designed and better-managed programmes and projects.

For Minions

For negotiations regarding *developmental* projects, government representatives must be in a position to make informed judgements about the merits of doctrinaire as opposed to non-doctrinaire approaches to problem analysis and resolution. In all of the cases discussed in this book, even if they had wanted to, none of the recipient governments concerned was in a position to make such judgements. Invariably, host governments relied on the technical know-how and (assumed) technical superiority of the LDI donor for this. This meant that in most of the cases discussed in this book, technical advice took the form of neoliberal dogma. In the few cases where alternatives to such dogma were presented to government, and agreed with them, project approval and implementation were always subject to the whim of the responsible donor official in the field. Several of the project examples discussed in the Samoan case illustrate this.

Our proposals are designed to encourage the consideration of alternatives to neoliberal design by recipient governments that are intent on using technical assistance wholly or partly for genuinely developmental purposes. The question then becomes, 'how best to do this?'

1. First, it will clearly be necessary for LDI donors to countenance such a possibility, which would be consistent with the 'For Masters' principle set out earlier that urges donors to assume that what is best for the recipient country, and for the planet, in the end, is best for the LDI donor country too. The ideology of neoliberalism, whose tenets LDI governments themselves have happily contravened during the COVID-19 pandemic, is unlikely to heal itself. Left to its own devices, it is likely to make things worse. Since the onset of the pandemic, the behaviour of stock markets and house prices in the major economies of the world demonstrates how. The trillions of dollars pumped into these economies by governments have been used by firms to buy back their own shares or to invest in property, wildly inflating already high prices for the benefit of the one percent, that is, worsening a social contract that was already 'alarmingly one-sided' (Tooze, 2021).
2. Second, recipient governments will need to become much more interested in, and informed and insistent about, alternatives to neoliberal standard practice. Even in recipient governments where non-developmental elite self-interests predominate, the urgency and magnitude of the climate crisis,

and the economic and social consequences of the COVID-19 pandemic and its successors, make it rational to examine alternatives to neoliberal dogma. The logic of the general argument applies equally to giver and receiver. If, as Tooze (2021) suggests, the pandemic has forced the governments in the LDI countries to acknowledge the hitherto Keynesian anathema, namely, that 'we can afford anything we can actually do', then this compels us to ask 'what can be done and by whom?'

With a few exceptions in Samoa, in none of the cases discussed in this book did recipient governments seem capable of, or interested in, asking these questions. The two constraints are of course inter-related. Interest is only likely to be sparked where the problems are understood in the first place. In the cases in Samoa where these questions were asked and projects were designed and implemented accordingly – until they were snuffed out by the donor – the importance of considering alternatives to 'conducive (neoliberal) investment climates' and 'privatisation' and so on were explained to the host government by the Programme.

3. A major responsibility of the PTL should be to help host governments to understand the necessity for alternatives to neoliberal design, what those alternatives might be, and what benefits could be realised. Considerable stress should be placed on this and, where necessary, additional expertise should be sought to make it happen. The establishment of such understanding should be a necessary and sufficient condition for the design of technical assistance projects or activities.[8]

Clearly, the rise of China as a global power and as an alternative source of development aid improves significantly the bargaining position of recipient governments who should therefore be able to push back in these vital respects more than they have done in the past.

Optimising the Fit Between Reforms and LDI Donor Institutional Arrangements

The haphazard messiness and structural violence of the LDI technical assistance discussed in Chapters 3 and 4 of this book demonstrate how much there is to be gained for global development from our proposals for the reform of such technical assistance. In principle, nothing that we have proposed is so complex technically or organisationally as to place it beyond the reach of any of the supply-side agents referred to in Table 5.2. For ideological and hegemonic reasons, the acceptability of our proposals is another matter of course. Another limiting factor that we need to consider is the extent to which the agencies in Table 5.2 stand to lose, or gain, organisationally from our proposals.

We are inclined to think that ideological and hegemonic walls of resistance will be more difficult to surmount in institutions with deep roots, a strong sense of self or of corporate identity, high levels of technical capability, and well-established (neoliberal) traditions, policies and practices. International financial institutions

(IFIs) like the World Bank and the ADB would normally be placed close to the top of any such list. However, we also surmise that because the management of LDI-funded technical assistance by IFIs is not part of their core business and, in some instances – as in the Indonesian case – it constitutes, at best, an optional add-on and sop to government that carries substantial reputational risk, the IFIs might be open to persuasion. They would listen most attentively of course to those LDIs at the top of the IFI's list of contributors.

Specialised LDI donor agencies like SDC perhaps stand to lose the most, as they would relinquish considerable responsibility for programme/project design and control to the CPD and the contractor-appointed PTL. Unlike the United Kingdom and Australia, where specialised development agencies have been absorbed by other government departments dealing mainly with foreign affairs, and our proposals would allow officials there to concentrate on their core business of diplomacy, for SDC our proposals would eat-in to, or eliminate, one of its principal lines of business. Nevertheless, our arguments for doing what we propose – as set out under 'For Masters' and 'For Messengers' – are unaffected by this. Indeed, because SDC already uses third parties to implement most of its programmes/projects of technical assistance, there would be considerable savings.

Whatever organisational form they might take, and wherever housed institutionally, under our proposals, the donor agencies responsible for LDI technical assistance would be able to divest themselves of the technically complex, risky and often messy business of programme/project design and implementation in favour of policy development and strategic management. As with much high-level government policy, to do this well, the best available talent will need to be drawn upon, wherever it may be found. To achieve development objectives that contribute to the global public good, it will clearly be necessary also for non-doctrinaire policy advisers to be well represented in such talent.

The logic of this is supported by an 'independent review' of the DFAT/AusAID merger conducted by Moore (2019, p. i), which found that it had produced a significant decline in the institution's capability to design and manage bilateral aid combined with 'idiosyncratic' policy compliance, and organisational systems that relied on a 'dwindling number of highly experienced officers'. Many professional staff felt that their capabilities and experience were 'not highly valued'. Also supportive of our suggestion – and findings – is Cook's (2020, p. 2) assessment of the merger, which found that it had resulted in the 'disillusionment of many staff' and that it had reduced the general effectiveness of the aid programme. Metherell's (2014) report of widespread dissatisfaction among AusAID staff following the merger adds to this. Such withering on the vine of professional motivation and morale, and the limited scope allowed for the utilisation of skills, knowledge, 'imagination' and 'critical thinking', could be said to comprise the ministering by the (neoliberal) system of bureaucratic structural ('spiritual') violence to subdue and discipline its own.

As with the absorption of AusAID by DFAT, Clare Short (2020), DfID's founding secretary of state, argued that the merger between DfID and the Foreign and Commonwealth Office (FCO) was a bad idea because the FCO's 'thinking is necessarily dominated by short-term political and trade interests' and, therefore, that it would always have its mind on things other than global development. Three former United Kingdom prime ministers – Gordon Brown, David Cameron and Tony Blair – also condemned the move. According to David Cameron, the abolition of DfID would significantly reduce expertise and voice for development 'at the top table' and the standing, and respect for, the United Kingdom abroad (Mitchell, 2020).

Major NGOs have been particularly vocal in their opposition to the abolition of DfID. For example, a joint statement issued by more than 100 charities, including Action Aid, Oxfam and War on Want, said that the move implied that the United Kingdom was 'turning [its] back' on the world's poor, as well as global challenges such as climate change and the prevention of conflict. And that the United Kingdom aid might simply become 'a vehicle for UK foreign policy, commercial and political objectives', when its principal aim should be to alleviate poverty (Honeycombe-Foster, 2019). The timing could not have been worse either. Kevin Watkins, the chief executive of Save the Children UK, asserted that the decision to effect the merger during the COVID-19 pandemic was 'reckless' and 'irresponsible' and a 'dereliction of UK leadership' that 'threaten[ed] to reverse hard-won gains in child survival, nutrition and poverty' (Stewart & Wintour, 2020).

However, despite the weight and breadth of criticism, it seems highly improbable that the British and Australian governments will restore the specialised development agencies that have been abolished. In the circumstances, our much less radical, and piecemeal, suggestions seem feasible. Less radical, and feasible, to the extent that one of our most profound suggested changes simply entails LDI donor countries committing to do as they (already) say and to displaying the same levels of transparency, integrity and fair dealing that they espouse and expect of others. In short, there is little to lose, by way of control, and much trust, goodwill, respect and development benefit to be gained from shifting away from a strategy of 'whatever we might say, we shall do as please' to one of 'we shall always strive to do as we say, in our own interests, and in the interests of the planet and the public good, which we acknowledge to be inseparable'. Likewise, the organisational and administrative arrangements that we propose reduce donor risk, increase the likelihood of mutual benefit and provide for honourable and fair dealing without conceding much in the way of control, or any at all.

We acknowledge that the examples of LDI historical structural violence that we set out in Chapter 3 – which demonstrate LDI preferences for 'fishing in troubled waters' – make the thread from which dangles the appeal to conscience a very slim one indeed. More plausible perhaps is the extent to which our arguments may serve to bolster and unify resistance, and pressure to reform, from below.

Notes

1 Note that in none of these cases was there any evidence to suggest donor or government misunderstanding of the notion of 'ownership' or which agencies were responsible for exercising it.

2 Our resort to hegemonic competition as a means for encouraging genuinely developmental assistance is itself a depressing comment on the condition of the global political economy.
3 This would reduce the financial costs to the donor and relieve it of the burden of having to 'manage' a wide variety of programmes in technical fields in which it has little or no expertise. It would have the added benefit of allowing donor officials in the field (who, for some LDIs, are diplomats) to get on with the business of diplomacy.
4 This method depends on informal communication to achieve the desired coordination of work. Control of work under mutual adjustment resides with the workers themselves. The method works best in relatively small and simple organisations. But it is also a method which is suited to coordination in some of the most complicated organisations. The reason for this is that at the beginning of highly complex projects nobody can be sure how, exactly, they are going to develop. Accordingly, the organisation needs to remain extremely flexible, able to learn as it goes along, and to adapt quickly. Mutual adjustment permits such flexibility (Blunt & Jones, 1992, p. 112).
5 This should make for greater consistency and encourage the donor to think through and develop clear policies regarding where red lines should be drawn and why. It would ameliorate or eliminate the 'donor official idiosyncrasy problem' that was so evident in the cases discussed in this book, where all too frequently 'red lines' were drawn or 'red flags' were raised according to the personal characteristics of the responsible donor official rather than clear, formal donor policy or strategy.
6 High power distance implies a high willingness on the part of less powerful individuals to accept an unequal distribution of power without question and to regard it as normal. Uncertainty avoidance refers to the extent to which people within a culture are made nervous by situations that they consider to be unstructured, unclear or unpredictable, and the extent to which they try to avoid such situations by adopting strict codes of behaviour and a belief in absolute truths. Low individualism is characteristic of collectivist cultures and implies that individuals, because of close-knit kinship relationships, belong to tightly woven 'ingroups'. The ingroup – whether extended family, clan or organisation – protects the interests of members and, in turn, expects loyalty. Masculinity/femininity is concerned with the extent to which roles for the two sexes in a culture are defined differently (Blunt & Jones, 1992, pp. 190–192).
7 Easier to the extent that this would be a contractual requirement for the contractor and could be emphasised more readily in the selection of CPDs, whose role would be similar across all of their programme responsibilities.
8 Whether this will be possible without the kind of revolutionary change envisaged by Engels (1925/1986, pp. 181–182) – given, above all, the strong pressures that, in accordance with the functioning requirements of the global market and related corporate interests, are imposed on poor and indebted countries by international financial institutions to adopt neoliberal measures in exchange for loans, bailouts and financial aid – is another matter: 'by long and often cruel experience and by collecting and analysing historical material, we are gradually learning to get a clear view of the indirect, more remote social [and environmental] effects of our production activity, and so are afforded an opportunity to control and regulate these effects as well. This regulation, however, requires something more than mere knowledge. It requires a complete revolution in our hitherto existing mode of production, and simultaneously a revolution in our whole contemporary social order'.

References

Blunt, P. (1991). Organizational Culture and Development. *International Journal of Human Resource Management, 2*(1), 55–71. https://doi.org/10.1080/09585199100000051

Blunt, P., Escobar, C., & Missos, V. (in press). Emergency Responses Under COVID-19: Development Assistance, 'Structural Violence', and 'Interpretive Labour' in Samoa. *Journal of Interdisciplinary Economics.*

Blunt, P., & Jones, M. (1992). *Managing Organisations in Africa.* Walter de Gruyter.

Chomsky, N. (2007, March 9). A Predator Becomes More Dangerous When Wounded. *The Guardian*. www.theguardian.com/commentisfree/2007/mar/09/comment.iran

Chomsky, N. (Author), Pollin, R. (Author), & Polychroniou, C. J. (Contributor). (2020). *Climate Crisis and the Global Green New Deal: The Political Economy of Saving the Planet*. Verso Books.

Cook, J. R. (2020, January 26). *Australia's International Development Assistance – Policy Submission*. www.dfat.gov.au/sites/default/files/jon-cook.pdf

Engels, F. (1986). *Dialectics of Nature* (C. Dutt, Trans., 2nd revised ed. reprint). Progress Publishers (Original work published 1925).

Honeycombe-Foster, M. (2019, December 17). *Abolishing DfID Would See UK 'Turn Its Back on Poorest', Charities Warn Johnson*. CivilService World. www.civilserviceworld.com/professions/article/abolishing-DfID-would-see-uk-turn-its-back-on-poorest-charities-warn-johnson

Metherell, L. (2014, May 29). *DFAT Survey Shows Dissatisfaction Among Former AusAID Employees With Merger*. ABC News. https://www.abc.net.au/news/2014-05-29/survey-shows-staff-dissatisfaction-over-dfat-ausaid-merger/5484860?nw=0&r=Interactive

Mintzberg, H. (1979). *The Structuring of Organisations*. Prentice-Hall.

Mintzberg, H. (1983). *Structure in Fives: Designing Effective Organisations*. Prentice-Hall.

Mitchell, S. (2020, June 19). *Bad News for the Poor? Why the Abolition of DFID Matters*. Joint Public Issues Team. www.jointpublicissues.org.uk/bad-news-for-the-poor-why-the-abolition-of-DfID-matters/

Moore, R. (2019, February). *Strategic Choice: A Future-Focused Review of the DFAT-AusAID Integration* [Independent Review]. Development Policy Centre, Australian National University. https://devpolicy.org/publications/reports/DFAT-AusAIDIntegrationReview-FullVersion.pdf

Prima, B. A., Urbinati, L., & Loi, V. (2019). *Our Land. Fact-Finding Mission Report on the Impacts of Mining on Defenders and Environment in Khentii and Dornod Provinces, Mongolia*. Asian Forum for Human Rights and Development (Forum-Asia). www.forum-asia.org/uploads/wp/2019/10/FFM-Mongolia-2019-Report.pdf

Robinson, N. J., & Chomsky, N. (2022, August 15). If We Want Humanity to Survive, We Must Cooperate With China. *Current Affairs*. https://www.currentaffairs.org/2022/08/if-we-want-humanity-to-survive-we-must-cooperate-with-china

Roy, A. (2003a, May 5). The Ordinary Person's Guide to Empire. *In These Times*, *27*(12). https://inthesetimes.com/article/the-ordinary-persons-guide-to-empire

Roy, A. (2003b, May 13). *"Instant-Mix Imperial Democracy" (Buy One, Get One Free)* [Speech audio recording]. Retrieved February 24, 2022, from http://jonsenglishsite.info/Class%20Docs%205/6_InstantMix.pdf

Short, C. (2020, June 16). *Opinion: On the Abolition of DFID*. Devex. www.devex.com/news/opinion-on-the-abolition-of-dfid-97497

Stewart, H., & Wintour, P. (2020, June 16). Three ex-PMs Attack Plan to Merge DfID with Foreign Office. *The Guardian*. www.theguardian.com/politics/2020/jun/16/foreign-office-and-department-for-international-development-to-merge

Tooze, A. (2021, September 2). Has COVID Ended the Neoliberal Era? *The Guardian*. www.theguardian.com/news/2021/sep/02/covid-and-the-crisis-of-neoliberalism

6 Conclusion

US Power and Global Development

Introduction

In the pantheon of Greek mythology, Nemesis[1] was the goddess of retribution and revenge. Her divine duty was to punish those who were guilty of hubris and extreme arrogance. One of her best-known victims was the excessively vain and self-centred Narcissus, who disdained even those who loved him. To punish him for his sins, the myth explains how Nemesis lured Narcissus to a pool of water where he became so enamoured with his own reflection, and so transfixed by it, that eventually he died there.

Does the hubris, vanity and narcissism of empires cause them to make the same fatal mistakes? Do empires, like narcissists, become so 'inebriated with the exuberance'[2] of their own power and the sycophancy of their functionaries and at least some of their subjects, and so blinded to their own mortal failings – their 'declining strength, ineptitude, and savagery' (Hedges, 2021b) – that self-destruction is inevitable?[3] Will climate catastrophe or nuclear holocaust be the nemesis of the US Empire, and ours? The resuscitation of our dying planet before it is too late and the prevention of nuclear conflagration hinge on the answer to these questions. They are, as we said at the beginning of this book, the most urgent and profound questions that human beings have ever had to face.

The United States is both the most powerful nation on earth and the self-proclaimed leader of the so-called free world, the 'good old boys' club whose most devoted members include most of the LDI donor countries discussed in this book. The behaviour of these nations will largely determine the course of global development and the fate of the planet. Among them, the expression of US power will be the decisive factor.

What will become of it in the next 10 to 20 years? How will the United States react to its declining influence and the rise of China and an increasingly assertive and bellicose Russia? An indication of the Establishment's frantic concern about the possibilities is the invitation extended in 2021 by *The Economist* magazine to a select group of 'the world's leading thinkers', asking them to express their views on this question and to examine 'the forces shaping the country's [USA's] standing'. 'Frantic' because the shortlist of invitees included Noam Chomsky and Arundhati Roy, 'leading thinkers' whose views on such

DOI: 10.4324/9781003284352-6

matters hitherto – conspicuously – *The Economist*, and the corporate-controlled media in general in the 'free world', had largely scorned.

In addressing the question here, our shortlist of the leading commentators on the way the world works comprises two citizens and two subjects of the US Empire whose credentials we do not need to extol: Chomsky, Hedges, Roy and Varoufakis.

A Volatile Mix: Military Dominance, Economic Decline, Domestic Turbulence and Social and Political Decay

The fate of US power must begin with an assessment of the relative state of the US's military strength. In 2020, US military spending was US$778 billion, more than three times that of second-placed China ($252 billion) and more than 12 times that of fourth-placed Russia ($62 billion).[4] In Chomsky's (2021) view, there are no credible direct security threats to the United States,[5] yet it has countries that it regards as its adversaries surrounded by more than 800 military bases, many of them nuclear-armed. At the time of writing, China had one military base, in Djibouti.[6]

The United States is clearly the dominant global military power and the 'gendarme' of the new imperialism (Prashad, 2018). To defend its hegemony against the real, imagined or fabricated threats posed by its main rivals, China and Russia, it possesses advanced weapons of mass destruction and maintains a ubiquitous military presence that gives it the capability to strike with overwhelming force anywhere. The challenge will be for the United States to maintain its military dominance over its rivals while keeping them as compliant members of the global economic and financial systems that it controls and benefits from (Prashad, 2018).[7] It is of course moot whether the 'madness' (Chomsky, 2021) of such a dominant position, and the military escalation and ever-present threat of universal nuclear annihilation that go with it, is an advantage.[8]

The trail of destruction and violence that has been the hallmark of US imperialism since the end of the Second World War leads here, but does it end here? If accountability for sins committed is an indicator of sins to come, the signs are not encouraging. According to Hedges (2021a):

> There is not a single case since 1941 when the coups, political assassinations, election fraud, black propaganda, blackmail, kidnapping, brutal counter-insurgency campaigns, U.S. sanctioned massacres, torture in global black sites, proxy wars or military interventions carried out by the United States resulted in the establishment of a democratic government. The two-decade-long wars in the Middle East, the greatest strategic blunder in American history, have only left in their wake one failed state after another. Yet, no one in the ruling class is held accountable.

Against such uniformly bleak precedent, where consequences have always been for Empire to inflict with impunity and others to endure, will US power behave any differently, even in this, our gravest hour of need? Is the United States capable of conceding the ground necessary for realising a sufficient level of cooperation with China and Russia to provide for an authentic global society, which is what the future of the world largely depends on, as Chomsky (2021) suggests? Will the United States be able to overcome its obsession with its distorted image of 'self' and its purblind belief that 'we are exceptional'[9] and 'to universalise issues', that is, to start abiding by the same codes of conduct that it demands of others, as Chomsky (2021) and we (see also Robinson & Chomsky, 2022), in this book, propose?

Hedges (2021c) thinks not. For him, in the United States, the stark choice is between oligarchy and autocracy, between the 'naked kleptocracy' of authoritarian rule and the 'hidden kleptocracy' of the oligarchs. For now, oligarchic control is entrenched in a two-party system separated by the 'narcissism of minor differences', but otherwise at one on all of the major structural issues such as excessive defence spending and military aggression; 'free' trade; taxation that favours corporations and the one percent; a corporate-controlled political electoral system that amounts to a form of legalised bribery;[10] austerity and deindustrialisation; a neglected and decaying physical infrastructure (Fleming, 2016); an unaffordable, inefficient and ineffective privatised system of health care; a brutalising and militarised police force; and 'the world's largest ["colour-coded" and partly privatised] prison system'. These conditions are laced with institutional racism (Bridges, 2020) and have produced grotesque economic and social inequalities and widespread poverty, leading to an increasingly alienated citizenry and delegitimised government (Moynihan, 2022; Robinson, 2022b).

Moreover, the 'normalisation' of far-right extremism, which is more pronounced in the United States than it is in other established state democracies (Mudde, 2022), indicates that the threat of authoritarian rule remains a stark reality. In late 2021, polls indicated that Biden and Trump were running neck-and-neck. According to Hedges (2021c), more than 25% of US citizens believe to varying degrees that the 2020 election was 'stolen' and that the current president is therefore illegitimate; 9% of US citizens consider the use of force to restore Donald Trump to the presidency to be justified.

At the same time, for Hedges (2021a, 2021b), the end of US imperialism is nigh, impaled by the latest – in Afghanistan – of a succession of catastrophic military invasions and occupations that 'herald [its] death'. Similar trajectories of military failure foretold the ends of the Chinese, Ottoman, Hapsburg, Russian, French, British, Dutch, Portuguese and Soviet empires. In all of these cases, military misadventures abroad were matched by severe and contemporaneous social and economic domestic problems. The parallels with the state of US power are striking, where, according to Hedges (2021a), all arms of government (legislature, executive and judicial) have been taken over by corporate power,[11] meaning that those committed to maximising profits for corporate and government elites rather than to the public good will continue to dominate national policy-making, leading the country into a *cul-de-sac*.

The sense of this brief commentary on the US Empire from within (Chomsky and Hedges) is that of a still immensely powerful and dangerous beast withdrawing reluctantly to its lair to lick its wounds: disgruntled, resentful, belligerent, paranoid, blinded to its own weaknesses, and ravaged by dissension and unrest among its own.

An ageing and tiring alpha predator at bay alarmed at the rise of China and made ever more anxious and watchful by the realisation that the safe haven of its own geography – 'of plenty of land and fresh water, no hostile neighbours, oceans on either side . . . [and] plenty of oil from fracking' (Roy, 2021) – is no more. Its security threatened by rising sea levels, forest fires, drought, hurricanes and floods, and rapidly depleting groundwater and reservoirs (e.g. Beaumont, 2022).

But even at its most vulnerable, the US's hubris and arrogance persist, as revealed in the AUKUS submarine deal and its narcissistic disdain and 'deliberate humiliation' of staunch allies like France and, 'by association', the rest of its European allies.[12] This, together with the US's reneging on the trilateral agreement to end Iran's nuclear programme,[13] helped to preserve 'America's financial and geostrategic hegemony over the West', and to remind everyone of who was still in charge (Varoufakis, 2021a).

However, these events were just as much a sign of the US's weakening grip on the world's financial system as they were a reassertion of control. For now, talk of a Eurobond is just that, talk. But the natives are clearly restless, realising all too well that, 'in any confrontation involving money', Europe will be vulnerable so long as the international payments system is controlled by the United States.[14] A Eurobond would change all of that, providing the basis of a payments system that the United States could not block. The chances of this happening are slim, but the threat is in the air (Varoufakis, 2021a).

More threatening still are the rising levels of poverty and inequality in the United States (and in Europe) and the mountains of public and private debt.[15] Following Varoufakis (2021b), savings have risen in tandem with inequality because the one percent are finding it increasingly difficult to spend their rapidly increasing wealth. As savings constitute the supply of money and investment constitutes the demand for it, the price of money falls to zero or close to it. The only way to 'break this vicious cycle of unbearable inequality and unnecessary stagnation' is for central banks to raise interest rates. To date, the fear of government bankruptcies and recession has prevented central banks from doing this.

As a counter, Varoufakis (2021b) proposes two policy initiatives. First, because debt restructuring is unavoidable, central banks should stop pretending otherwise. He argues that, by maintaining interest rates below zero, the European Central Bank and the Federal Reserve are simply extending indefinitely the insolvency of countries like Greece and Italy and a large number of 'zombie' firms, none of whom ever seem likely be able to repay its debts. Instead, such unpayable state and corporate debts should be restructured and interest rates increased so as to reduce the likelihood of further unpayable debts being incurred in the future.

Second, quantitative easing should continue. However, rather than being channelled to commercial banks and corporations (which typically use it to buy back their own shares), it should be used to fund a universal basic income and a 'green' transition. Inflation can be kept in check by taxing the basic income of the upper and middle classes more heavily, and by the outcomes of 'green' investment.

Rotten at the core, torn between oligarchy and autocracy, and increasingly paranoid about challenges to its hegemonic position in the world, the likelihood that the United States will seize the opportunity to do the right thing, by adopting the progressive monetary policies advocated by Varoufakis (2021b), seems somewhat fanciful. A prospect made more so by what will be perceived in the United States as the threat posed by the rapidly growing gap between the sizes of the Chinese and US economies. According to the World Bank (n.d.a), in 2020, China's GDP was over 15% greater than that of the United States, about US$23 trillion versus US$19.9 trillion in terms of purchasing power parity (in constant international dollars).[16]

Flashpoints: Ukraine, Taiwan and the South China Sea

Will the United States accord China the respect it believes it has earned, and some, like Keating (2021), think it deserves, or will it maintain its confrontational and belligerent stance and blunder into a war in Taiwan or the South China Sea? Will it (and NATO) continue its brinkmanship with Russia in Eastern Europe?

The war that began on 24 February 2022 with the invasion of Ukraine by Russia, and its aftermath, will aggravate global geopolitics, constrain economic and trade relations, and significantly increase the likelihood of nuclear war. The biggest war in Europe since Second World War will be an historic watershed in the relations between the United States and its allies and their principal adversaries, China and Russia. The aetiology of the invasion and Empire's behaviour regarding it have the all-too-familiar hallmarks of the imperialist historical structural violence discussed in this book, as demonstrated briefly in the following.

According to international law, Russia's invasion of Ukraine was illegal, a crime of less magnitude but of similar type to that of the US-led invasion of Iraq and Afghanistan and many other US and US-led military escapades and US-sponsored bloodbaths. The invasion was also a widely predicted response by Russia to the threat posed by the eastward expansion of NATO (e.g. Carpenter, 2022), which contravened clear and unequivocal assurances given to Russia in 1990. An expansion motivated largely by the 'multi-billion-dollar bonanza' that it created for arms manufacturers and the consolidation of US hegemony (Hedges, 2022a, 2022b). The expansion of NATO meant that four of its members (three of them former Soviet republics) – Latvia, Lithuania, Estonia and Poland – had shared borders with Russia. Analogous to Mexico being a member of a Chinese-led military alliance, carrying out military exercises with the People's Liberation Army, and allowing Chinese weapons to be aimed at the United States from Mexican soil (Chomsky in Polychroniou, 2022d). Unsurprisingly, the phalanx of NATO members on its north-western border increased Russia's trepidation at the realistic prospect of Ukraine's joining NATO and was one of the main reasons for the invasion.[17]

Following the invasion, support to Ukraine from the United States and its allies was provided in the form of arms and munitions[18] combined with the modern weapons of war, principally Russia's almost total exclusion from the international financial system and the imposition of wide and punitive economic sanctions. The latter always calibrated against the maintenance of Empire's own economic interests, some major ones of which – such as energy – were intricately intertwined with those of Russia and therefore double-edged.[19] Apart from the progress of the war itself, such measures, and how they were managed, defined the extent to which Putin was backed into a corner and whether there would be enough of a face-saving 'escape hatch' left to avoid wider conflict and the 'terminal war' that this could lead to (Chomsky in Polychroniou, 2022a). Important also were the reactions of countries like Sweden and Finland and whether, prompted by the war, they joined NATO, the likelihood of which increased significantly as the war progressed (Brennan, 2022).

The hypocrisy of Empire's outrage at the invasion, its own iniquitous track record and its disparagement of opponents or critics as 'useful idiots' and 'stooges' of the tyrants and regimes that it has supported or overthrown at its convenience are well summed up by Varoufakis (2022a). He depicts these behaviours as a distinctive pattern of Empire's opportunism and double standards, a pattern that is plainly discernible in our discussion of historical and bureaucratic structural violence in Chapters 3 and 4 and in the under-reporting and misreporting by the Western corporate-controlled media of wars or occupations outside of Europe, like those in Yemen, Palestine and Syria (e.g. Barrishi, 2020).

Indeed, Empire's double standards – such as its studied indifference to the immorality of 'approved' wars and their (particularly non-European) casualties and refugees[20] and its flaunting disdain of international law – are such central, taken-for-granted features of US exceptionalism and hegemony that they are rarely mentioned in the corporate-controlled media (Chomsky in Polychroniou, 2022b).

The unfolding tragedy in Afghanistan is the latest example of this and one of the most egregious.[21] There millions of people face starvation because the United States and Europe refuse to release Afghan funds held in their banks, pushing the country towards total collapse (Chomsky in Polychroniou, 2022e; Johnson, 2022a). The Biden administration led the way, issuing an executive order that authorised the permanent seizure of all Afghan assets held in the United States and imposing crippling economic sanctions, the combination of which could kill more civilians than 20 years of war (Johnson, 2022a).[22] There is little or no discussion of Afghanistan's fate in the corporate media.

None of this is to say, of course, that, while decidedly less ambitious in scale, Russia's imperialist aims and methods are any different in principle to Empire's, or any less reprehensible.

Critical questions arise, some of them existential. Will the Russian occupation of all or some of Ukraine become a long-running Syria-like quagmire maintained indefinitely by a US-supported insurgency and an insatiable (US) arms manufacturing industry? Will a long war in Ukraine, which also suits the purposes of a 'fossil fuel industry that can scarcely suppress its joy [at] the new opportunities the invasion has provided' (Chomsky in Polychroniou, 2022c), accelerate and make inevitable the breaching of irreversible tipping points for global warming? That is to say, despite the immense human toll and the damaging spill-over effects on climate and the world economy,[23] are the geopolitical, military and corporate interests of the US Empire – which include the desire for regime change in Moscow and a weakened Russia, and which converge with such force in Ukraine – best served by a drawn-out proxy war? A war that some members of the US Congress and their aides surmise could last for months or even years (Hansler & Atwood, 2022) or could become a 'perpetual war' (e.g. Lieven, 2022a)?

Evidence to corroborate such a conclusion includes the US's refusal to participate in or support negotiations, or to rescind or soften the belligerent policy of the joint statement issued by the White House on 1 September 2021 referred to above. Indeed, the general tenor of the US and NATO responses to the invasion was one of antagonism and what amounted to the incitement of both protagonists, making escalation and prolongation of the conflict much more likely than a negotiated settlement. Incitement achieved by the imposition of the wide-raging punitive sanctions on Russia mentioned earlier and the increasing supply of weapons and military equipment to Ukraine;[24] by urgings for Ukraine to fight on that included assertions by the Pentagon and NATO that a Ukrainian victory was possible and that Russia would only negotiate seriously if it faced defeat on the battlefield (e.g. Hansler & Atwood, 2022); by declarations such as that of the Democratic Chair of the House Permanent Select Committee of Intelligence, Adam Schiff, which advocated that aid to Ukraine should mean 'that we can fight Russia over there, and we don't have to fight Russia here' (Chomsky in Polychroniou, 2022h); by the alleged supply of military intelligence to Ukraine that had led to the deaths of 12 Russian generals by early May 2022 (Lieven, 2022b); and by Biden's inflammatory public statements about Putin, which, among other things, accused him of genocide and of being a war criminal, thereby exposing himself to the charge that 'it takes one to know one' (Chomsky in Polychroniou, 2022c, 2022e, 2022f).

Sentiments faithfully echoed in the United Kingdom by Prime Minister Johnson, who said that peace talks with Russia were 'doomed' because Putin behaved like a 'crocodile when it's got your leg in its jaws', and that the 'strategy' of uninterrupted supply of longer-range and more lethal weapons to Ukraine should therefore be maintained (MacAskill, 2022). Senior ministers in his government quickly rallied round, expanding significantly the range and severity of provocation. For example, the United Kingdom's defence minister asserted that it was 'not necessarily a problem' if the weapons supplied by the United Kingdom were used against military targets in Russia (Durbin, 2022). Soon thereafter, in late April 2022, the United Kingdom's foreign minister went further, announcing that victory for Ukraine was now a 'strategic imperative' for the West and that Russia should be pushed out of all of the territories it had occupied, including Crimea and parts of the Donbas region, which it had seized years before. She added that weapons supply to Ukraine should include 'heavy weapons, tanks and aeroplanes', and that production should be increased accordingly (Landale, 2022). The circumstances thus created are starkly put by Chomsky when he says that

> the U.S. [and its allies are] dedicated to [a] grotesque experiment . . . avoid any way of ending the conflict through diplomacy and see whether Putin will slink away quietly in defeat or will use the capacity, which of course he has, to destroy Ukraine and set the stage for terminal war.
>
> (Chomsky in Polychroniou, 2022g)

Meanwhile, a compliant Zelensky government had banned left-leaning opposition parties that wanted peace and taken harsh measures – allegedly, including kidnap and murder – against mayors and other officials who argued for a negotiated settlement of the war or were perceived to have collaborated with the Russian forces (Blumenthal & Krishnaswamy, 2022).

All of this against a corporate media backdrop – in the United States and elsewhere – that fanned the flames of rampant militarism by its incessant and simplistic portrayal of the war in Ukraine as a battle between the forces of good and evil, a result of an 'unprovoked' attack by Russia (whereas, for example, the attack by the United States on Iraq was virtuous and provoked) (Chomsky in Polychroniou, 2022g). A chorus that fed and 'endlessly reproduce[d]' the myth that portrays the United States and its allies as the sole custodians of 'moral righteousness' and as the saviours of the Ukrainian (and other oppressed) people (Giroux, 2022).

In this highly charged atmosphere, will those who argue for a negotiated solution that provides face-saving concessions to Russia and the conditions for a lasting peace be vilified and discredited as Putin apologists and side-lined, or simply be censored or condemned as treasonous (Brenner in Scheer, 2022b; Hedges, 2022e)? Will the ranks of Empire's warmongers be swollen by those who would normally be its critics thereby intensifying a generalised subordination to power and undermining citizen opposition to policies that make nuclear war and climate catastrophe more likely (e.g. Chomsky in Polychroniou, 2022e; Jaffe *et al.*, 2022)?

Backed into a corner and left with no palatable way out, will a weakened, desperate and humiliated Russia spark a wider (nuclear) conflict by formally declaring war on Ukraine; by using chemical weapons; by attacking arms' supply routes in neighbouring (NATO) countries; or by invoking its 'de-escalation doctrine' and carrying out a 'tactical' nuclear strike (Sokov, 2022)?[25] That is to say, could the destruction of

Ukraine and the slaughter and displacement of its people and the impoverishment and starvation of tens of millions of others around the world ultimately become the most self-destructive of Empire's many sacrifices to the gods of war?

And even if Ukraine turns out not to be the usher of the apocalypse, will the consequences of the war and the frailty of the doctrine of 'mutually assured destruction' simply postpone what increasingly seems like the inevitable? That is to say, as geopolitical tensions rise and nuclear and conventional rearmament escalates, will deliberate or accidental terminal responses by Empire or its adversaries in Eastern Europe or in places like Taiwan and the South China Sea become less and less avoidable? Responses made more likely by the perception in the West that the war in Ukraine unified and gave common purpose to the United States and its allies, allowing an emboldened United States to reclaim its mantle of 'world leadership', to re-emphasise its role as principal *agent provocateur*, and to make the most of the opportunities so afforded for it to seem 'great again' (Hedges, 2022f)? Opportunities that might entail attempts to destroy or enfeeble the Russian state (Lieven, 2022b). Will the casting of Russia as a pariah state make for interminable hostilities after the war in Ukraine ends? Our analysis here, and that of others – notably, for example, Chomsky in Polychroniou (2022i) – suggests that the answers to these questions are unlikely to have happy endings.

Implications for Global Development

All empires die. The questions are 'when' and 'how' and what will be the ramifications for climate change and global development? We have argued that a critical factor in any such assessment is the extent of the US's ubiquitous military presence and its overwhelming military superiority over its rivals, namely, the second- and fourth-placed military powers, China and Russia.[26] Its long history of aggressive and unprovoked military adventurism and massive military spending, which have fuelled domestic economic growth – a kind of 'military Keynesianism' (Hedges, 2021b) – seem unlikely to diminish in the face of a rising China and a beleaguered and more chauvinistic Russia that, like China, persists in its refusal to do as it is told, that is, to acquiesce to the largely US-devised so-called rules-based global order. The conditions for perpetual war set in stone by the invasion of Ukraine and its aftermath, by the demonisation of Russia and, despite the exposure of its military limitations in Ukraine, by its portrayal by the United States as a serious threat to NATO (Hedges, 2022f).[27]

At the same time, US society is divided and riddled with dissension and antipathy, caused principally by the ever-widening gap between rich and poor and by grave social and economic injustices that are borne disproportionately by so-called people of colour (Fukuyama, 2021; Hedges, 2021a; Robinson, 2022b).[28] For the first time, the United States has a genuine economic rival – China – which it openly regards as an adversary and which it plans to 'encircle' with an 'unbroken chain of U.S.-armed sentinel states' (Japan, South Korea, Australia, the Philippines, Thailand, Singapore and India) (Chomsky in Polychroniou, 2022d).[29] Its safe-haven geography has been shattered by climate change (Roy, 2021). Irretrievably tarnished by its chronic militarism, invasions, sponsorship of coups and dictators, and blatantly hypocritical 'soft power', its image abroad has been deteriorating for years, and is in tatters (Chomsky, 2021). Decades of imperial conquest have turned more and more countries against it. Yet, like the Narcissus of Greek mythology, 'despite its numerous defeats, fiascos, blunders and diminishing power', it seems constitutionally incapable of changing its ways, of preventing itself from 'striking out irrationally like a wounded animal' (Hedges, 2021b). Stupefied by a belief in its own omnipotence and civilisational superiority – its exceptionalism – and controlled by self-serving corporate and government elites consumed by greed and rejuvenated by pyrrhic 'success' in Ukraine, the US Empire, like empires before it (e.g. Elkins, 2022), seems unlikely to shrink from its mission to control and exploit the world and make it in its own image, to go 'gently into the night'. More likely, as ageing and weakened alpha predators tend to, it will fight to the bitter end, lashing out wildly at its real or contrived challengers and tormentors, 'raging against the dying of the light'.

These conditions do not bode well for military restraint or the avoidance of nuclear conflagration; for the moderation of the plundering of the earth's resources; for reductions in inequality and bold and progressive economic policy initiatives such as those proposed by Varoufakis (2021b); for the universalisation of issues; or for Empire's observing the same standards that it expects of others, which Chomsky (2021), and we, regard as necessary conditions for the profound changes that are needed to prevent climate catastrophe and to reform LDI technical assistance. In short, they do not bode well for the abandonment or complete redesign of Empire's neoliberal doomsday machine (Roy, 2020b), outcomes that can only be achieved when there is a better match than exists today between Empire's morality and its intelligence and technical capability (Chomsky in Polychroniou, 2022i). Already, it seems as if Empire will only begin to treat the terminal threats of climate catastrophe and nuclear holocaust with the seriousness that they require and deserve when it is too late (Roy, 2020a).

In Chapter 5, we suggested that the best-case scenario for the reform of LDI bilateral technical assistance would be that the proposals for change set out in this book would constitute a small but significant part of more fundamental and far-reaching reform of the main drivers of climate change and inequality by the major powers. Our gloomy assessment in this chapter makes that possibility seem highly unlikely. But the heavy dependence of our proposals on LDI donor willingness to 'universalise issues' and on empathy and fair dealing, that is, a willingness to treat others as we would have them treat us, also casts a dark shadow over even our worst-case scenario. This consolation prize, where the implementation of our proposals renders some kind of palliative care to the recipients of technical assistance in the hope that policies directed at the root causes will be developed and applied before it is too late, also seems unlikely. In the circumstances, perhaps the best that we can hope for is that some LDI donors in some places will do as we recommend for the reasons that we suggest, and that, forlorn as it may seem, sufficient pressure is put on them by recipient governments and by an 'organised public'[30] to force policy-makers to devise and implement measures that forestall a climate or nuclear apocalypse (Chomsky in Pâkzâd & Magnussen, 2021).

Notes

1 From the ancient Greek verb *νέμω*, which means 'to distribute' and implies divine intervention for the purpose of redistributive justice.

2 Taken from a longer passage by the nineteenth-century former British prime minister, Benjamin Disraeli (1804–1881), about the 'verbosity' of his contemporary and rival, William Gladstone (1809–1898).

3 Questions that have seeped into the mainstream media (e.g. Cooper, 2021).

4 According to the Stockholm International Peace Research Institute (2021a, 2021b), even as the global economy contracted during the first year of the COVID-19 pandemic, sales of weapons and military services by the world's top 100 arms corporations amounted to US$521 billion, an increase of 1.3% in real terms over the previous year. US firms dominate the industry, accounting for 54% of sales among the top 100 companies. Global military spending rose to US$1981 billion in 2020.

5 It has long been held that the threat of war has been used primarily by major powers like the United States to serve domestic political and economic purposes (e.g. Robinson, 2022a). The flimsy cover to stories concocted regarding such threats is most thoroughly exposed when the threats are said to come from countries that are clearly incapable of posing any serious military challenge and are weak economically and technologically. But the US quest to maintain its global suzerainty extends to other, so-called first world powers, as well, as Gill (1996, p. 661) makes clear.

6 Other reports suggest that China is planning to establish more bases abroad, for example, in Equatorial Guinea (Tanchum, 2021) and in places like Cambodia and Tanzania (Singleton, 2021).

7 A dominant position made more so by the fact that, in 2020, defence spending by three of its NATO allies combined – the UK, Germany and France – was about three times that of Russia (Stockholm International Peace Research Institute, 2021a). Moreover, following the invasion of Ukraine by Russia in February 2022, a number of European countries – notably, Germany, Sweden, Poland and Denmark – declared their intentions to increase their defence spending significantly, in Germany's case by more than 100% (*From Germany to China*, 2022). At the same time, Germany lifted its ban on exporting weapons (Hedges, 2022b). In late March 2022, the Biden administration proposed a US$31 billion increase in military spending over the previous year and an emergency appropriation of an additional $14 billion for military support to Ukraine (Robinson, 2022a).

8 The growing risk of war with China arises because it does not follow (US) orders. That is, the 'threat' posed by China stems from its disobedience, not from its military presence or actions. The United States is clearly much more of a military threat to China than China is to the United States. China is surrounded by dozens of nuclear-armed US military bases. By this measure alone, the US's stance is highly antagonistic towards China (and towards Russia). The same cannot be said of China (Pâkzâd & Magnussen, 2021; Robinson & Chomsky, 2022). The United States, of course, expects to get its way and has a long track record of punishing recalcitrant nations militarily. However, the threat posed by China is not just a function of its economic power and its refusal to obey orders. Perhaps just as tellingly, it arises from its mere existence as a highly successful alternative model of political economy, which casts doubt on the presumption of US exceptionalism and its self-representation as the pinnacle of human endeavour and achievement. Empires have always found it difficult to resist the temptation of using military force as a (usually vain) means of addressing such perceived threats to their hegemony (Robinson, 2022a).

9 A belief in US exceptionalism presumes that the values, society and political and economic systems of the United States are unique, superior to those of other countries and peoples, and deserving of universal admiration. It presumes further that such pre-eminence entitles the United States to be above international law, and to intervene at will – militarily and in other ways – in the affairs of other countries on the pretext that it is for their own good (Walt, 2011). As noted earlier, it also means that the United States believes that it has the right to establish a global network of hundreds of military bases – and that no other country should have such rights.

10 For example, it is estimated that over the last 20 years in the US weapon manufacturers have spent US$2.5 billion lobbying Congress, US$177 million in 2021 alone (Ludwig, 2022). Aided and abetted by what Hedges (2022d) refers to as 'the pimps of war', that is, a 'cabal of warmongering pundits, foreign policy specialists and government officials' who are the puppets and cheerleaders of the Pentagon.

11 The relentless persecution of whistleblowers by the US government and by US corporations, and corporate influence on the judicial and prosecutorial systems of the United States, are evident in (among many) the cases of Julian Assange (Hedges, 2021d) and of Steven Donziger (Hedges, 2020). For 27 years, Donziger has been embroiled in a bitter struggle with Chevron on behalf of indigenous communities and peasant farmers in Ecuador. The might of Empire's unwillingness to forgive or forget is evident in the resources it marshals in its persecutions. Chevron has used its immense wealth (of more than US$260 billion in assets) to employ about 2,000 lawyers from 60 law firms to implement its campaign against Donziger (Hedges, 2021b). Released in April 2022 after 993 days of detention – said to be the longest ever for a misdemeanour charge – he continues to be pursued by Chevron in the civil courts (Johnson, 2022b).

12 The United Kingdom and Australia were all-too-eager accomplices, pawns in a grand strategy designed to prevent China from acquiring 'a second-strike nuclear capability' against the United States (Keating, 2021). At the time, the disequilibrium of submarine capability was heavily loaded in favour of the United States. According to Chomsky (in Pâkzâd & Magnussen, 2021), China had relatively few submarines, which were 'old' and 'nonnuclear' and 'easily detected'. The United States, on the other hand, had a 'fleet of advanced [nuclear] submarines', armed with Trident missiles. Each (US) submarine was capable of striking 'about two hundred cities all over the world'. The AUKUS submarine deal made an arms race in the region seem inevitable.

13 One of Trump's main reasons for reneging on the deal was to put Germany in its place. Chancellor Merkel's declaration that EU corporations would pay no heed to the sanctions imposed on Iran by Trump was simply ignored by German corporations who, because they did not want to lose access to the US market and Trump's corporate tax concessions, said they would stop trading with Iran (Varoufakis, 2021a).

14 Following the invasion of Ukraine, the exclusion of Russia from the international payments system drove home the seriousness of this threat and the vulnerability of central banks everywhere to the whims of Empire.

15 The indebtedness of non-financial corporations rose by 12.5% during 2018–2020, significantly more than in the ten years leading up to the declaration of the COVID-19 pandemic in March 2020. The war in Ukraine made many of these 'zombie firms' even more liable to failure (Roberts, 2022a).

16 Moreover, China's economy has been growing at a consistently faster rate than that of the United States. According to World Bank's (n.d.b) data, from 2010 to 2020, the annual percentage growth rate of China's GDP at market prices (based on constant local currency) was, on average, a little over 7%, whereas that of the United States was less than 2%.

17 A major provocation had been the 'Joint Statement on the U.S.-Ukraine Strategic Partnership' signed by the White House on 1 September 2021. The statement declared that Ukraine was free to join NATO and proposed a framework for enhanced strategic defence and security cooperation between Ukraine and the United States. This

included the supply of advanced anti-tank and other weapons and training programmes and military exercises (Chomsky in Polychroniou, 2022d).

18 The volume, sophistication and deadliness of weapons supplied by the United States and its allies increased significantly as the war progressed, eliciting from Russia thinly veiled threats of nuclear retaliation. Not since the Cuban Missile Crisis in 1962 had a nuclear power threatened another nuclear power with nuclear attack.

19 But no matter how careful the 'calibration' of the sanctions imposed on Russia may be, they will not be able to prevent massive disruptions to the world economy including the economies of the United States and its allies as well as Russia (and China). The full extent of these disruptions will only be revealed as the sanctions – and Russian retaliatory measures – take effect. These effects are likely to multiply in unpredictable ways and to last for years (see, e.g., Roberts, 2022b). It seems just as likely that the chronically deteriorating economic and social conditions at home that these disruptions will produce for all protagonists will only increase the chances of a drawn-out war in the Ukraine and of other military confrontations in places like the South China Sea and of escalation to nuclear war (Robinson, 2022a).

20 A view endorsed by the Director General of the World Health Organisation, Tedros Adhanom Ghebreyesus, who accused 'the world' of 'not treating the human race in the same way', saying that only a fraction of the attention given to Ukraine is afforded to other equally or more-deserving humanitarian emergencies (*WHO Chief*, 2022).

21 Another example is the inhumane treatment of Julian Assange. Had his tormentors been Chinese, Russian or Iranian, it is not difficult to imagine the endless chorus of pious and banal political and media outrage that would have ensued. Likewise, Hedges (2022c) observes that Empire has 'one set of standards' for 'white Europeans' and another for everyone else, noting that the Western media lionises as heroes European and US volunteers who go to fight in Ukraine while Muslims from the West who volunteer to fight against foreign invaders in the Middle East are branded as terrorists.

22 In early 2022, this was the subject of the world's largest-ever humanitarian appeal of US$4.47 billion, more than quadruple what was needed at the beginning of 2021. UNICEF estimates that more than one million children will need treatment for severe acute malnutrition and that a total of 13 million children will need humanitarian assistance. Ninety-five percent of the Afghan population was said not to have 'adequate nutrition' (Johnson, 2022a).

23 For example, before the invasion, the World Food Programme obtained 40% of its wheat from Ukraine. According to 2019 data, Ukraine and Russia supplied 64% of global Sunflower oil exports, 23% of wheat exports, 19% of barley and 18% of maize exports. The countries most reliant on such exports are in the global South. For example, in 2019, Uganda obtained over 99% of its wheat from Ukraine and Russia (Ritchie, 2022). At the same time, the costs of delivering food aid are at an all-time high and the gap between humanitarian need and funding is growing, with appeals achieving on average only 6.5% of requested levels (Maxwell, 2022).

24 On 10 May 2022, the US House of Representatives approved a US$40 billion (predominantly) military and humanitarian aid package to Ukraine. This followed the approval a few weeks before of US$13.6 billion in emergency military aid (Edmondson & Cochrane, 2022).

25 Some analysts assess the chances of nuclear war as being higher now than they have ever been, higher even than during the Cuban Missile Crisis (e.g. Postol in Scheer, 2022a).

26 The principal author can attest to Empire's reach into some of the remotest places on earth. In 2002, while on a short-term consultancy (funded by an LDI through an NGO) for the rebel government-in-waiting in Rumbek, South Sudan, alongside the town's murram airstrip, he shared a tented camp with a group of US special forces equipped with high-tech 'listening' equipment. A short time before, commercial deposits of oil and gas had been discovered in South Sudan (Blunt, 2003).

27 This is a striking illustration of power's propensity for Orwellian double-think – the ability to hold and believe two clearly contradictory ideas at the same time, a capacity

that is most pronounced in totalitarian states. That is to say, the United States adopts and proclaims the view that Russia poses a serious military threat to the 'free world' and, at the same time, argues that it (the United States) must 'arm [itself] to the teeth to protect [itself] against the demonic plans of [what it also believes to be a] paper tiger' (Chomsky in Polychroniou, 2022i).

28 In 2018, more than one-half of global wealth was controlled by the richest one percent of humanity while the bottom 80% controlled a mere 5%. In the first two years of the COVID-19 pandemic, the ten richest men in the world doubled their wealth, from US$700 billion to US$1.5 trillion, while the incomes of 99% of humanity fell and an additional 160 million people became impoverished (Robinson, 2022b).

29 In 2022, the US Indo-Pacific command was said to be planning to enhance the encirclement, 'doubling its spending in fiscal year 2022' to include a network of 'precision-strike missiles' (Chomsky in Polychroniou, 2022d).

30 In a world where a startling 80% of the global population live on less than US$10 a day and control less than 5% of the world's wealth, there has been a global upsurge in popular anti-capitalist and anti-government protests and union action. Yet (so far) these movements are too uneven, fragmented and disorganised and lack a sufficiently coherent and comprehensive counter-argument to mount a serious challenge to the prevailing order (Robinson, 2022b).

References

Barrishi, A. (2020, July 10). Underreporting on the Crisis in Yemen, the Complicity of the British Government, and What we Can Do to Help. *Varsity*. www.varsity.co.uk/opinion/19596

Beaumont, H. (2022, May 5). *California Declares Unprecedented Water Restrictions Amid Drought*. Al Jazeera. www.aljazeera.com/news/2022/5/5/california-declares-unprecedented-water-restrictions-amid-drought

Blumenthal, M., & Krishnaswamy, E. (2022, April 17). "One Less Traitor": Zelensky Oversees Campaign of Assassination, Kidnapping and Torture of Political Opposition. *The Grayzone*. https://thegrayzone.com/2022/04/17/traitor-zelensky-assassination-kidnapping-arrest-political-opposition/

Blunt, P. (2003). Governance Conditions, Roles and Capacity-Building Needs in the Rebel-Held Areas of Southern Sudan. *Public Administration and Development*, *23*(2), 125–139. https://doi.org/10.1002/pad.272

Brennan, D. (2022, March 3). NATO Issue in Sweden, Finland Pits Anxious Public Against Cautious Politicians. *Newsweek*. www.newsweek.com/nato-sweden-finland-public-politicians-russia-ukraine-1684621

Bridges, K. M. (2020, June 11). The Many Ways Institutional Racism Kills Black People. *Time*. https://time.com/5851864/institutional-racism-america/

Carpenter, T. G. (2022, February 28). Many Predicted NATO Expansion Would Lead to War. Those Warnings were Ignored. *The Guardian*. www.theguardian.com/commentisfree/2022/feb/28/nato-expansion-war-russia-ukraine

Chomsky, N. (2021, September 24). The Future of American Power: Noam Chomsky on the Cruelty of American Imperialism. *The Economist*. www.economist.com/by-invitation/2021/09/24/noam-chomsky-on-the-cruelty-of-american-imperialism

Cooper, R. (2021, August 25). The Hidden Costs of American Imperialism: Man Cannot Live on a Vicarious Sense of Power Alone. *The Week*. https://theweek.com/afghanistan/1004092/the-hidden-costs-of-american-imperialism

Durbin, A. (2022, April 27). *Ukraine War: Russia Accuses UK of Provoking Attacks on its Territory*. BBC News. https://www.bbc.com/news/uk-61235301

Edmondson, C., & Cochrane, E. (2022, May 10). House Passes $40 Billion More in Ukraine Aid, With Few Questions Asked. *New York Times*. www.nytimes.com/2022/05/10/us/politics/congress-ukraine-aid-questions.html

Elkins, C. (2022). *Legacy of Violence: A History of the British Empire*. Knopf.

Fleming, S. (2016, May 11). US Infrastructure Decay Forecast to Cost Trillions. *Financial Times*. www.ft.com/content/6aa759f8-16c0-11e6-b197-a4af20d5575e

From Germany to China, How Russia-Ukraine Conflict Is Forcing the World to Ramp Up Defence Budgets (2022, March 8). Firstpost. www.firstpost.com/world/from-germany-to-china-how-russia-ukraine-conflict-is-forcing-the-world-to-ramp-up-defence-budgets-10440251.html

Fukuyama, F. (2021, August 18). The Future of American Power: Francis Fukuyama on the End of American Hegemony. *The Economist*. www.economist.com/by-invitation/2021/08/18/francis-fukuyama-on-the-end-of-american-hegemony

Gill, L. (1996). *Fondements et Limites du Capitalisme*. Editions du Boreal.

Giroux, H. A. (2022, April 13). Nonstop Corporate News on Ukraine Is Fuelling Support for Unchecked US Militarism. *Truthout*. https://truthout.org/articles/nonstop-corporate-news-on-ukraine-is-fueling-support-for-unchecked-us-militarism/

Hansler, J., & Atwood, K. (2022, April 15). *No Short-Term End in Sight in Russia's Invasion of Ukraine, Western Officials Say*. CNN. https://edition.cnn.com/2022/04/15/politics/ukraine-russia-protracted-war-us-european-officials/index.html

Hedges, C. (2020, August 25). Chris Hedges: How Corporate Tyranny Works. *Scheerpost*. https://scheerpost.com/2020/08/25/how-corporate-tyranny-works/

Hedges, C. (2021a, April 19). Hedges: The Unravelling of American Power. *Scheerpost*. https://scheerpost.com/2021/04/19/hedges-the-unraveling-of-the-american-empire/

Hedges, C. (2021b, August 30). Hedges: The Empire Does Not Forgive. *Scheerpost*. https://scheerpost.com/2021/08/30/hedges-the-empire-does-not-forgive/

Hedges, C. (2021c, September 27). America's Fate: Oligarchy or Autocracy. *Scheerpost*. https://scheerpost.com/2021/09/27/americas-fate-oligarchy-or-autocracy/

Hedges, C. (2021d, October 28). Hedges: The Most Important Battle for Press Freedom in Our Time. *Scheerpost*. https://scheerpost.com/2021/10/28/hedges-the-most-important-battle-for-press-freedom-in-our-time/

Hedges, C. (2022a, February 26). The Ukraine Catastrophe and How We Got Here: Chronicle of a War Foretold. *Salon*. www.salon.com/2022/02/26/the-ukraine-and-how-we-got-here-chronicle-of-a-foretold/

Hedges, C. (2022b, March 14). Hedges: Waltzing Toward Armageddon With the Merchants of Death. *Scheerpost*. https://scheerpost.com/2022/03/14/hedges-waltzing-toward-armageddon-with-the-merchants-of-death/

Hedges, C. (2022c, March 24). The Dangerous Myth of American Innocence: Only Our Enemies Commit "War Crimes". *Salon*. www.salon.com/2022/03/24/the-myth-of-american-innocence-only-our-enemies-commit-war-crimes/

Hedges, C. (2022d, April 12). Pimps of War: Neocons Who Fuelled 20 Years of Carnage in the Middle East Are Back for More. *Salon*. www.salon.com/2022/04/12/pimps-of-war-neocons-fueled-20-years-of-carnage-in-the-middle-east-are-back-for-more/

Hedges, C. (2022e, April 18). Hedges: American Commissars. *Scheerpost*. https://scheerpost.com/2022/04/18/hedges-american-commissars/

Hedges, C. (2022f, May 2). Hedges: The Age of Self-Delusion. *Scheerpost*. https://scheerpost.com/2022/05/02/hedges-the-age-of-self-delusion/

Jaffe, A., Levenson, Z., & Wills, V. (2022, April 14). A Hunger Within the US Left for "Action" on Ukraine Is Driving Us Astray. *Truthout*. https://truthout.org/articles/a-hunger-within-the-us-left-for-action-on-ukraine-is-driving-us-astray/

Johnson, J. (2022a, March 30). Biden Won't Release Afghanistan's Central Bank Assets, Even in Face of Collapse. *Truthout*. https://truthout.org/articles/biden-wont-release-afghanistans-central-bank-assets-even-in-face-of-collapse/

Johnson, J. (2022b, April 25). Steven Donziger Walks Free After 993 Days of 'Completely Unjust' Detention. *Common Dreams*. www.commondreams.org/news/2022/04/25/steven-donziger-walks-free-after-993-days-completely-unjust-detention

Keating, P. (2021, November 10). 'It Would Make a Cat Laugh': Key Moments From Paul Keating's National Press Club Appearance. *The Guardian*. www.theguardian.com/australia-news/2021/nov/10/it-would-make-a-cat-laugh-key-moments-from-paul-keatings-national-press-club-appearance

Landale, J. (2022, April 27). *Push Russia Out of Whole of Ukraine, Says Truss*. BBC News. https://www.bbc.com/news/uk-61251698

Lieven, A. (2022a, April 27). Potential US Proxy War in Ukraine Could Be Disastrous. *Common Dreams*. www.commondreams.org/views/2022/04/27/potential-us-proxy-war-ukraine-could-be-disastrous

Lieven, A. (2022b, May 5). Giving Ukraine Intel on Russian Generals Is a Risky Gamble. *Responsible Statecraft*. https://responsiblestatecraft.org/2022/05/05/giving-ukraine-intel-on-russian-generals-is-a-risky-gamble/

Ludwig, M. (2022, April 15). Ukraine and Yemen Wars Highlight US's Role as Biggest Arms Dealer in the World. *Truthout*. https://truthout.org/articles/ukraine-and-yemen-wars-highlight-uss-role-as-biggest-arms-dealer-in-the-world/

MacAskill, A. (2022, April 21). *UK PM Johnson Says Ukraine Peace Talks are Doomed Because of "Crocodile" Putin*. SWI swissinfo.ch. www.swissinfo.ch/eng/uk-pm-johnson-says-ukraine-peace-talks-are-doomed-because-of – crocodile – putin/47531952

Maxwell, D. (2022, May 1). War in Ukraine is Pushing Global Hunger to Worst Level in this Century. *Common Dreams*. www.commondreams.org/views/2022/05/01/war-ukraine-pushing-global-hunger-worst-level-century

Moynihan, D. (2022). Delegitimization, Deconstruction and Control: Undermining the Administrative State. *The ANNALS of the American Academy of Political and Social Science*, *699*(1), 36–49. https://doi.org/10.1177/00027162211069723

Mudde, C. (2022). The Far-Right Threat in the United States: A European Perspective. *The ANNALS of the American Academy of Political and Social Science*, *699*(1), 101–115. https://doi.org/10.1177/00027162211070060

Pâkzâd, P., & Magnussen, B. (2021, November 19). Noam Chomsky: Ending Climate Change 'Has to Come From Mass Popular Action', Not Politicians. An Interview with Noam Chomsky. *Jacobin*. www.jacobinmag.com/2021/11/noam-chomsky-climate-change-afghanistan-anarchism-china

Polychroniou, C. J. (2022a, March 1). Noam Chomsky: US Military Escalation Against Russia Would Have No Victors. *Truthout*. https://truthout.org/articles/noam-chomsky-us-military-escalation-against-russia-would-have-no-victors/

Polychroniou, C. J. (2022b, March 8). Noam Chomsky: A No-Fly Zone Over Ukraine Could Unleash Untold Violence. *Truthout*. https://truthout.org/articles/noam-chomsky-a-no-fly-zone-over-ukraine-could-unleash-untold-violence/

Polychroniou, C. J. (2022c, March 14). Chomsky: Peace Talks in Ukraine "Will Get Nowhere" If US Keeps Refusing to Join. *Truthout*. https://truthout.org/articles/chomsky-peace-talks-in-ukraine-will-get-nowhere-if-us-keeps-refusing-to-join/

Polychroniou, C. J. (2022d, March 24). Chomsky: Let's Focus on Preventing Nuclear War, Rather Than Debating "Just War". *Truthout*. https://truthout.org/articles/chomsky-lets-focus-on-preventing-nuclear-war-rather-than-debating-just-war/

Polychroniou, C. J. (2022e, March 30). Noam Chomsky: Russia's War Against Ukraine Has Accelerated the Doomsday Clock. *Truthout*. https://truthout.org/articles/noam-chomsky-russias-war-against-ukraine-has-accelerated-the-doomsday-clock/

Polychroniou, C. J. (2022f, April 7). Chomsky: US Policy Toward Russia Is Blocking Paths to De-escalation in Ukraine. *Truthout*. https://truthout.org/articles/chomsky-us-policy-toward-putin-assures-no-path-to-de-escalation-in-ukraine/

Polychroniou, C. J. (2022g, April 28). Noam Chomsky: Propaganda Wars Are Raging as Russia's War on Ukraine Expands. *Truthout*. https://truthout.org/articles/noam-chomsky-propaganda-wars-are-raging-as-russias-war-on-ukraine-expands/

Polychroniou, C. J. (2022h, May 4). Chomsky: US Is Prioritizing Its Jockeying with Russia, Not Ukrainians' Lives. *Truthout*. https://truthout.org/articles/chomsky-u-s-is-prioritizing-its-jockeying-with-russia-not-ukrainians-lives/

Polychroniou, C. J. (2022i, May 11). Chomsky: To Tackle Climate, Our Morality Must Catch Up With Our Intelligence. *Truthout*. https://truthout.org/articles/chomsky-to-tackle-climate-our-morality-must-catch-up-with-our-intelligence/

Prashad, V. (2018, March 1). *In the Ruins of the Present*. Tricontinental Working Document No. 1. https://thetricontinental.org/working-document-1/

Ritchie, H. (2022, March 24). *How Could the War in Ukraine Impact Global Food Supplies?* Our World in Data. https://ourworldindata.org/ukraine-russia-food

Roberts, M. (2022a, March 20). Ukraine-Russia: Like an Earthquake. *Michael Roberts Blog*. https://thenextrecession.wordpress.com/2022/03/20/ukraine-russia-like-an-earthquake/

Roberts, M. (2022b, September 4). Energy, Cost of Living and Recession. *Michael Roberts Blog*. https://thenextrecession.wordpress.com/2022/09/04/energy-cost-of-living-and-recession/

Robinson, N. J., & Chomsky, N. (2022, August 15). If We Want Humanity to Survive, We Must Cooperate With China. *Current Affairs*. https://www.currentaffairs.org/2022/08/if-we-want-humanity-to-survive-we-must-cooperate-with-china

Robinson, W. I. (2022a, April 24). Global Capitalism Has Become Dependent on War-Making to Sustain Itself. *Truthout*. https://truthout.org/articles/global-capitalism-has-become-dependent-on-war-making-to-sustain-itself/

Robinson, W. I. (2022b, May 14). Mass Protest Is Rising–Can It Confront Global Capitalism? *Truthout*. https://truthout.org/articles/mass-protest-is-rising-can-it-confront-global-capitalism/

Roy, A. (2020a, February 12). *The Graveyard Talks Back: Arundhati Roy on Fiction in the Time of Fake News* [Text of the 2020 Clark Lecture in English Literature, Trinity College, Cambridge]. Literary Hub. https://lithub.com/the-graveyard-talks-back-arundhati-roy-on-fiction-in-the-time-of-fake-news/

Roy, A. (2020b, April 3). Arundhati Roy: 'The Pandemic Is a Portal'. *Financial Times*. www.ft.com/content/10d8f5e8-74eb-11ea-95fe-fcd274e920ca

Roy, A. (2021, September 3). The Future of American Power: Arundhati Roy on America's Fiery, Brutal Impotence. *The Economist*. www.economist.com/by-invitation/2021/09/03/arundhati-roy-on-americas-fiery-brutal-impotence

Scheer, R. (2022a, March 25). T. Postol: Nuclear War With Russia? 'A Wall of Fire That Encompasses Everything Around Us at the Temperature of the Centre of the Sun'. *Scheerpost*. https://scheerpost.com/2022/03/25/ted-postol-what-you-really-need-to-know-about-the-threat-of-nuclear-war/

Scheer, R. (2022b, April 15). Michael Brenner: American Dissent on Ukraine Is Dying in Darkness. *Scheerpost*. https://scheerpost.com/2022/04/15/michael-brenner-american-dissent-on-ukraine-is-dying-in-darkness/

Singleton, C. (2021, July 7). Beijing Eyes New Military Bases Across the Indo-Pacific. *Foreign Policy*. https://foreignpolicy.com/2021/07/07/china-pla-military-bases-kiribati-uae-cambodia-tanzania-djibouti-indo-pacific-ports-airfields/

Sokov, N. N. (2022, March 8). Russian Military Doctrine Calls a Limited Nuclear Strike "De-Escalation." Here's Why. *Bulletin of the Atomic Scientists*. https://thebulletin.org/2022/03/russian-military-doctrine-calls-a-limited-nuclear-strike-de-escalation-heres-why/

Stockholm International Peace Research Institute. (2021a, April 26). *World Military Spending Rises to Almost $2 Trillion in 2020* [Press Release]. www.sipri.org/media/press-release/2021/world-military-spending-rises-almost-2-trillion-2020

Stockholm International Peace Research Institute. (2021b, December 6). *Business as Usual? Arms Sales of SIPRI Top 100 Arms Companies Continue to Grow Amid Pandemic* [Press Release]. www.sipri.org/media/press-release/2021/business-usual-arms-sales-sipri-top-100-arms-companies-continue-grow-amid-pandemic

Tanchum, M. (2021, December 14). *China's New Military Base in Africa: What It Means for Europe and America*. European Council on Foreign Relations. https://ecfr.eu/article/chinas-new-military-base-in-africa-what-it-means-for-europe-and-america/

Varoufakis, Y. (2021a, September 23). *Europe's Latest Humiliation*. Project Syndicate. www.project-syndicate.org/commentary/european-leaders-to-blame-for-subordination-to-america-by-yanis-varoufakis-2021–09

Varoufakis, Y. (2021b, October 28). *A Progressive Monetary Policy Is the Only Alternative*. Project Syndicate. www.project-syndicate.org/commentary/progressive-recipe-for-monetary-policy-tightening-by-yanis-varoufakis-2021–10

Varoufakis, Y. [@yanisvaroufakis] (2022a, March 3). *Hideous War after Hideous War, the Pattern Remains the Same . . .* [Tweet with text image]. Twitter. https://twitter.com/yanisvaroufakis/status/1499350037947727875?ref_src=twsrc%5Egoogle%7Ctwcamp%5Eserp%7Ctwgr%5Etweet

Walt, S. M. (2011, October 11). The Myth of American Exceptionalism. *Foreign Policy*. https://foreignpolicy.com/2011/10/11/the-myth-of-american-exceptionalism/

WHO Chief: World Treats Crises Differently Depending on Race. (2022, April 13). Al Jazeera. www.aljazeera.com/news/2022/4/13/who-chief-says-world-treats-crises-differently-due-to-race

World Bank. (n.d.a). *GDP, PPP (Constant 2017 international $) – United States, China* [Data set]. World Bank Open Data. https://data.worldbank.org/indicator/NY.GDP.MKTP.PP.KD?locations=US-CN

World Bank. (n.d.b). *GDP Growth (Annual %) – United States, China* [Data set]. World Bank Open Data. https://data.worldbank.org/indicator/NY.GDP.MKTP.KD.ZG?end=2020&locations=US-CN&start=2010

Index

Note: Page numbers in **bold** indicate a table on the corresponding page. Page numbers followed by 'n' indicate a note.